RUBIES IN MY EARS, OBSESSION TO SUCCESS

SIX COUNTRIES, SIX ADVENTURES. ONE RELENTLESS OBSESSION : SUCCESS

SANJIV T LALL

Copyright © Sanjiv T Lall
All Rights Reserved.

ISBN 979-888521751-4

This book has been published with all efforts taken to make the material error-free after the consent of the author. However, the author and the publisher do not assume and hereby disclaim any liability to any party for any loss, damage, or disruption caused by errors or omissions, whether such errors or omissions result from negligence, accident, or any other cause.

While every effort has been made to avoid any mistake or omission, this publication is being sold on the condition and understanding that neither the author nor the publishers or printers would be liable in any manner to any person by reason of any mistake or omission in this publication or for any action taken or omitted to be taken or advice rendered or accepted on the basis of this work. For any defect in printing or binding the publishers will be liable only to replace the defective copy by another copy of this work then available.

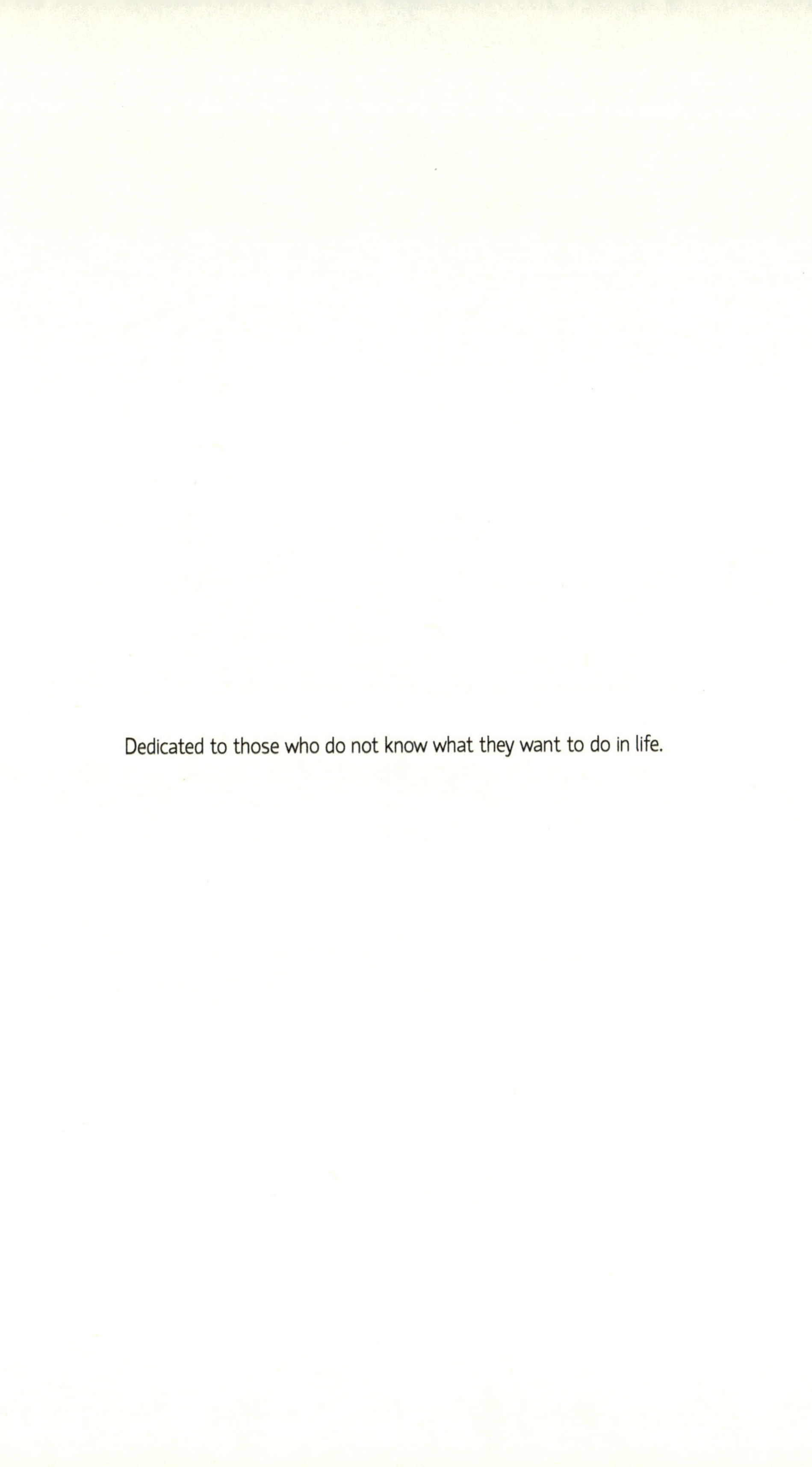

Dedicated to those who do not know what they want to do in life.

Contents

1. Introduction — 1

2. The Seminal Years — 3

3. Sanawar — 8

4. Calcutta — 13

5. Job Hunting — 21

6. Sea Land, Tehran, Iran — 27

7. The Great Union Of Soviet Socialist Republics - Ussr — 53

8. Glorious Scandinavia — 65

9. The Alzey Wine Festival — 70

10. Wonderful Madrid — 83

11. Sea Land Spain — 88

12. Jumping The French Border — 95

13. Back To India — 100

14. Trador Inc — 104

15. Sakshi — 110

16. Tusks And An Elephant Gun — 115

17. Redec — 118

18. Hong Kong — 126

19. Elephant Walk — 128

20. Zoee — 133

21. The Dream Merchants — 137

22. Sapcorp Inc — 148

23. The Australian Nullabor — 173

24. Orange County And Sunny Sirohi — 176

25. Laguna Beach Misery — 180

26. Meeting President Clinton — 182

27. Stlcorp — 185

28. A Life To Live — 190

Contents

29. Yunca 192

30. Kaleidoscope Of Thoughts 194

31. Mongolia 197

32. Goa 201

33. Jeeps 204

34. Sap Revisited 205

35. Reflections 207

36. Afterword 210

CHAPTER ONE

Introduction

A few months short of my 59th birthday, I decided to write a book. I must admit that I had often toyed with the idea of writing a book; I just had not done anything about it. But I knew that when the time came, I would take it up vigorously. I guess the time is here.

I do not know the vagaries of writing a book; in fact, I hardly read any books. I used to read fairly voraciously when I was at college in Calcutta; I mostly read "boys" books, especially thrillers, like those by Alistair Maclean and James Hadley Chase.

In my later life, I gave up reading books almost completely. I do, however, read a lot on the net, both from the perspective of my work as well as for pleasure. Writing a book is a whole new experience for me, one I never imagined I would ever embark upon. But here I am!

I view myself as an ordinary person with an ordinary upbringing, certainly not academically inclined, as my grades in school and college would testify. In school, I was pretty much at the bottom of the academic rung! However, despite my being a 'C' grade student, the picture was quite different in my professional life: I routinely had 'A' grade students reporting to me. This was a buzz in itself, as it proved to me that academic qualifications are not everything in achieving success. In life, success can also come without any qualifications whatsoever, as my own experience has shown.

Throughout my working career, I continually searched for new opportunities and was quite happy and adept at working on different projects at different levels simultaneously. You could say that I could juggle several balls in the air!

I never viewed my "not knowing" what to do in life as a disadvantage, or as a low point in my career, as I knew that something different and new would always come along to captivate me. This certainly proved to be true for me, time and again. I seized the opportunities as they came along or rather, seized the bull by the horn one could say, and made the most of whatever came along.

This book is dedicated to those people who are in a perpetual quandary; those who do not know what to do and when. In the course of my life, I have encountered innumerable boys and girls, men and women, who have been lost, be it in their personal or professional lives. This book is for them.

This is the story of my life, a story that I hope will communicate this simple axiom: "If I can do it, so can you."

CHAPTER TWO

The Seminal Years

I was born Sanjiv Tandan (Bablu), 22 September 1955, in New Delhi. My mother was all of 19 at the time. She had three children, my twin sister, Mala (Babli), me, and our older sister, Gita (Kunkun).

I don't remember very much of my life before I was 10 years old.

The memories are a bit jumbled, but they are happy. I recall carefree memories of my mother and father, my grandmother and great-grandfather on the maternal side, and my grandfather on the paternal side. We called my grandmother Didima. There was also my mother's sister, Billy Masi, and her brothers, Uncle Reggie and Uncle Kenny, and of course, my own two sisters.

My father, Major Surinder Nath Tandan, was a cavalry officer in the Indian Army in the Central India Horse (CIH) stationed at Ferozepur, Punjab. He was the "B" Squadron Commander of CIH. He stood six feet tall, a slim and elegant man; he loved reading books and spoke fluent English and French. He was always very well dressed and fond of the finer things in life.

One of the earliest and most vivid memories I have is standing at the wrought-iron gate of our house in Ferozepur, watching my father drive a jeep, leading his "B" squadron out to war. It was 7 a.m. on a still and clear September morning. I remember my father driving an olive-green, left-hand drive, open-top Willys jeep with a trailer, followed by a long convoy of Army jeeps, trucks, troop carriers and tanks. I was captivated.

The Willys jeep has a low body, more evident when the canvas top is removed and the glass visor is put flat down on the bonnet; the steering column majestically protrudes above the bonnet. My father, being tall and slim, towered over the steering column and was visible from afar; it was quite a sight to behold. The vision of my father driving an olive-green Willys jeep, leading a long convoy of Army vehicles, as it turned out, had a very big impact later in my adult life.

Around this time, just before my tenth birthday, my parents had taken me to Mayo College, Ajmer. Founded in 1875 by the Sixth Earl of Mayo, it is one of the oldest public schools in India. Here, I met the headmaster, the formidable Mr. Gibson, and did some kind of an entrance test, which I passed.

En route to the Ajmer railway station, my parents took me to the Ajmer Sharif Dargah, which is the second most visited mosque in the world after the holy shrine in Mecca and Medina and amongst the few mosques in the world that allow people from all faiths to visit without any questions. I vividly remember walking around the filigreed marble mausoleum of the inner sanctum wondering why so many people came here.

At the Ajmer railway station, waiting to board the train that was pulling into the platform, a tall man with a flowing black beard, wearing a long coat, came up to my father and asked him if he was the military man, to which my father, who was in civvies, said yes. The bearded man gave a *tabiz* (a locket typically given by Muslim saints for protection) to my father and said that he must wear it when he went to war.

My father asked him which war, to which the man said that he knew nothing; he had simply been asked to give the tabiz to my father. That done, the mysterious man walked away. We never got to know who he was or who had asked him to give the tabiz to my father.

Pakistan declared war on India some 10 days later. I remember seeing my father helped by his batman (army valet), removing his epaulettes and insignia from his uniform. I asked him why he was doing that. He said it was to confuse the enemy. I asked him how he would recognize the enemy? He told me that they wore khaki uniforms whereas the Indian soldiers wore olive-green uniforms.

My father left his batman behind to look after my mother, my two sisters and I. He, too, removed all insignia from his uniform. At home, all the windows were covered in newspaper to prevent the light from being seen by the prying eyes of the enemy.

The batman had dug a trench just in case we needed to jump inside during an air raid. It was night, and I was sitting on the toilet with my shorts around my ankles when I heard a tap on the window. I looked out and froze to death. I saw a man in khaki uniform, gesticulating wildly with his hand; he seemed to have something in his hand and kept pointing fingers at me. All I could see was his khaki uniform in the poor light.

It took me a few minutes to realize that it was the batman asking me to put out the light, and not the enemy at my door! Needless to say, we survived the war.

On the night of 11th September 1965, the jeep in which my father and his Commanding Officer were driving was blown up by the enemy's antitank mine, close to the Icchogil Canal, Barki, Lahore. The Commandant of CIH was very seriously injured and passed away a couple of days later. My father miraculously got away with a fractured shoulder, making me wonder if it was the tabiz that he was wearing around his neck, given to him a couple of weeks earlier by the mysterious man on the railway platform, that had indeed saved him from certain death.

Following the outbreak of war between India and Pakistan, my two sisters and I, along with our Lhasa Terrier Fifi, were sent to Delhi to my grandmother's house, as Ferozepur was now decidedly unsafe. I remember sitting in a first-class compartment with my mother and my two sisters with about 10 other people, including some men who were returning from the front lines.

Upon arriving in Delhi, my sister Mala and I were duly dispatched to Bareilly to be with my maternal great-grandfather, Raja Charanjit Singh of Kapurthala. Whilst in Bareilly, jumping off a windowsill of my great grandfather's house, I fell backwards and fractured my hand.

I was brought back to Delhi for treatment at the military hospital where I saw my father with his full upper torso and right hand in plaster, jutting out at a 45-degree angle. My father and I were in the same hospital for a few days, though I was in the children's ward. I was taken to meet him once a day.

I could see my father was distinctly uncomfortable but, thankfully, alive and well. When his shoulder wound finally healed, he found his right hand was shorter by about an inch than his left hand. He was also in constant pain; it could have been that the shoulder ball joint was not set properly in the military hospital. Whatever the cause, his one hand became shorter than the other, which would have technically graded him medically as "C" category or unfit for field duty. "C" category officers are kept for administrative work and cannot get promoted. At the time of his injury, my father was a Major. It would have meant that he remained a Major for the rest of his Army life; that was not something my father wanted or desired. Secondly, his shoulder had been wrongly set to begin with. This had to be set right.

A rather simple, straightforward surgery was suggested to reset the shoulder and extend the upper arm by an inch by way of a steel plate. With both arms of the same length, my father would be declared fit for field duty.

Six months later when my father was being wheeled into surgery to fix his shoulder, the nurse on duty removed the tabiz from around his neck. The good luck charm that had saved my father's life in war, not once, but twice, was gone. My father had been wearing the locket around his neck for the last six months.

What should have been a relatively simple surgery went horribly wrong; the anesthetist administered an overdose of anesthesia. The surgery was traumatic and what should have lasted about an hour took more than six hours.

My father never really recovered; his body went into traumatic shock and started shutting down. My grandmother contacted a pious Muslim saint, someone in whom she had great faith and asked for my father's life.

The saint asked me to go to the local mosque where I was given four white pigeons, which I had to take with me to the hospital. "Get your father to touch the pigeons with his hands and take them out and let them fly away," I was told. My father was delirious, slipping in and out of consciousness. He apologized to me for not buying me a bicycle for my tenth birthday as he had promised he would. I reminded him that he had already bought me a bike for my birthday and asked him not to worry. He then told me that he wanted me to see the "lights"; to this day, I do not really know what he meant.

I took each pigeon out individually and touched them one by one to my father's hand. He did not quite know what was going on. Seeing so many machines and tubes, I was quite scared. I distinctly recall bringing the pigeons out of the hospital room. They were in a little cane basket. I lifted the cover, but the pigeons refused to fly away. I waved my hands at them, and they flew only about eight feet and went and sat on the balcony's wooden rafters just outside my father's room. A few hours later that very evening, 3ʳᵈ March 1966, my father passed away.

The Army provided a moving funeral for my father. His body was carried on a gun carriage, bedecked with flowers, and he was given a touching three-gun salute at the cremation ground.

After my father's death, my mother had to make a living, as until then she had been a housewife. My father's pension being quite modest, my mother had no option but to go out and work.

She learned to drive a car and type, did a secretarial course and eventually got herself a job with the French embassy in New Delhi.

I was studying at Mrs. Bob's Garden School at Jangpura Extension, New Delhi. I used to walk to school. In a class of three pupils, I stood third!

In 1967, my sisters and I joined the Lawrence School in Sanawar, a co-ed boarding school, the only one of its kind in India at that time.

CHAPTER THREE

Sanawar

On 28 February 1967, my sisters and I were dispatched to Sanawar. Yes, dispatched it was: I don't think there is any other way to put it!

I do not quite know why my mother sent my sisters and I to Sanawar. I, for one, was most certainly not ready for boarding school.

Before going to Sanawar, I thought of myself as a happy and confident young boy who could handle things. Boy, was I proved wrong at Sanawar! I did not relish life at Sanawar one bit, but there was nothing I could do about it. The first year was torture; there are no other words to describe it.

Sanawar was founded in 1847 as the Lawrence Military Asylum to provide education to orphans and the children of soldiers serving or having served in India. Children of pure European parentage got preference over those of mixed race parentage.

The school was subsequently renamed the Lawrence Royal Military School and, finally, The Lawrence School, Sanawar, as it was known when I was there and continues to be today. Being a former military school, it was very strict on discipline and very hard on those boys and girls who took time to conform to a regimented form of school life.

Sprawling across some 120 acres of landscaped undulating land, the school is located in the beautiful Himalayan hills at about 5,600 feet altitude. It is about three kilometers from the cantonment town of Kasauli, which is where we would go for an outing on Sundays to take a break from the harsh school life.

Starting out as I did when I was 11 years old, life at Sanawar was rigid, to say the least. Getting up at the crack of dawn, a grimy cup of tea with "dog-style" hard biscuits followed by arduous physical training or PT as we called it, was really hard.

Then, a quick change into classroom uniform, followed by an inspection of our beds, school uniform, shoes, stockings, etc. If anything was out of line, which included the bed and the wooden locker being unaligned with your neighbor's bed and the locker's on either side, we were in trouble. There were about 30 boys per dormitory.

Sanawar was divided into four houses - Himalaya, Nilgiri, Siwalik, and Vindhya, all named after the majestic mountain ranges of India. I was in Siwalik House. I joined in class VI, and was in the junior dormitory, along with another 29 boys or so. Each house had three prefects. Typically, there was one school (senior) prefect and two house (junior) prefects. The school (senior) prefect was always in the senior dormitory.

Sanawar functioned like a regimented military school. I vividly remember getting up each morning around 5 a.m. to go to the "bogs", as that was the only time they were clean. At 6:30 a.m. was PT, which was always treacherous under the command of Mr. Jagdish Ram.

The dormitory inspection and general daily monitoring of the boys were conducted by the prefects. Punishment was regularly meted out and was largely driven by the temperament of the prefect of the day. Some prefects were pure sadists and mean, whereas others were relatively kind.

It was a very tough and arduous grind for the first year, getting bullied by the senior boys, losing all sense of self-respect, literally battling one's way forward from day to day. The smallest misdemeanor such as shoes not being properly polished or stockings not held up or not tying one's turban properly (in the case of young Sikh boys) or the bed not being made properly or the bed and locker being out of alignment incurred the harshest of punishments, which usually meant being hit by towering prefects, who typically would be in their final year in school, literally hammering young kids aged 10, or in my case 11, black and blue.

A particularly sadistic prefect once put me up against a friend of mine and said, "I am not going to punish you myself tonight; you two slap each other." I proceeded to gently slap my friend on his cheek. "Harder," said the prefect. So, I slapped him a bit harder, but the sadistic prefect was not satisfied. "I will show you what a hard slap means," and he came across to me and slapped me so hard that my face spun around. I then proceeded to slap my friend hard, who, in turn, slapped me back even harder. After three rounds of slapping each other, my friend and I were told to go to bed.

The prefects became devils, and at 7:30 a.m., when a prefect uttered the dreaded, "Sanjiv, see me tonight," I would be petrified the entire day, wondering what kind of punishment lay in store for me that night. It was quite difficult to concentrate in the classroom knowing fully well that you had a thrashing in store for you in the evening. Some prefects were moderate and reasonable, but some were downright mean and vindictive.

The punishments were always very physical in nature. Legs up, hands down meant going against a wall and putting your feet up with your hands on the ground at a rather steep angle. The steeper the angle, the more difficult it is to maintain this position for longer than a minute, as all the blood from the body drains out to your head; you feel dizzy. Even when you stand erect, one minute later you feel woozy. However, as punishment, this was preferred by many, as it was over in less than five minutes as opposed to other types of physical abuse which could be 15 to 20 minutes of pure hell.

Some of the staff members, too, were authoritarian and punitive. I recall one occasion when I was hauled up for talking during prep. Mr. Abraham called me outside the classroom and slapped me so hard with the heel of his palm that I literally saw stars. Till then, I had only heard and read about seeing stars. Honestly, I would put it down to a mild form of concussion.

Like almost all the boys I knew, I would question why our parents had sent us to this hellhole. But there was nothing we could do about it. It was almost a major achievement not to get hauled up by a prefect for not being punctual or not doing what I should have or what was expected of me. That perhaps was the first lesson of life that I learned rather early on, to face adversity head-on.

Year two at Sanawar was a bit better as one had learned "how to cope" trying to be good and perfect, I would say. Studies took a backseat as your whole focus was not to make any mistake for the fear of being punished.

Year three, or upper four, things started to get a bit better; maybe the new kids on the block took our place and we were able to move forward.

Life in the senior dormitory was much easier; also, as I got older, the prefects were typically friends. This helped the days to pass.

In class X, I opted for humanities, or English, History, and Hindi.

Other than English and History being a piece of cake, I was also in a class with 16 girls and just two boys. This made the last two years of school great fun. We would both sit in one corner, with all the girls on our left, so that we could see them all!

These were good bonhomie times, too; lasting friendships were made, boys became adults and young girls became fine ladies.

In October 1967, my mother remarried. Mr. Shoy Lall lived in Ranchi on a beautiful 12-acre farm called Tikratoli. I did not even know where Ranchi was. To me, it somehow sounded like Karachi.

My mother brought Mr. Shoy Lall to Sanawar to introduce us to our future stepfather and tell us about the wedding plans. The first thing I recall about him was that he was wearing dark glasses and boots, which I remember thinking was quite cool.

I recall I was dressed in "home clothes", waiting at the quad, close to Napi's, the barber shop for Suraj Ram, Didima's driver, who had driven up from Delhi to pick up my sisters and I for the wedding, when Mr. Bhalerao saw me and asked, "Where are you going, lad?"

"I am going to Delhi, Sir, to attend a wedding."

"Whose wedding are you going to attend?" asked Mr. Bhalerao. "My mother's, Sir," I said with a straight face, leaving Mr. Bhalerao looking rather confused.

In the first term or semester, we went home to Delhi; from the second semester onward, we were part of the "Calcutta Party". From there we would go to Ranchi and Tikratoli.

Years four, five and six were good fun at Sanawar. Maybe I had learned to cope, maybe I had simply graduated to a higher level, but whatever it was, life was fairly good and steady.

In upper five (Class X), in November, three friends and I (all from Siwalik House) decided to take a shortcut during the morning road works/ boxing run. While taking the shortcut, we were noticed by one of the dining room bearers whom none of the boys liked. He went and reported the matter to Mr. Jagdish Ram.

At the end of the run, all the boys were lined up at Gaskell Hall, and Mr. Jagdish Ram commanded us to tell him which boys had taken the shortcut. He said if we did not own up, all the boys would be severely punished. No one moved. I put my hand up and indicated to Mr. Jagdish Ram that I was one of the culprits.

Out came the Malacca cane. I was whipped as I had never been whipped before. The first blow landed exactly behind my right knee; the next three were on my buttocks, but they were somewhat easier to handle. (The vicious and ugly-looking welts remained behind my knees and legs for weeks.)

Then came 20 push-ups, which were relatively easy, though I do remember my backside and knees reeling in pain.

Then it was one minute in the boxing ring with an acclaimed school boxer. I was not much of a boxer and had to negotiate the punches being thrown at me. I daresay a few full-blown punches hit me slap bang on my face, head and torso.

Finally, we had to run the "long back". Running was never my forte, but that day I ran flat out, without stopping.

Amidst all the punishments, I also did NCC (National Cadet Corps) for four years, another tough regimented training. I finally made it to Lance Corporal, wearing crisply starched shorts that could stand on their own with the amount of starch they had in them! The NCC uniforms were very old hand-medowns and I am sure would probably have been worn on the Founders Day for at least the last 50 years!

Founders Day was always a fun time, as it was followed by a three-day break when the kids were allowed to go home.

My latter years in Sanawar were better. The sixth form was great. We were allowed to wear trousers instead of shorts. I had become a senior student.

My memories of Sanawar are vivid. The first year was full of pain. It was harsh with punishments meted out by prefects, older boys and teachers. This impacted my studies and leisure activities. I was not a good academic student and neither was I a sportsman. What I would say is, that I was an average student. But what I could do, was think on my feet and speak good English.

My life at Sanawar did instill in me some sense of discipline and a sense of survival. Because of my experiences at Sanawar, I developed the ability to face adversity and to get things done, which I firmly believe always stood me in good stead later in life. That, in itself, was a fine takeaway from six years of being in Sanawar. All in all, barring the initial years, Sanawar was good fun. I came away with a second division in academics.

CHAPTER FOUR

Calcutta

Calcutta being in close proximity to Ranchi was where my sisters and I were sent to college. My sisters got into Loreto College while I was admitted to St. Xavier's College, Park Street (both Catholic institutions).

I opted for the easiest course, Political Science, and it was indeed easy, actually a cakewalk. That was the first time I thought that I was not quite the duffer I had believed I was. I thrived in a punishment and bullying free educational environment.

Life at the St. Xavier's boy's hostel was great fun. Initially, I was in a room with two other boys. But in the second year, I got a single room. Hooray!

Classes were only from 9:50 a.m. to 1:50 p.m.; so, before and after we could do what we liked. Sitting outside the girl's hostel at varying vantage points was a meaningful pastime. Sitting at Flury's, sipping coffee and eating at the best patisserie in Calcutta, every second day, courtesy my dear friend, Alex, was quite grand.

In 1975, St. Xavier's organized a fete to raise money for a charitable cause. Father Mathew, the hostel superintendent, was the chief organizer. I was put in charge of the Coca-Cola stall. A very simple job. I had to sell a few hundred bottles of Coke. At the end of the day, I had to either return full bottles of Coke or one rupee (Eight US cents) per empty bottle.

My friend Suheil had the 'throw a hoop and win a prize' stall. The first prize was a bottle of Golden Eagle beer. Suheil said, "You come to my stall and I will give you a beer. In turn, you give me a couple of bottles of Coke." A fair exchange, I thought.

I went to Suheil's stall once I found someone to look after the Coke stall. True to his word, Suheil declared to all and sundry that I had won a bottle of beer, which was duly presented to me. I took the beer and put it in the icebox with the bottles of Coke and drank it with Suheil, half an hour later. For his magnanimity, Suheil was given three bottles of Coca-Cola!

I am not exactly sure what transpired while I was away. I had left the Coke stall in what I thought were trustworthy hands, but at the end of the day, I was 72 rupees short. Even given the few freebies, a shortfall of 72 Coke bottles was a bit much.

"Tandan," growled Father Mathew. "This is very simple. You sold the bottles of Coke and took the money. How are you short of 72 rupees?"

"I do not know, Sir."

"Get out of my office; I do not want to see you today."

"Yes, Father," was all I could say in the meekest possible tone.

A couple of weeks later, my grandmother, Smt. Naina Devi, who was an acclaimed Indian classical, ghazal, and thumri singer, had come to Calcutta from Delhi to perform at the Kala Mandir on Theatre Road. I was told to attend the concert by my mother. I thought I had better do the right thing and go to the concert. I went to Father Mathew's office and told him that I wanted a pass to go out that evening.

"Where are you going, Tandan?"

"I am going to Kala Mandir," I said, "for a classical music concert. I know some of the Indian classical artistes singing there tonight."

"Oh really," said Father Mathew, "who is singing?"

"My grandmother, Father."

"Tandan, do you have to tell such outrageous lies every time?"

"It is my grandmother, Father. I am not lying. Here is the program. Smt. Naina Devi is my grandmother."

Father Mathew was taken aback. "Go, go, enjoy yourself," he said.

In my second year at college, I was given an individual room. Life was beginning to get better and better. Midway through my second year in college, in November 1975, my stepfather passed away. For the second time in nine years, my mother had lost a husband, and my sisters and I a stepfather who had been very good to us.

Death brings everything that has been ticking along to an abrupt halt. My father's pension after his death was about INR 75 or USD 9 per month; that was totally unlivable for my mother and her three children. My grandfather (paternal) chose not to give my mother what was her due, as he should have. He was a very wealthy man but having married for a second time, his second wife made sure no support, financial or otherwise, came our way.

My stepfather, too, had no money in the bank, but he did leave behind a beautiful property in Ranchi. My mother was once again in a position where she had to earn a living. Whilst my sisters and I continued with college, my mother began to explore possible business ventures in Tikratoli. We were young and oblivious of the pressures on my mother at the time.

One day, in early 1976, when I was in my final year, I noticed some commotion from across my room. I went to have a look. The room opposite mine belonged to Suresh. I saw Jyoti, a fellow student, standing there, and asked him what was going on. Jyoti said, "It seems the woman in the house opposite is a nymphomaniac, and Kalyan is trying to fix her up."

I stuck my head out to see Kalyan signaling the lady furiously. This charade took place for a few minutes. Then, in disgust, the lady went inside her room and shut the window.

The lady was dark as pitch, with long oily black hair. The next day I went to Suresh's room and saw the lady in black combing her hair. I started signaling; a few minutes later, she responded. I was trying to tell her that I wanted to come across to meet her. She signaled her approval but asked me to come at 11:30 p.m. I was trying to convince her to allow me to come at 10 p.m., but she kept refusing, asking me to come at 11:30 p.m. instead. A few minutes later, she disappeared.

By this time, Deepak was standing next to me, as were Jyoti and Suresh. "Who wants to get laid tonight?" I asked. Deepak put up his hands. We agreed to meet at 10 p.m. Since it was our final year, we were allowed to keep our lights on till 10:30 p.m.; which is why I wanted to go to the lady's house before 10:30 p.m., as movement thereafter was restricted.

"How do I get across to the woman's house?" I asked. "I have seen Kalyan doing it," said Jyoti. "He climbs onto the flat roof of the house opposite hers; then he climbs the tree and goes to the tip of the branch and swings like Tarzan to the woman's window. The other way is to climb the wall to the woman's house, but for that you need two people."

Since I had no intention of doing the Tarzan act, we decided to shinny up the wall to the woman's window.

That night at 10 p.m., Deepak and I met outside the hostel. We walked behind it, clambered up to the roof of the flat building, quietly ran along the entire length of the roof, and came up against the big tree on the right and the woman's window, straight above, about 12 feet up from where I was standing. I looked to the left to see both Jyoti and Suresh grinning from ear to ear, egging us on.

The floor of the roof had small pebbles, which had been embedded in coal tar. Deepak knelt down, as I clambered on his shoulders. Deepak slowly got up and I stood up to my full height, holding the wall in front of me.

I could just about look into the woman's room. I saw her standing there, combing her hair, as she always did.

As soon as she saw me, she came up to the window and started talking softly. "I told you to come at 11:30 p.m. Why have you come now?"

"Please let me in," I said. "We have come so far."

"What is she saying?" Deepak asked. "Go inside and pull me up."

"I cannot do that. She is asking me to come back at 11:30 p.m."

"No, go in now," Deepak said.

Just then the woman turned and said, "My husband is coming now. He is a sergeant, he will shoot you."

"Let me down, Deepak. Her husband is a goddamn sergeant. He is coming home any minute."

The next second, Deepak slipped, and I went for a toss, landing with a noisy thud on the rough roof with stone pebbles.

I immediately picked myself up as the tenants of the house I had fallen on came out running and screaming, looking for the miscreants. Deepak and I sprinted across the roof, and like Tarzan, both of us leaped across the short brick wall and landed at the back of the hostel compound

Fortunately, we landed on grass and did not get hurt.

I told Deepak, "First I will go, then you follow." I walked around the building and approached the hostel from the front, as if I were walking in from Park Street.

"Hello, Tandan," boomed the hostel superintendent. I was totally shocked. I had not even seen him. "Coming back from a walk after studying all day?"

"Yes, Father, I went out for a walk."

Fortunately for me, I was standing in the dark. Father Mathew could not see that I had bruised shins and was bleeding. I never attempted to visit the woman's house again; neither did Deepak. Life at the university continued with its adventures and trials. In 1976, I shifted out of the hostel and moved in with Alex, a great friend of mine living in Khairu Lane, behind the Broadway Hotel, just off Chittaranjan Avenue.

Alex had a two-bedroom apartment on the second floor in an old tenement building that had been rented by his father since the late 1940s. The rental in 1976 was INR 175 per month. Since the rickety building was adjacent to the police station, it meant that the electricity was never cut. In a city of regular power shortages, we had no electricity problems whatsoever.

The entrance to the apartment was up a dirty, smelly staircase, which was home to several street vagrants at night. At least two to three people slept on each step, leaving a small space for the tenants to use the stairs.

When I moved in, I decided that I wanted some color in my life and that this would be a great place to start my post-college life.

The main door was painted post office red. The two front rooms, living and dining rooms, were painted peach, with white ceilings. The two bedrooms at the back, for Alex and me, were both painted a light lilac with white ceilings.

We had a young boy, Nando, to cook and clean for us; he would sleep in the dining room, which was fine with us because we rarely used that room. Nando's wages were fixed at INR 20 per month plus food and clothing, circa 1976.

We had a colorful apartment and a telephone landline, a real luxury in those days! All that was lacking were the girls.

I persuaded my mother's cook, Aziz, who was on leave, to swing by Calcutta to teach Nando how to cook. Aziz spent a couple of days with Nando, teaching him how to make some of my favorite dishes. By the time Aziz left, Nando had turned into quite the cook, and he could even make a beefsteak.

Since both Alex and I were perpetually short of funds, we decided to do without furniture. The main bedroom was converted into the air-conditioned bedroom cum sitting room. Mattresses were laid on the floor, 40-watt bulbs were put in, and the louver shutters were purposely kept shut at all times.

This meant that every time guests or girls came to the room, they had to sit or recline on the floor on the mattresses, in a rather dim lighting. As a young man, what more could I want?

It had been an unfulfilled dream thus far to have an affair with a married woman. I am not quite sure where that came from; perhaps it emanated from knowing at least the girl would know how.

A brief affair with a married woman ensued; a beautiful, well-spoken, well-attired Anglo-Indian lady, working in Carit Moran, a tea trading company in Calcutta. I will remember the gentleness of this forever. I still recall the smell of Ponds powder on her. It all started with my great friend Suheil getting the wrong telephone connection. Quite strange, but that's exactly the way it happened.

Meanwhile, Alex was totally infatuated with a young girl, Sapna. Unfortunately, Sapna was far too young to go out alone; she would only go out with her two sisters. Alex was dead keen that Suheil and I go out with the three sisters together. I was not too keen, but to humor Alex, I did go to a party the girls were having. Those were orange squash party days! I met the girls and their spunky friend, Yuti. I had a dance with Yuti, but that is as far as it went, as she was rather quiet.

I told Alex, "I am not going to sit here drinking orange squash." I was learning German those days, and just to show off, as I walked past Yuti, I said, "Guten nacht, fraulein," smiled at her and walked out. Alex came out a little later saying Yuti was most upset.

"What did you tell her?"

"I said good night in German. That's all I said."

"Oh, then I had better go and tell her that," said Alex. "She thought you made some smart-alecky comment."

"Please assure Yuti I only wished her good night."

The next day around noon, Alex called me from his office.

"What are you doing this evening," he asked. "Are you going out?"

This was not usually the kind of thing Alex asked. "Why?" I said. "Something up?"

"No, I just wondered. What are you doing?" Alex asked. "Yuti had called, and she wanted me to meet her."

"Really?" I said. "Wow, that's great. Is she coming to the flat?"

"No. I asked her to meet me at the Grand Hotel." So, we agreed, if Yuti were coming back with Alex, he would call me from the hotel reception, and I would disappear from the apartment.

Alex came to the apartment, spruced up and left at 3 p.m. to go to the hotel all keyed up. He replaced his Wills cigarettes with the expensive India Kings brand to impress Yuti and off he went. I waited for Alex to call me, but no call came. Finally, around 5 p.m., Alex came stomping into the apartment.

What happened?" I asked. "Did Yuti not show up?"

"No, she came." "Then what happened?"

"She does not want to see me. She wants to meet you," said Alex.

I burst out laughing. "But yesterday she thought I was abusing her in German," I said. "Where is she?"

"She is waiting at the end of the road for you," Alex said.

I quickly changed and went downstairs to the end of the road. Yuti was standing there looking very nervous. "Hello," I said. "Why did you not tell me directly yourself?" I asked.

"I was nervous," she said honestly.

I brought Yuti back to the apartment and calmed her down.

Thereafter, Yuti would often come to the apartment; she was the first girl I truly had a relationship with. The relationship didn't last very long. I shall always remember Yuti with very fond memories.

Alongside the love trysts, University life continued. At Calcutta University, in those years, the exams were always delayed, and a three-year curriculum almost always extended to four years. My final BA exams in political science were held in November 1976 and went off without a hitch with fairly limited studying. After the Political Science papers were done with, I got myself half a bottle of rum, assuming that Deepak, Suresh or Jyoti would partake in the celebrations. But none of them did. What the heck, I downed the whole bottle of rum myself.

I am not quite sure what happened afterward, but I could not stand for the next three days; every time I did so, I felt giddy. I had to get special permission and do my subsidiary papers lying in bed! I finally graduated with a BA in mid-1977. Following graduation, whilst looking for a job, I spent time between Tikratoli and Calcutta

In late 1976, whilst home for the holidays in Ranchi, some friends visited. They brought a friend with them from Calcutta called Barfi. We got along from the minute I set eyes on her; she was an Irish Bengali and very cute.

I took her for a walk outside Tikratoli. As the sun set, we walked hand in hand, as if we had known each other for years. We decided to meet when I returned to Calcutta.

On New Year's Eve 1976, Suheil managed to get a car from his friend Mayank, an Ambassador, with a full tank of petrol. Suheil and Udit were sitting at the back. I was driving with Barfi beside me. Udit and Suheil had a bottle of rum at the back, which they kept swigging from.

It was about 11:30 p.m. when we reached the Ballygunge Club a strictly ticketed event, with all the tickets having been sold out. We arrived at the barrier specially set up for the evening and were stopped by the Gurkha guard.

Suheil got out of the car and barked at the Gurkha, "Don't you recognize me? I am Captain Chatterji."

"Sorry, Sir," said the Gurkha.

"Don't say sorry. Lift the barrier," he said.

"Yes, Sir," said the Gurkha and with a salute he let us inside the club.

Udit and Suheil immediately went about finding someone to buy us drinks, and the drinks soon arrived. Around 12:30 a.m., Suheil came to me and asked me whether I wanted another drink, and I said yes.

"But who is going to sign?" I asked. Cash service was not allowed.

"Just wait," said Suheil and proceeded to order two whiskeys and a packet of India Kings cigarettes.

"We only have Gold Flake Kings," said the bartender.

"Okay, give me two packets," said Suheil before taking the pen and signing for the drinks and cigarettes with a flourish.

"The bartenders are on contract; they do not know or recognize any of the members," explained Suheil. Thereafter, Udit and Suheil signed for booze and food like they were going out of style.

Afterwards, Udit and I walked into the secretary's room. Udit picked up the phone and made a "lightning" call to Ghazipur and spoke to someone at home in Bhojpuri. He wanted to speak to his mother and wish her a happy New Year, but I think she was asleep.

We left Ballygunge Club around 2 a.m. and drove to the Centaur Hotel at Dumdum. I left Udit and Suheil at the Centaur and drove off with Barfi to an isolated part of the Dumdum Airport and parked the car.

We did not make love that night, but barring that, oh boy, was it a wild wild night. We came back to the Centaur to pick up Udit and Suheil around 5:30 a.m.

I took Barfi to her house, when she suddenly said, "Look at my trousers." The zipper had been ripped and was hanging to one side. She smiled and said, "Don't worry, it's only my trousers. I had a fabulous time tonight, my best ever New Year's Eve."

When we reached home, the petrol tank was empty; we had driven all over Calcutta that night and had emptied the tank.

From November 1976 to June 1977, it was like being on holiday in Calcutta, making the most of the Khairu Lane apartment. It was quite easily the most stress-free and fun period of my life, perhaps the only time when I did not have to earn a living, but I knew that time would surely come.

CHAPTER FIVE

Job Hunting

When I was in college in Calcutta, I used to often think of what I would like to do in life. I examined several options.

My mother tells me that when I was young, I wanted to be a railway engine driver; I was mesmerized by those guys hanging out of the railway engine, tooting their horns when they passed railway crossings. I thought that to be quite cool. At the beginning of my third year in college, I was thinking about different career options. I seriously considered joining the Merchant Navy. An uncle of mine was the director of Mckinnon and Mackenzie in Bombay. At the time, my stepfather, who was still alive, gave him a call, and he asked me to come over to Bombay for an interview.

To get to the interview, my stepfather asked someone in his Calcutta office to buy a railway ticket from Calcutta to Bombay for me. That done, my stepfather came to Howrah Station to see me off. I discovered that my name was not to be found in the first-class coach but in the AC first-class coach. By mistake, the clerk had booked me in the higher category. I went to Bombay in style!

In Bombay, I interviewed with Mckinnon and Mackenzie. I passed the interview with flying colors, the only snag being that they wanted me to pass trigonometry, which I knew nothing about. Mckinnon and Mackenzie were willing to wait a few months for me to pass the trigonometry test, but I was not going to have any of that!

Closer to graduation, I once again thought about what I really wanted to do in life. I thought of the Army but immediately decided it wasn't for me. I did consider becoming a tea planter. I had been told that as a young planter, one had a huge house to live in with several servants, the downside being that most tea planters ended up hitting the bottle, and some married their help out of sheer loneliness, none of which I wanted for my life.

I then thought about the hospitality industry and got the syllabus of the Pusa Institute of Hotel Management, New Delhi. I thought I would go into hotel management. The hitch was that people suffering from leukoderma (depigmentation of the skin) were not allowed on the course. That pretty much threw cold water on that one.

Meanwhile, back in Calcutta, Alex, Suheil, and I frequented the Oberoi Grand Hotel every other day to have a beer or drink, mostly courtesy Alex, and sometimes, Suheil. It had become a ritual. The Chowringhee Bar at the Grand Hotel was an upmarket bar, tastefully done, with a piano in one corner.

Alex was a big drinker; I was always playing catch up with him and could never match him drink for drink, but I was not ready to admit that. One day, when Suheil had dropped by, the conversation turned to booze, and Alex told me that I could not hold my drink. That got me going, and a lively debate ensued as to who could drink more. To put this to the acid test, it was decided that we would go to the Chowringhee Bar and have a drinking contest.

The rules of the contest were that Alex would pay for the drinks, and if it were a draw, or if Alex won the contest, I would recompense Alex over a period.

To keep a neutral eye on the contest, our good friend Suheil was made the drinking referee, but he would not be allowed to drink that evening since money was short. As per the contest rules, the drinking session would start with an alcoholic cocktail, to be followed by a large bottle of beer, to be followed by hard spirits, 60 ml each of rum, vodka, gin, brandy, and whiskey.

So, the three of us set off for the Chowringhee Bar. We started, as we had agreed, with an alcoholic cocktail; I had a planter's punch, and Alex opted for a Bloody Mary. That was followed by a bottle of beer each. Thereafter, we graduated to 60 ml spirits; it was decided that we could have the spirits in any order as long as the drink was not repeated. I was on my first spirit when I noticed a man sitting at the bar who was intentionally being ignored by all the waiters. I called the captain, Mr. Majumdar, and asked him why the man was not being served.

"His name is Mr. Romi. He comes in here regularly, gets drunk, and does not pay his bill," he told me. "So that's why we do not serve him alcohol." I looked at the man and told Mr. Majumdar to give Mr. Romi a large whiskey and that I would pay for it. A whiskey was put in front of Mr. Romi, and he was told that I had bought him a drink. We raised glasses and toasted. A little while later, I saw that Romi's glass was empty and asked the captain to give Mr. Romi another round. Romi came up to me and asked me my name and where I was from. Having established my lineage, he turned around and said, "You come from an established family, young man. What are you doing with yourself?"

"I have just finished my BA and am looking for a job."

"What kind of a job do you want?"

"Any kind, Sir, in a company," I replied. "Please give me my briefcase," Romi said. "Open it. Take out those photos and tell me which one you like."

One photograph was of tramlines crisscrossing each other; the other was of an old building. I was unsure of what I could possibly like in those photographs.

"Young man, I am about to build a large building. Which of these two sites do you prefer?" he asked.

I explained to Romi that at the moment Alex and I were in a drinking contest.

"Why don't you join me at the Calcutta Club tomorrow for some Bloody Mary and lunch?" Romi asked.

By this time, Alex and I were on the last round of spirits, and the contest was beginning to get a bit noisy, but it was evident there was not going to be a single winner that evening, so Alex decided to call it a draw. I was okay with that, as I realized I could not have managed much longer anyway.

As we were breaking up, Romi came up to me and said, "Young man, now it's my turn to buy you a drink, at Prince's, the fine dining restaurant at the Grand Hotel."

I readily agreed and trotted off with Romi to Prince's, and Alex and Suheil retired to the coffee shop to have something to eat.

At Prince's, I ordered a Brandy Alexander, in line with keeping each drink different that evening. "Get the young man whatever he wants," Romi told the barman. "I will be back in a jiffy."

The live band that was playing at Prince's had taken a break. I could see them walking back to the floor. Romi went up to the crooner in his crisp white kurta pajamas and started talking animatedly with her. The next thing that happened was that Romi grasped the microphone, switched it on, and started singing in an offbeat, slurry voice.

When I saw this happening, I gulped down my drink and decided that I needed to get the heck out of there before this guy made a total monkey of himself. I was not sure whether he had the money to pay for the drinks or not; I didn't care.

I went to the coffee shop to find Alex having a beer, "I won the contest," he said, "because I had a beer after you left."

"Not so fast, Alex. I just had a Brandy Alexander. We are back to a draw."

The entire evening, Suheil, who was keeping count of the drinks, kept telling us how unfair we had been in keeping him out of the contest, and we should not repeat it in the future. The more we drank, the more we chided Suheil, who told me that he had just about had enough of us that night.

We were walking back toward the lobby and were passing the Chowringhee Bar when Suheil slipped on something and fell on his right toward me. I took Suheil's weight on my left shoulder and tried to prevent myself from falling backward toward the glass windowpane; involuntarily, I put up my right hand to break my fall. The big steel *kara* or bangle that I was wearing on my right hand hit the glass pane. The next second there was a sound like a bullet, a loud bang. I ended up sitting on the two-foot-high ledge, bleeding from deep cuts and gashes, covered with shards of glass. The glass windowpane, four feet by seven feet, was completely shattered. All the alcohol that I had drunk instantly left me.

Fortunately, the cuts and gashes were not life-threatening; it looked far worse than it was. I brushed off the glass on my clothes and was walking out of the hotel when the lobby manager came running up to us.

"You cannot leave, Sir," he said.

"Why not?"

"You have broken the glass. It's very expensive!"

"How much does it cost?" I asked.

"I do not know."

"If you do not know what it costs, what do you expect me to do? I have to go to the hospital right now."

Alex interjected and said that we would return to the hotel at 6:30 p.m. the next day and meet the general manager. With that, we left the Grand Hotel.

It was 2 a.m. by the time we left. I jumped onto a rickshaw, went home, and went to sleep. I did not think the gashes and cuts were deep enough to warrant immediate attention.

I was woken up the next morning by the shrill sound of the telephone ringing. I picked up the phone and heard someone I knew but whose voice I could not immediately place.

"Is that Bablu?" spoke the voice.

"Yes, it is." "Are you okay, Bablu?"

"Yes, I am."

"Are you really okay?" the voice asked again. By this time, I recognized the caller as Viki, my first cousin. "Yes, I am okay, Viki, but why do you ask?" I said, a little puzzled.

"Well," replied Viki, "I got a call from Grandmother (that is, my step father's step mother) this morning. Apparently, Romi had arrived at their house at 4:30 a.m. and woke them up. He told them that he was with you at the Grand Hotel last night. He said that you ended up in fisticuffs with someone and that you had been thrown through a glass window and had lost your right arm, and you were bleeding profusely."

Viki continued, "Romi said he saw this himself. Grandmother did not believe him and told him, 'Romi, you are drunk. Go to sleep.' But at 6:30 a.m., Romi woke her up again, insisting that he was not drunk. 'Your grandson has met with a serious accident and has lost his arm,' he said. I was called and asked to go from hospital to hospital, looking for you," explained Viki.

I downplayed the events of the evening and told Viki that it was, in fact, Romi who was drunk. I did walk through a large glass pane at the Grand and had suffered some minor injuries, but nothing serious. Viki went and relayed the message to Grandmother.

At 6:30 p.m., Alex, Suheil, and I walked into the Grand Hotel. They were waiting for us. The lobby manager followed us to the coffee shop and saw Alex having a beer while I sipped on a cup of tea.

"What, at it again?" he said. "I have been told how much you boys drank last night. You will have to pay for the glass pane."

"How much does it cost?" I asked. "Without labor, it comes to INR 850. Would you mind paying for the damages you caused?"

"Yes, I do mind," I said.

"What do you mean you mind? You broke the glass pane because you were drunk."

"Glass pane?" I asked. "Really, is there a glass pane there? I did not see anything. Did you write, 'Glass, do not walk through'?"

"No, of course not. It's glass; everyone can see that."

"I did not, and you did not caution me by writing a warning.

Now, you need to pay my medical bills instead. Please fix a meeting with your general manager. Tell him I am not going to pay for the damages; instead, you have to pay my medical expenses."

With that, the three of us walked out. I was never charged or asked to pay a single cent toward the damages. This was one of my early lessons in life; I came to know firsthand that, if you challenge with authority you get results.

As you can imagine, I did not go to the Calcutta Club for some Bloody Mary and lunch with Mr. Romi. I really did not wish to work for a total nutcase. However, I did find out that Romi was once a genius, who had headed a very prestigious tea company in Calcutta when he was in his early 40s before he went totally off the rails. He was admitted to the Institute of Psychiatry in Ranchi, which was once, one of the biggest mental asylums in the country.

On one occasion, he escaped from the asylum, arrived at the Ranchi railway station and put a gun to the stationmaster's head. He did not allow the Ranchi–Howrah overnight train to depart for 10 minutes, all along holding the gun to the stationmaster's head, telling him that he had just escaped from the loony bin and would not hesitate to kill him if the train moved. After 10 minutes of intense drama, he jerked the gun away from the stationmaster's head and pulled the trigger, which released soapy bubbles!

"Fooled you, fooled you!" said Romi. "That was a joke."

I do not think that the stationmaster saw it that way at all! Some five years later, I heard that Romi had hung himself from a ceiling fan and died.

Other than the Grand Hotel, the other place Alex, Suheil and I used to frequent regularly was Flury's, the famous café on Park Street. Flury's was a great place to meet; it was at the corner of Park Street and Middleton Row where the girls from Loreto College would emerge and was, therefore, a good vantage point for us.

We started going there so often that we got friendly with the waiters. One day, Suheil asked me if I would like some chicken sandwiches. That was followed by some pastries and coffee.

"How are we going to pay for this?" I asked Suheil.

"Don't worry, it's all under control," he said. He had worked out an arrangement with the waiters whereby we could eat and drink whatever we wanted and walk away with paying only 50% of the billable charges! While this was great fun, it only lasted for a few months as the owner cottoned on!

Meanwhile, amidst all this revelry, the search for employment continued.

CHAPTER SIX

Sea Land, Tehran, Iran

In my search for a job, various friends and family tried to help. This included my paternal uncle Naresh. I was in Delhi for a few days and Uncle Naresh was trying to persuade me to get a corporate job.

"How about hotel management with ITC?" he asked.

"I can give it a try," I said.

"I will speak to Ajit, my university batch mate tomorrow," he said.

Next evening, when I met Uncle Naresh, I asked him if he had spoken to Mr. Ajit.

"Yes, I did," he said. "It was rather embarrassing. I have not seen Ajit since Benares Hindu University (BHU), 40 years ago. I did not know what to say, so I just said, 'Ajit, what happened to the girl you used to chase at BHU?' You know some light banter to break the ice! He replied, 'She became my wife, Naresh, and has been for 35 years now!'"

Needless to say, I did not get the ITC job.

I went back to Calcutta and met up with my local guardian, Mr. Khokhan Bose. Uncle Khokhan, as I knew him, was a confirmed bachelor, a great person, with his feet firmly planted on the ground. I would often visit him whenever I was at a loose end for a drink or just to be with him to talk about my job search woes.

In those years, I had just discovered booze. Uncle Khokhan used to serve me either whiskey or rum, which I would greatly relish. His younger brother, Baby Bose, was a flamboyant man with a handlebar mustache. Uncle Baby was married to a Turkish lady. Each time I went to the Bose household, Uncle Baby would try to goad me into going abroad to work. "The best time of my life was when I was in Paris," he would say. "If I were you, I would go to Iran."

"What would I do in Iran?" I asked.

"Work there," said Uncle Baby.

"Where would I work? Who would give me a job?"

"I will ask my agent in Tehran, Mr. Sharni Chopra, to give you a job. You can travel all over Iran selling bicycles."

"Where will I stay in Tehran?"

"You will stay with Sharni in his house. You have nothing to worry about. They will take good care of you."

Uncle Baby used to work in those years for Sen Raleigh; they used to export bicycles to Iran, to Mr. Sharni Chopra, who generated good business for them.

"The Iranian girls are great looking. You will have a wonderful time. Even if you do not find a job, sweep the streets if you have to. That is what I used to do in Paris and look at me now."

I was sold on the idea of going to Iran. My head was spinning with pretty Iranian girls, and the idea of selling bicycles in the desert quite appealed to me.

My final year BA exams were held in June 1977. Thereafter, I went to Ranchi and announced to my mother that I was going to Iran to work. My mother thought that I would get over the idea and did not deter me from going. She believed that just like a hangover, the idea would diminish and go away in time.

Around this time, my brother-in-law to be, Mr. Ajai Chowdhry, had started a computer hardware manufacturing and marketing company in Delhi, along with five of his colleagues from DCM Data Products. Mr. Shiv Nadar, who was married to my first cousin, Guddu, headed the company.

Ajai asked me whether I would like to work for HCL. I said I would think over it, but he urged me to at least come for an interview. An interview was arranged for me in Delhi, which was a piece of cake, and I passed quite easily. The second phase was some kind of a psychoanalysis test wherein we had to complete sentences by filling in the blanks.

"On a Sunday afternoon, I..."

"Like to have a bottle of beer," I wrote. Whatever stupid thoughts came into my head, I wrote down.

This was reported to Ajai, who went and told my sister (they were not married then), "Look what kind of answers your brother wrote!"

In spite of the strange answers, I got through the interview. The next round comprised a group discussion. It was dead easy; since most of the other boys kept their mouths shut!

I qualified for the third round of interviews conducted by Mr. Subhash Arora.

"Why do you want to join marketing?" he asked me.

"I don't really," I said. "Then what are you doing here?"

"I was asked to come for the interview."

"What kind of a job do you want?"

"In administration."

"But this is a marketing position interview."

"I am not interested in this position," I said and walked out.

When Ajai heard that, he was even angrier. The point was that I had no intention of working for HCL, so I was making up answers to all the questions as they came along, thinking they would reject me. I just wanted to put the HCL chapter behind me, which I did, with finality.

At Ranchi, I would spend a lot of time with my stepfather's brother-in-law, Brigadier Dilip Chaudhuri, who, incidentally, was also my godfather. Brigadier Dilip Chaudhuri was the "Colonel" of CIH, and my father had asked him if he would become my godfather. This discussion, I assume, must have occurred over several rounds of drinks. Brigadier Dilip Chaudhuri agreed, and I became his godson.

Little did either of us know that in a few short years, destiny would bring us together. Brigadier Dilip Chaudhuri, Uncle Dilu as I knew him, and his wife, Aunty Tunu, had retired at Ranchi. They had built a large house, one kilometer from Tikratoli. Whenever I visited Ranchi, and I was on my own, I would go across to their house, Kolambi, for dinner. Uncle Dilu would always keep a bottle of Sea Pirate rum handy for me.

Uncle Dilu was fascinating. He would captivate everyone with his stories of life in the British Indian Army and subsequently in the Indian Army. He had the distinction of being in the first batch of the Indian Military Academy in 1934, his IC (India Commission) number was 20. His elder brother General J.N. Chaudhuri, (Muchu), led the annexation of Goa to the Union of India, on 19th December 1961, setting the sun on 451 years of Portuguese rule in India, in an armed action called Operation Vijay. General Chaudhuri went on to become the Chief of Army Staff, India, and was the Chief, in 1965, during the India-Pakistan war in which my father was critically wounded. My father was commissioned in the Indian Army in December 1948, he was in the third course of the Indian Military Academy, his IC number was 3959.

In August 1977, I had made up my mind to go to Iran to sell bicycles. I made the announcement to my mother and Uncle Dilu. My mother gracefully agreed to give me 8,000 rupees, the cost of an air ticket from Delhi to Iran.

I went to Delhi and asked Uncle Kenny's wife, Meena (my aunt), to help me get a visa for Iran. At that time, there was nothing known as a visitor visa for Iran. I went to meet the Iranian ambassador in New Delhi, along with my aunt, Mrs. Meena Singh. The ambassador asked me why I wanted to go to Iran. I said I wanted to just look around and perhaps travel through Iran to Turkey and on to the UK. I got my visa for Iran!

Off I went to Uncle Baby and told him that I had a visa and a ticket for Iran. Uncle Baby told me that in all probability he would be going to Tehran, too, and I could go with him. So, that's how I arrived in Tehran, in tow with Uncle Baby and the export manager from Sen Raleigh, Mr. Roy Chaudhry.

Mr. Roy Chaudhry was a pain. During the flight, he continually questioned me about why I was going to Iran, whether I had a job in hand, whether I had made any prior inquiries about job prospects, and whether I had any special skills. I told him that I had done none of these and he said, "Look at me. I could easily get a job as I have a pilot's license, but you do not even have that."

I told him I had a driver's license. Mr. Roy Chaudhry was not amused by my rejoinder.

All in all, even before I had landed at Tehran International Airport, I was feeling very depressed, wondering whether I had made a monumental mistake by borrowing 8,000 rupees from my mother, who could ill afford to give me the money at that time.

Upon arrival in Tehran, we were met by Mr. Jessie Chopra (Sharni's younger brother), who came in a white Mercedes. Uncle Baby introduced me to Jessie. "Sanjiv is the person I had spoken to Sharni about."

I had been led to believe that I was going to stay with the Chopra`s. I assumed that is what would happen when I got into the car. All I had was USD 300 in my pocket. I was quite worried, what with all the things I had heard from Mr. Roy Chaudhry. Jessie stopped the car about 20 minutes from the airport, in front of a hotel, and said that I would be staying there.

"What about Uncle Baby and Mr. Roy Chaudhry?"

"They will be staying at a hotel just down the road from here."

So, here I was in Tehran, thinking that I had a job and would be staying with the Chopra's, but was summarily dumped at a hotel. I checked into the hotel, which cost me USD 60. It came as a rude shock, as all I had with me was USD 300.

For dinner that day, my first meal in Iran, I ate at a Korean restaurant in the hotel. For the first time in my life, I had kimchee. Interesting dish, I thought, but so expensive!

The dinner cost me USD 25. Before the night was out, I was down to USD 215. Boy, was I depressed?

I made inquiries at the front office for cheaper accommodation. Someone recommended a working persons' hostel not too far away. The next day I went to the hostel and made inquiries on whether they had any vacancies.

On hearing that they did, I rushed back to the hotel, checked out of there and checked into the hostel. Here I was in a room of six boys, five of whom were from India. The room had three double-decker steel beds. I opted for a top-deck bed, which, luckily for me, was empty.

It was a bit like perpetually sleeping on a train, the advantage being that one could sit up quite comfortably. We were not allowed to cook in the room; neither were we allowed to bathe in the restroom down the corridor. Showers were provided in the *hammam*, which cost 10 cents!

For the next three days, I had all my meals at Uncle Baby's hotel, where I had to listen to Mr. Roy Chaudhry's nonstop nonsense.

In all the time that I was in Tehran with Uncle Baby, neither of the Chopra brothers spoke to me about a job; all they told me was not to worry. However, the more they said that the more I worried!

To be on the safe side, I booked my return ticket on the same flight as Uncle Baby on BOAC. Uncle Baby, with due credit to him, advised me that I should sweat it out. "Life is not a bed of roses, things will eventually work out, the Chopras will help..." he said.

On Uncle Baby's last day in Tehran, Sharni Chopra invited him and Mr. Roy Chaudhry to lunch at the Maharaja, an Indian restaurant. I was at the hotel and tagged along for the lunch; my bags were packed and ready to go. My ticket and passport were with me for my flight to Delhi, scheduled at 6:30 p.m.

While we were having lunch, Sharni Chopra mentioned that Maharaja Captain Amarinder Singh of Patiala was sitting across the room. My ears perked up as my family knew the Maharaja of Patiala. I got up and went across to the Maharaja; he was having lunch with three other people. I introduced myself, referring to my late father, my mother, and my uncle, who was very friendly with Maharaja Amarinder Singh.

"What are you doing here?"

"Looking for a job," I said.

"A job? What kind of a job?"

Then my Iranian story unfolded. I told the Maharaja that I had come to Tehran looking for a job and sheepishly asked him if he could help me.

Maharaja Amarinder Singh turned around and introduced me to Sardar Sahni and asked him if he could help me with finding a job. Sardar Sahni briefly asked me what I was doing earlier. I told him I had just graduated from college in Calcutta and was looking to join a company in Tehran.

"Can you type?"

"No," I said. "Can you send a telex on tape?"

"No."

"Fine. Please come and meet me on Monday in my office, and I will see what I can do."

The Maharaja of Patiala asked me to come to his hotel in the evening for a drink. "Come to the Hilton at 7 PM tonight," he said.

There went my plans to fly back to Delhi that evening. I could not be at the airport and the Hilton at the same time!

I went back to Uncle Baby and told him what had happened. "You must stay and see this through. Sweep the streets if you have to."

Sharni Chopra was quite awed that I had met HH Patiala and that he had introduced me to Sardar Sahni. "He is a partner of Mr. Hinduja. Sardar Sahni has a direct link to the Shah of Iran. He is very powerful."

So, chuffed and excited that I had some openings, I decided to continue my stay in Tehran. I returned to the hotel and wished Uncle Baby and the creep, Mr. Roy Chaudhry, goodbye and walked back to my hostel.

At 7 p.m., I went to meet HH Patiala. He was with Mr. Khanna, his accountant. They offered me some wine. I had never had wine before in my life; I simply did not know what it was. I nervously said yes, and flowing red wine was poured into a glass and handed over to me.

HH Patiala had been invited to Tehran personally by the Shah, with the mandate of converting large tracts of desert into a green oasis of land, the supposition being that if it could happen in Punjab, why not in the deserts of Iran!

I asked HH Patiala if I could work on the project. He said that the project had not been approved and was in the nascent stages. He suggested that in the interim I should meet Sardar Sahni and see what might come of that. HH

Patiala said that he would personally speak to Sardar Sahni about me before he left.

Monday morning, I presented myself to the Hinduja office, to Sardar Sahni's chamber. He politely sat me down and said that since I did not have any office qualification it would take some time for him to find me a job and that I should come back the following week.

My stomach churned. I was down to USD 150; I had very little money.

I had no option and readily agreed to come back to Sardar Sahni's office the following week.

Being close to Sharni Chopra's office, I dropped by and met Sharni.

He said they were participating in an International Trade Fair and asked if I could help with his stall, to which I immediately replied in the affirmative.

Sharni's company was selling water pump sets and electric motors imported from the USA. I would diligently walk to the trade fair every morning and hand out leaflets to potential customers. I could not speak Farsi, but because I spoke fluent English, I, surprisingly, had no problem.

Every evening, at the end of the day, between 6 and 7, was the happy hour; free booze was provided. What could be better than that? Two or three quick whiskeys down, I would slowly walk back to the hostel and pick up something to eat, which almost always turned out to be either a burger of some sort or a piece of meat or cheese wrapped in Iranian bread. I could only afford one meal a day.

For the 10 days that I worked at the International Trade Fair, Sharni did not pay me a cent. However, I was okay with that, at least I had something to do. On day two or three into the trade fair, I had asked Sharni for a loan, which he had readily given me. I took this as my payment for working, and the fact that I was not formally paid for my time at the trade fair was fine with me.

Subsequently, I asked Sharni if I could meet his father.

"Go and meet Sharni's father. He came to Iran from Punjab, and look at his sons now," Uncle Baby had said. So, I thought I might as well meet the old man; I had nothing to lose. A meeting was set for me to meet Sharni's father.

He was sitting on a *charpai* (string bed), sipping a cup of tea. He asked me if I would like some tea, and a mug of milky tea was promptly brought to me.

"I understand you are looking for a job. What kind of a job do you want?" the old man asked me in Punjabi.

I do not speak Punjabi, but I can understand the basic gist of it.

I answered in Hindi that I was looking for a job in a company. The old man asked me, "Are you willing to work with your hands? Are you willing to work hard?"

"Yes, Sir, I am willing to work hard."

"I can put you in the sawmill. You will live at the sawmill and eat with the other workers. It is hard, backbreaking work, but you will have a job."

I did not quite believe whether I had heard him right. The old man, judicious and self-made as he was, in his wisdom, was offering me a job in the sawmill as a laborer! My life in Sanawar, Calcutta, St. Xavier's, the raucous time I had had there, wine, women and song flashed past me in a flicker of a second. I had read about this in books, but it sure as hell was happening to me right there and then, sipping milky tea, listening to the old man giving me worldly advice.

"Well, what do you think? Should I tell the sawmill you would be coming?"

"Sir, can I just think about this for a day or two and get back to you? This is not something I was looking at."

I thanked the old man for the tea, hurriedly left, and thought to myself: "Where the heck have you arrived chum, a sawmill?" I was quite dumbfounded. Back at the hostel, I stood in front of a mirror and tried to imagine myself working in a sawmill, wearing kurta pajamas and covered head to toe in sawdust. Somehow, the picture did not fit. That was most certainly not an option!

When the trade fair ended, I went to meet Sardar Sahni to inquire if he had found a job for me, as he had promised he would. He told me that he had been very busy with his business and asked me if I could return the following week. He also said that it would be very difficult for me to get a work permit, but he would see what he could do.

After two straight meetings with Sardar Sahni, I began to realize that the man had no interest in finding a job for me. I finally asked him, "If I find a job myself, would you please help me with my work permit?"

"How will you find a job?" he asked. "You have no qualifications."

I reiterated my question: "If I do find myself a job, will you help me with my work visa?"

To this, Sardar Sahni looked at me in the eye and said, "Yes."

There was a boy from Sri Lanka, Raja, in my room at the hostel, he gave me a few tips: "Do not ask anyone where they are working, be vague in your questions, and should you get a job, do not tell anyone where you are working."

I asked him why.

"Because there are several boys like you looking for a job, and sometimes they go to the same company and offer their services at considerably lower wages than those being paid to the existing staff, thereby pulling the carpet from under the other person's feet," he replied.

Raja Ayathuray was an accountant from Sri Lanka. He and I got along well, perhaps better than the other boys because the other four boys spoke no English at all. One was working as a driver; the other three were doing some other kind of blue-collar work.

Speaking to Raja, I narrowed down my search to jobs such as advertising, shipping, freight forwarding, etc. Raja told me that he worked for a company called Sea Land, a company in the shipping industry; he did not tell me where Sea Land was or what exactly he did there.

Walking down a road in Tehran one morning, in my one and only suit, armed with my CV, I came across a brass plaque that read: Sea Land.

Oh, I thought to myself, what a coincidence. This is where Raja works, the shipping company. That was all I knew. I did not know that at that time Sea Land, Inc. was the world's largest containerized shipping company!

I wondered whether I should go in and decided that I had nothing to lose. So, I opened the door and walked into the reception.

"Yes, can I help you?" the receptionist asked in Farsi.

"Do you speak English?" I asked.

"A little," she said. "What do you want?" "I want a job," I said.

The receptionist looked me up and down and said, "Please wait here," and disappeared inside.

A few minutes later she came out and asked me to wait.

A man with closely cropped hair, wearing a light blue polo sweater and a jacket stepped out with a paper in his hand that looked like my CV, which I had handed to the receptionist moments ago.

He looked down at my CV and said, "Sanjiv Tandan Lall, where are you from? I have never heard of the name Tandan Lall."

"My name is Sanjiv Tandan. Upon my mother's marriage to Mr. Lall, I assumed my stepfather's family name and became Sanjiv Tandan Lall."

All right, Mr. Lall, tell me about yourself. What are you doing in Tehran?"

Until that time, no one had ever called me Sanjiv Tandan Lall; it had always been Sanjiv Tandan. Most people found it difficult to say my full name; it sounded a bit cumbersome. Thus, on a cloudy autumn day in Tehran, Sanjiv T. Lall was born, circa September 1977.

Is he Indian? That was my first thought about the man questioning me. I hoped not and wondered if he would believe my story.

"Are you looking for a job?"

"Yes, I am!" I replied. "Sir, if I may, who are you?" I politely asked.

"My name is Kar Sakhuja. I am the CFO of Sea Land, Iran. I think there may be an opening on the Operations side. What is your work experience? Have you worked before?"

I looked Mr. Kar Sakhuja in the eye and said, "Yes, I have worked before at an import/export company in Calcutta."

"Really? What was your job in the company?"

"Import/export, mostly export of jute and coir products."

"What was the name of the company you worked at?" Mr. Sakhuja inquired.

With a straight face, looking directly at Mr. Sakhuja, I told him that the company was called Vaikath Brothers of Calcutta.

"I have not heard of the company. What did you say the company did?"

"Import/export, mostly export of jute and coir products."

"Do you have a work permit to work in Iran?"

"No, I do not have a work permit; however, once I have a job I will get a work permit."

"How can you be so sure you will get a work permit?"

"I know some really connected people who have promised to help me with the work permit once I get a confirmed job."

"I will speak to Mr. Hans Herdingh. Why don't you drop by and meet Hans tomorrow morning at 8:30 a.m.?"

I went running out of the office, totally excited. I met Raja and told him that I had gone to Sea Land and met Kar Sakhuja.

Raja's face fell. "I told you that in confidence. How could you do this to me? Kar Sakhuja is my boss! Did you give him my name? Did you tell Kar you knew me?"

It took quite a while for me to pacify Raja. Eventually, he saw reason and relented. Once he realized that his own job was not under any threat, he was quite happy for me. He made me promise that I would not do anything stupid.

The next day, I arrived at the Sea Land office at 8:30 a.m. sharp, dressed in a suit and tie. Fortunately, the suit was not too crumpled and dirty. Mr. Hans Herdingh met me a few minutes later. A Dutchman, slim built, in early thirties, medium height, with light brown hair, Hans asked what I had been doing prior to coming to Iran. I told him I was working at an import/export company and had recently graduated.

Hans asked me if I had a work permit to work in Iran. I replied that I did not but that I could get one if I had a confirmed job, to which Hans said that was simply not possible, as Sea Land was only allowed to employ people with legal status in Iran. He went on to say that he was not willing to file my application for a work permit with the immigration authorities, as that would take far too long, and secondly, I would not get a work permit in any case, as they were only given to people with an engineering degree. Since I only had a BA, I would not get one.

I told Hans that I had a very influential connection who knew the authorities and had assured me that he would get me a work permit as long as I had a confirmed job with a company.

Hans thought about it and said he just could not take the risk of employing someone without a work permit.

I was desperate for a job. I pleaded with Hans, literally begged him to give me a chance. I told Hans, "Please give me an opportunity, just for 30 days. If I do not produce a work permit in that time, I will leave of my own accord. You will not have to fire me or anything of the kind. I will just leave on my own."

Hans must have seen the desperation and determination in my eyes and body language. I was trying to remain calm, but I do think my voice gave me away. Hans asked me why I was so desperate for a job. I told him I needed one, I had come from India, and going back empty-handed was simply not an option for me.

Hans looked at me long and hard, and said, "So if you do not have a work permit in 30 days, you will leave?"

"Yes, I will, sir, unconditionally," I said.

Hans asked me to wait for a few minutes, while he consulted the head of Finance and Administration, Mr. Kar Sakhuja, whom I had met the day before. They spoke for a few minutes, and then Kar came to me and said, "You do know that it is very difficult to get a work permit, and if you do not get one in 30 days, you will have to leave Iran."

I said I would.

Kar asked me, "Why don't you return to India? At least you have a valid visa and air ticket."

I again reiterated that going back to India at that stage was simply not an option for me anymore, and I was ready to take my chances. Moreover, I personally knew someone very high up and influential who knew the Shah of Iran himself and had assured me that he would get me a work permit once I had a confirmed job offer.

Hans asked me to wait. He returned about 15 minutes later. I was wondering what was going on, hoping that they had not changed their minds. I was so nervous sitting there, sipping a glass of water.

Hans came back with a letter, addressed to Sanjiv Tandan Lall in his hand, my appointment letter. I almost passed out in my excitement. "You will get a wage of 4,500 Iranian Riyal per month. If you do not produce a work permit within 30 days, the employment offer will be automatically withdrawn. Is that clear?" said Hans.

"Yes," I said, "it's clear to me."

"You can start tomorrow morning. Please be here by 8:30 a.m."

I thanked Hans profusely. I thanked the Iranian lady at the reception desk for offering me a glass of water and went running out of the office. I wanted to go and meet Raja and tell him that I had got a job but thought better of it, as he could get into trouble.

The first thing I did was to go and have breakfast, two eggs cooked with butter, one tomato, Iranian bread and a glass of black tea. I was famished, and it tasted so good!

At that time IRR 4,500 amounted to about INR 5,000 per month. I thought to myself it was more than what my stepfather used to draw as a director of a company in Calcutta!

I immediately went to meet Sardar Sahni. He was not in his office. I was told he never came in before 11 a.m. I waited for him till he arrived. He was a bit surprised to see me sitting there.

"I thought I had told you to come next week."

"Yes, you did, Sir, but there is a development. I have a job."

"What job? What are you talking about?" he asked me a bit suspiciously.

"I have got a job with an American shipping company called Sea Land."

"Really? How did you get the job? They are not allowed to employ anyone without a work permit."

"That's it, Sir, they have given me a job on the condition I get a work permit within 30 days. Here is the letter."

Sardar Sahni read the letter and said, "What kind of an employment letter is this? It's only for 30 days. The Immigration Department will not give you a visa if you have a job only for 30 days."

"Yes sir, that may be true, but you did assure me that if I got myself a job, you would help me get my work permit. This was the only way Sea Land was willing to give me the job offer."

"Okay, okay. Leave a copy of your letter, and I will see what I can do. It will be difficult."

"When should I come, Sir?"

"Come back next week."

The next day I reported for work at Sea Land, my first day. I was taken to Hans's room, and he introduced me to the Operations team which was headed by a beautiful Iranian lady named Brigitte and her junior, a young boy, a few years older than me, from Sri Lanka.

They showed me a whiteboard with slots; each slot had a piece of paper. Hans plucked off one piece of paper and said, "This is a container. This is the number, this is the name of the consignee, and this is the city where it is going for delivery."

Basically, the whiteboard was a container tracking board. It tracked the container from arrival in Iran by ship until delivery, and then from being an empty container until it was sent to an export company, filled and ready for export.

We would get the report from the container yard on the location of the containers; that information was then transferred to the whiteboard. It was easy to read and grasp once the container cards were correctly slotted. It was easy to identify how many containers were en route to Bandar Abbas, or Shiraz or Isfahan.

My job was to keep the container board up to date. At the end of the first day, I came back to the hostel with my right hand a little stiff from slotting cards in the whiteboard. But it felt so good to have a job.

The job itself was dead easy; there was nothing to it. The cards were written by someone else; all I had to do was to correctly position them on the board so that, at a glance, the senior management could check the inward and outward position of their containers. The manual tracking system without computers actually worked really well.

Sea Land, Iran, was full of Dutchmen. Hans's boss was from Holland, Mr. Dijksmann, and his boss, the country head of Sea Land, Iran, was also from Holland, a fine man, Mr. Mathew Quartel or Matt, as he was called.

I had very little interaction with Mr. Dijksmann but kept bumping into Mr. Kar Sakhuja, CFO, and Mr. Charles McCarthy, an Englishman, also in Finance. Charles was formerly with American Express where he had retired as Finance Director and taken up the position with Sea Land, Iran, after his retirement.

Kar Sakhuja and Charles McCarthy lived together.

I would frequently meet Kar and have a chat with him now and then. One evening, Kar invited me over to his house and offered me a drink. He produced a bottle of vodka from the freezer. I had never seen anyone ever do that. I did not know that vodka was best served chilled. I did recall that when Sharni Chopra had taken Uncle Baby out to dinner, and I had tagged along, a bottle of Russian vodka had been served in a vase of ice, which also was new to me.

So, chilled vodka with tonic was the order of the day at Kar's house and it tasted darn good. Kar told me that Charles and he had to fly to Rotterdam in a few days and asked if I would like to stay in their house. My eyes almost fell out. "And if you like, you can drive my car."

So, now I had a three-bedroom house with a swimming pool, plus a car, a Ford, and a booze cabinet stocked with Johnny Walker Black Label, all for me. Kar actually got a bottle of Black Label for me, plus, of course, several bottles of Stolichnaya Russian vodka stocked in the freezer with endless bottles of tonic water.

"We trust you," said Kar. "Please look after the house and enjoy yourself."

I was very careful from day one, so much so that I only had one drink a day and did not bring anyone over to the house. Raja came for lunch only one weekend, the second time I was housesitting for Kar and Charles.

Every Wednesday I would go and meet Sardar Sahni, who had the same reply for me: "I have been very busy, come next week." This "come next week" began to sound a bit ominous; it reminded me of "see me tonight" at Sanawar, the ruination of a good day.

Hans asked me one day, "Sanjiv, how's your work permit coming along? You do not have much time."

"It's happening, Sir," I said. "I have been told it will happen," I said with as much of a deadpan face as I could muster!

Week three, I was beginning to get a bit frustrated after "come next week" had been reiterated yet again. "Mr. Sahni, I only have 10 days to get my visa," I told him.

"I have told you I would try. I am trying. It is not easy getting a visa," he said in response.

On my way out of the office in the lift, I bumped into one of the younger Hinduja brothers who asked me why I was coming so often to meet Sardar Sahni. I told him Sardar Sahni had promised to get me a work permit.

"A work permit?" he enquired.

"Yes. That's why I keep coming here since my arrival in Iran."

"You will not get a work permit. Has a work permit even been filed and applied for?"

This shocked me. So, I went back to Sardar Sahni's office and asked him, "Sir, has my work permit been formally applied for?"

"What kind of a question is this? I told you I have been looking into this; it's not easy getting a work permit."

"But, Sir, I have not even signed any application forms, and I only have 10 days left."

"Please leave me. Can't you see I am busy? Come back next week."

I realized the futility of the whole thing; I left the office cursing Sardar Sahni. He should have been upfront with me. I could have tried some other means to get a work permit. The fact that no work permit had been formally applied for really did me in.

I knew it was very difficult to get the permit. I had inquired from the person in charge of immigration requirements at the Sea Land office. He told me what I already knew that without an engineering certificate a work permit was impossible. Engineers in Iran were called *mohandish* and given an elevated status.

I had been led on a wild goose chase by Sardar Sahni and it left me totally exhausted and angry. What angered me the most was how much I had believed in him. I was very quiet for the rest of the week; I told Raja that my work permit was not happening; he tried to cheer me up, but that only made matters worse.

The next week, I worked diligently. On Wednesday, I made my last visit to Sardar Sahni, hoping that he would pull off a miracle. It was a routine meeting, nothing different.

I returned to the office and at 5 p.m. I went and met Hans and told him, "Sir, my work permit is not happening. As per my agreement, I will not come to work on Monday." I apologized profusely for letting him down.

Hans did not say a word; he just looked at me. I was trying to talk slowly and purposefully, but, somehow, I don't think I was coherent; it was an emotionally charged moment for me. Hans told me that he had enjoyed working with me and that he would speak to Kar Sakhuja. He asked me to come the next day to clear my accounts.

I had already told Kar that I was unable to get my work permit; he knew that something was wrong but did not know the full details.

I really did not know what to do or what to say. Should I apologize to Kar for not telling him the truth up front? I thought better of it and went to his office and told him that my work permit was definitely not happening and that I had informed Hans, who had asked me to come the next day to clear my dues.

Kar asked me if I would drop by his house for a drink. "Cheer up," he said. I declined as I was far from a cheerful mood.

The next day, I dressed as usual for work and was there on the dot at 8:30 a.m., as I was every day. I saw Kar and Hans talking together and looking at me.

"Well, I guess this is it," I said to myself. "So much for Iran."

Hans asked me into his office; he looked at me and said, "Sanjiv, you have done a good job the last month; we are pleased with you. I have decided to raise your wages to IRR 5,000 per month."

I didn't quite believe what I was hearing. "But sir, I do not have a work permit. I cannot work," I said.

"I know that," said Hans. "However, we have decided to keep you without a work permit."

I jumped up from the chair and wanted to hug Hans, but I controlled myself and shook his hand, thanking him profusely.

I immediately went to Kar's office and told him that Hans had given me a raise.

Kar looked at me with a bemused smile and said, "Sometimes things do not turn out the way they look."

I do not know for certain, but I do think Kar had a big role to play in Sea Land hiring me to work permanently without a work permit. All that I was told was not to tell anyone that I did not have a work permit and to keep it to myself.

I never visited Sardar Sahni again. I was secretly harboring the thought that one day I would meet him in a dark alley so that I could punch him in the face; he had caused me a lot of pain and grief.

Now that I had become a permanent employee, albeit without a work permit, life became somewhat easier and things fell into a pattern of work and housesitting for Charles and Kar Sakhuja.

It was November 1977, my elder sister Kunkun was getting married in New Delhi. Because I did not have a work permit, I could not travel, and, as a result, I decided not to attend her wedding. I was totally charged with trying to sort my life out in Iran, so the decision not to attend my own sister's wedding was an easy one to make.

On 26th November, the day of the wedding, I purchased a bottle of Vat 69 for an in-absentia wedding celebration, along with Amarjit, a friend who had called me over for a chicken curry dinner. Amarjit and Raja, both of whom had work permits, were my two friends in Tehran. Raja was a quiet, conscientious accountant whereas Amarjit was a gregarious architect who loved to live it up. It was a great balance, though, as you can imagine, I spent more time with Amarjit.

In Farsi, girls are called *duktar* and boys, *pesar*. Amarjit would often come to me and say, "Let's do some *duktar bazi* (let's go get some girls)." Not that we could do so, but it was a good pastime thinking and ruminating that we could and what if we could.

In those years, the taxis in Tehran were Datsun Paykan, orange and white, dusty, beat-up cars, and they were driven as shared cabs. They offered a cheap and efficient way to get around.

Kar and Charles would travel to Rotterdam at least once a month, and, at times, twice a month. Each time they went away I had the run of the house. During the third time that I was housesitting, I invited Raja and Amarjit over. They were quite astounded. From a bunk-style bed to a bungalow with a pool and a bar stocked with booze!

On one occasion, I was backing Kar's Ford out of the basement garage and the rear fender nicked the landlord's old Peugeot (one with the long headlight). Just at that time, the landlord, an irate and grumpy Iranian, came down to the basement and went ballistic. He started screaming at me. The more I tried to pacify him, saying that I would pay for the headlight repair charges, the more he screamed, "You bloody Indians."

The landlord stomped off fuming, "This will cost IRR 900."

"I will pay it, it's my fault," I said.

"You do not know how to drive," and on and on the man ranted about bloody Indians.

I met Kar and Charles at Tehran Airport and drove them home. On the way, I told Kar what had happened and went on to say that the landlord got very annoyed at me and shouted, "You bloody Indians!" The moment I said that Kar got visibly upset. "Why did he say that? Why should he say that? That's got nothing to do with it. It's only a goddamn headlight, that, too, of a very old Peugeot for goodness sake."

When we got home, the Peugeot was not there. The next day I went to the landlord's house, and he gave me the bill for repair, IRR 875. I told him I would pay it the next day.

At the office, Kar asked me if the Peugeot had been fixed. I told him that it had been fixed and that I would pay the bill. "Give it to me; let me see it." I gave the bill to Kar who glanced at it and said, "Leave it here. I will take care of it."

The bill was picked up by Sea Land, and, thankfully, I didn't have to pay anything! The next day, whilst thanking Kar, he told me that the next time something like that happened, and anyone said bloody Indians, I should not take it lying down.

One day, Matt Quartel, the national manager for Sea Land, Iran, walked into the operations room, and told Hans, "It's very difficult for me to know what to do when I don't know how many containers were dropped at Shiraz over the last six weeks."

Hans said that it was difficult, though he could hazard a guess. I was standing right there, listening, and offered my help.

"How can you help?" Matt asked.

"I will pull out the old container cards and tell you," I said.

"Can you do that?" he asked.

"Yes," I said. "I can do that, but it will take some time."

"How long will it take you?" "Well," I said, "if the cards are all there, it should not take more than a day or two."

"Really? Hans, please give Sanjiv the old cards," said Matt. So, now I had a new job, finding out how many containers were dropped at Shiraz over the last six weeks. The job was laborious but dead easy; all I had to do was to find the containers destined for Shiraz over the last six weeks. Two days into the job, I went to Matt and asked him if I should categorize all the containers city-wise.

"Can you do that?"

"Yes, of course, I can."

"Can you tell me where the containers were dropped over the last six weeks?"

"Well," I said, "I should be able to go back the last six months if you want and give you a city-wise breakdown."

"Can you do a city-wise breakup for containers being loaded in Iran?"

"Yes," I said, "that's far simpler as the cities involved are fewer."

So, now I had a new mandate to give a city-wise breakdown of the container delivery in Iran, as well as a similar city-wise breakdown of the containers destined for export from Iran.

"I need a big desk to place all the container cards," I told Hans.

So, I was given an appropriate desk and all the stationery items I needed. I had never done anything like that before, but I thought to myself how difficult it could be. After all, it was just categorizing the cards.

The job was very laborious. Steel trunks, one after another, were brought to my desk. The problem was that as soon as I thought the job was finished, suddenly an old card would emerge, and I had to include and categorize that by destination, month, and year.

The job took three weeks to complete; each week I would go and give Matt a written update. He was highly impressed.

"No one has ever given me this information before. I will inform Rotterdam. I do not know if they have such a system."

Three weeks later, I compiled the detailed report in longhand because I could not type and gave it to Parveen (Matt's spunky secretary) to type.

Thereafter, life became quite good. Matt would stop and chat with me in the corridor. None of the other boys including Raja ever spoke to Matt other than to wish him "good morning".

One day, Raja asked me, "What does Matt talk to you about?"

"Nothing in particular," I replied.

In December 1977, I went up to Hans and asked him if I could be transferred to the container terminal (depot).

"Why do you want to go there? It's dirty, there is nothing to eat or drink, and whenever I go there, I leave within an hour. You will not like it there," he said.

"No Sir, I would like to go there. It's more relaxed."

"It's not all office work. You will have to spend time in the yard, checking the containers, talking to the drivers. Are you sure you want that?"

I was transferred to the container terminal that was 25 kilometers outside Tehran. It was headed by a Sikh boy from Delhi, Ranjit Singh Sanand. Ranjit would come to the head office each day with the daily update of container movement around 3:30 p.m. or 4 p.m. He would spend a few minutes and leave for the day. I kind of liked that concept and the fact that it was not a desk-bound, office job.

We had to be at the container terminal by 7 a.m. It meant I had to wake up at 5 a.m., which was fine by me as I had the washroom to myself at that time and could cheekily have a bath (which was not allowed). The company car would pick me up about one kilometer from the hostel, which meant a brisk early morning walk, which was good.

Often, I would wait for the car, which was rarely late, munching on a piece of delicious, freshly baked Iranian bread with feta cheese. For the first time, I saw the huge tractor trucks that hauled the containers.

At the terminal, there was Dawood and Mahmud and, of course, Ranjit and I. The job meant mingling with the container drivers, a rough but cheerful lot. There were some drivers from Bulgaria, huge guys, with big beer bellies, who would drive overland to Europe, and had the capacity to drive large distances without stopping.

Each container would have to be checked and re-checked for damage before it left the terminal and again on its return. On cold mornings, this was always a problem, but it had to be done.

Sometimes I got to drive the company car, a Toyota fourwheel drive. There were times when I got to keep the Toyota for the weekend. On one occasion, Raja and I drove to Tabriz, a holiday resort town on the Caspian Sea. Since neither of us was interested in spending money to stay the night at Tabriz, we had some lunch, saw the Caspian Sea, and drove back to Tehran the same day.

There were no girls to meet as such in Tehran; the only ones we saw were the ones in the office. In those years, it was more or less forbidden for a girl to be in the company of a man who was not her husband, father, or brother. If ever a girl checked into a hotel with a man, they would have to produce their marriage certificate!

Strangely enough, it was permissible for a man and woman to cohabit together as man and wife, for as little as a day with a temporary marriage license. If you wanted to have fun with a young lady, all you had to do was to get married temporarily; then you could do whatever you wanted.

A virgin girl was in high demand; all the Iranian boys wanted virgins. Coming as I did from India, this was not much of a surprise. After the nuptial night, blood-stained sheets were often displayed on the balcony as proof that the bride was indeed a virgin. I was told that this was why pig's blood was a premium commodity, as it is closest to human blood in color, tone, and texture.

As time went on, I became very friendly with Kar and Charles; they would often invite me over for barbecues or on the weekends to use their pool. Kar had a table-tennis table where we regularly played with each other. On one occasion, Kar invited several people from the office, senior management with their secretaries. I was the only young person there. My job was to man the bar and play table tennis with the young ladies. I was hugely pleased about that.

The American embassy was a big client; they would import several containers per month. I would often go to the American embassy to drop off urgent containers. They would import ice cream, cheese, and other exotic food products from America in refrigerated containers called reefers. I had never seen anything like that before. Reefers were urgent cargo; they had to be driven nonstop to Tehran from Bandar Abbas, which was the port of entry for the large container ships in Iran, a distance of almost 1,300 kilometers.

In the hostel where I stayed, there were several boys from Pakistan and a few from Afghanistan. They would tell me that it was possible for boys without legitimate visas for Iran to travel to Pakistan via Afghanistan. This was done over the Iranian mountain ranges on horseback.

On the Afghanistan border, two Afghans would take one person at a time riding on a motorcycle squashed in the middle between the two huge riders. There would be a night stop in an Afghan village. The cardinal rule was never to look at any woman in the eye. You did that, and you were history. The next day the person would continue their journey on either horseback or motorcycle, escorted by the Afghan hosts to Peshawar, Pakistan.

I actually met some boys who had taken this route to Pakistan and back to Tehran. I looked at them incredulously; they did not think much about it. For them, it had to be done, period.

It was also possible to "gatecrash" into Turkey taking the northern mountain route, being escorted by Turks. Many years later, I saw a film, Not Without My Daughter. It was the true story of an American lady who escaped to Turkey via the northern mountain land route with her young daughter.

In Iran, we could not openly talk about the Shah of Iran, Mohammad Reza Pahlavi. We were told he had secret service informers at every corner and that people got picked up at random, never to return. Thus, we tended to keep our mouths shut; see no evil, speak no evil, and hear no evil was the motto of the day.

Amarjit became a good friend; we would spend a lot of time together planning where we would go and what we would do once we left Iran, which we all knew would happen sooner or later.

By September 1978, Matt Quartel's tenure at Tehran as country manager was coming to an end. Matt had been appointed the country manager of Sea Land, Spain, and was slated to commence his tenure in Madrid in October. He had purchased a Chevrolet Blazer that he was going to drive overland to Europe with his wife and two young daughters.

Exactly two weeks before Matt left Tehran, I got a call from Parveen, asking me to stop by the office. Parveen ushered me into Matt's office. He was standing beside his table with a sheaf of papers in his hands; he looked at me and sat down.

"I don't know how to say this, so I will say it straight. The Iranian government has sent Sea Land a circular asking us to declare if we have anyone working here without a legitimate work permit or visa."

I just looked at Matt, and he went on to say, "Look, I do not want to do this, but if I don't, then I, as the country manager of Sea Land, Iran, could be hauled up. Heck, I only have another 10 days or so left in this country."

"No, Sir, of course not. I fully understand," I said, though when I said that, I had not completely understood the ramifications of this latest development. I had not quite completed one year at Sea Land, and I had been eagerly looking forward to that as it would have meant a substantial raise; unfortunately, that did not happen.

He then asked me to go and meet Kar and see if the immigration cell could resolve my problem. I immediately went and met Kar and told him I had just met Matt. He looked at me and said, "I know. Sit down."

Kar explained that there was no way that Sea Land could officially withhold information from the government. They had to divulge the truth; if there was a person working without a work permit, they had to be told.

Kar went to explain that the Shah's secret police were behind this move as they were trying to quell the uprisings that were beginning to happen in Iran. The winter of discontent had silently crept upon the Iranian people. People were unhappy with the Shah, the functioning of the government, how he ran the country, as if it were his own personal fiefdom. The secret police were checking up on the immigrant population, trying to isolate and neutralize the issues that until then had been left alone.

"We will try officially to see if we can get a work permit for you. Bring your passport tomorrow. I will personally see if this is possible," said Kar.

The next day I gave my passport to Kar who had already spoken to Ahmed, the Iranian immigration consultant. I knew Ahmed; I used to see him at the office all the time with passports of various colors in his hands. We used to acknowledge each other.

The immigration consultant told Kar that it would be difficult, but he would see what he could do. He also informed Kar that since I had already overstayed my visitor visa by almost a year, the immigration authorities would not take it lightly. "Pay whatever you have to," Kar said, "Get the work permit." He looked at the worried expression on my face, and added: "The company will pay, don't worry."

The immigration consultant said it would take three to four days and he would get back to Kar. For the next few days, I was on tenterhooks, wondering what would happen, what I should do, or not do, and where I should leave in the event my visa was declined.

On the third day, Ahmed, the immigration consultant, came back to Kar and said that it was just not possible to get the work visa; he said he had tried hard, and offered up to IRR 50,000, but no one was willing to touch the case. He said the Immigration Department had received strict instructions from the government not to regularize any person who had overstayed their visa period. He went on to say that he was surprised that this was happening.

When Kar told me the work permit could not be had, it did not come as a surprise. I was kind of expecting it.

"How will I get out of the country?" I asked Kar. "I have overstayed my welcome by almost one year."

I most certainly did not want to return to India. I could not use the Afghanistan route, as that would take me to Pakistan; the only option I had was to take the northern overland route to Turkey, across the mountains.

Kar told me that Ahmed would get me an exit visa. When Ahmed was called he said that it would be very expensive as there was a penalty for each day that one overstays. "I cannot say what the Immigration Department will say, and what it will cost," he said.

The time had come for Matt to leave and there was a small office farewell for him. I was standing at the door when he came down the hallway, shaking hands with everyone. When he came to me, he said, "Sanjiv, I am truly sorry that you have to go. If you are ever close to Madrid and looking for a job, come and look me up."

I smiled at him and shook his hand. "I might take you up on your offer, Sir."

"Yes, please do," he said.

Two days after Matt left Iran, I formally gave my passport to the immigration consultant for the exit visa. This was purposely delayed by a few days to allow Matt to leave the country.

Three days later, Kar called me. Ahmed had brought my passport back with the exit visa, and along with it, a very stiff penalty. The document was written entirely in Farsi. I could not make out a thing.

"Do I have to pay the penalty at the airport at the time of leaving?" I asked. "No, the company has already paid it on your behalf," I was told.

"Really?" I said incredulously. "Yes, really. You have worked hard for Sea Land for almost a year, that is the least the company can do for you, but sit down," Kar said. "There is one little problem."

Now what, I thought to myself.

"Have you thought where you are going to go?"

"No, Sir, I have not. I am not going to India, that's all I know."

"I think you might have to go to India."

"Why?" I asked.

"Well, your exit visa is valid only for 72 hours."

"72 hours?" I said. "What does that mean?"

"It means that you have to leave Tehran within 72 hours."

I was shocked. "But that's only three days!"

Kar looked at me and said, "Please plan carefully, you do not have much time. I will prepare your final wages tomorrow."

I had not quite turned 23, and my stint in Iran was fast coming to an end. I went back to the hostel and immediately spoke to Amarjit as he had traveled to Dubai and Turkey. I had never been anywhere.

There were not many options. I could fly to London without a visa; in those years, Indian passport holders could get a visa on arrival in the UK. Some countries in Europe were not possible without a visa per se. Turkey, I was not keen on.

I had always been kind of fascinated by Scandinavia, by the tall, beautiful blondes. That's where I wanted to go, I told Amarjit.

"Go to Moscow, and take the train from there to Helsinki. Indian passport holders do not need visas for Scandinavia. You will need a visa for Moscow, but they like Indians, you will get a visa," he said.

So that was decided, I would fly to Moscow. The next day I went to Iran Air, booked myself a one-way ticket for Moscow and went to the Russian embassy to apply for my visa.

"Apply for one week's visa for Moscow," Amarjit said. "See a bit of Moscow and then go to Finland." That was the plan.

By noon, I had submitted my application for my one-week Russian visitor visa. I was asked to come back at 4 p.m. to collect my passport.

When I went to collect my passport, I was the only person there. I met someone and gave him my visa slip; he disappeared inside the gate and came back with my passport. The visa was written in Russian.

I looked at the visa and breathed a sigh of relief; at least now things were beginning to come together. The Russian guy could not speak English. "Is my visa valid for one week?" I asked. I held up one finger; he looked at my visa and smiled, holding up his thumb.

I trotted off to meet Kar, told him the happy news that I was off to Moscow the day after next. He looked at me quite happy and said, "Well done. Come home and have a drink."

The next day I went to the bank and withdrew all my savings. I converted my entire savings of Iranian Rials into Deutsche Marks, Swiss Francs, British Pounds and US Dollars.

I went to the office after lunch and met everyone. Many people were not aware I was leaving and were wondering what was going on. I thanked Hans, Kar, and Charles profusely.

It was Fernando who moved me a bit. Fernando was a Sri Lankan boy in the shipping department. A clean-cut young man in his mid-20s. I knew Fernando but had little dealings with him.

As I was leaving the room, Fernando came to me and said, "Sanjiv, if you need any money, please let me know." I was very surprised and touched. I smiled and thanked Fernando and vigorously shook his hand.

I was almost in tears. There was pin-drop silence in the room with about 20 people standing around. By this time, Ranjit and Dawood had also arrived from the terminal. Going around shaking everyone's hands was an emotionally charged moment.

I remember Kar standing outside his office, in the polo-neck sweater he always wore, looking at me. At the door, I turned around, waved at him, and left.

My last evening in Tehran, I spent at the hostel; both Amarjit and Raja were with me while I was packing.

I had a black leather Duckback suitcase which Uncle Khokhan had given me; I had brought it with me from India. I had purchased a brown Samsonite briefcase, a fancy Casio calculator, and a blue nylon ski jacket from Amarjit.

I had two suits with me which I had brought from India. One lightweight and one heavy wool. As I did not want to carry a huge amount of stuff in my suitcase, I left the rather natty, dark navy woolen three-piece suit hanging in the closet in Tehran. I am not sure what came of it. I hoped Raja would take it.

Many years later, I met Amarjit. He said one day shortly after I had left, he went to the hostel and found the suit still hanging there. He asked Raja if he could take it for me, as he was returning to India. Raja refused, and that's where the matter ended. After that, as things turned out, Amarjit said he never went back to the hostel again.

The next morning, Raja went off to work. I never saw him again. Around noon, I took a taxi to the airport.

Amarjit came to the airport to see me off; he was really a sweet guy. We chatted about a few things; I was a bit tense wondering whether I was doing the right thing, going off to Europe.

In 1978, the rumblings of discontent with the Shah of Iran fueled events that took place all over the Middle East, which is now being played out with Syria, Iraq, Israel, Turkey, and Russia. The Arab Spring, the Afghanistan Spring, Saddam Hussein, Iraq, Osama Bin Laden, Al Qaida, Taliban, ISIS, all happened post the exile of the Shah of Iran and the storming of the US Embassy in Tehran in 1979. It was post-Tehran 1978, where it all started, and I was there. The events in Iran changed global politics forever. Working in Iran certainly changed my life.

CHAPTER SEVEN

The Great Union of Soviet Socialist Republics - USSR

It was early evening when my flight touched down in Moscow, 5th September 1978. I had been quite apprehensive and pensive throughout the flight, thinking back upon my time in Iran, and particularly, Sea Land, where I had worked. I thought about Kar, Mac, and Matt Quartel, all the people who had been so good to me, and Hans, who had given me my first job ever at Sea Land, with perhaps a little persuasion from Kar Sakhuja. I took comfort that I had my USSR visa, that I had sufficient funds to get me across USSR and Europe. The last three days in Tehran had been a bit overwhelming. I felt totally drained emotionally. I was looking forward to checking into a nice hotel in Moscow. As we walked down the steps of the aircraft, I saw a Russian guard wearing a typical Russian greatcoat and cap, standing at attention with a rifle and bayonet.

Next to him was a portly Russian lady in a blue uniform checking each passenger's passport and boarding card.

When my turn came, the lady glanced at my passport and asked me to step aside, which I did. Slowly all the passengers walked inside the terminal building; I was the only passenger left standing on the tarmac. The Russian lady asked me to follow her to the terminal. As we passed through the double-glazed doors of the terminal building, the lady asked me to wait there and disappeared. A few minutes later a person came to me, saying he was the Persian translator. Whilst I could speak pidgin Farsi it was nowhere the fluency required for this interaction. I requested for an English translator and waited there.

I could see the passengers queuing up at the immigration counter. 15 minutes later, all the passengers had cleared immigration, and I was once again on my own. About 10 minutes later, the English translator arrived and asked me what I was doing in Moscow; I told him I was going to Helsinki.

"How will you go to Helsinki?" he asked.

"By train," I said.

"Do you have a train ticket to Helsinki?"

"No," I said. "I thought I would spend a few days in Moscow and purchase a ticket for Helsinki. What is the problem? Why are you not allowing me to go through immigration?"

"Your visa for Russia is only for one day, and you do not have a train ticket to Helsinki, so that is the problem," the interpreter replied.

"Can I buy a ticket to Helsinki today?" I asked worriedly.

"Yes, you can," he said and walked me to the immigration counter.

I cleared immigration, with leave to stay for just one day in Moscow. I really did not know what was happening and just wanted to get the heck out of the airport as fast as I could.

Having cleared immigration, I now arrived at Russian customs. There was a customs inspector wearing a dark navyblue uniform. I was asked to put my bag on the big stainlesssteel table.

The customs inspector spoke fluent English. He asked me if I had anything to declare, such as narcotics, drugs, pornographic material, arms, ammunition, etc. I answered "no" to each question he asked.

"Have you filled in the currency declaration?"

"Yes," I said and gave it to him.

He looked at all the currencies that I had listed and asked me where I was going. I told him I was going to Helsinki.

"Open your bags, please," he said, and asked again, "Do you have anything to declare? Any pornographic material?" I again said "no".

The customs inspector lifted the lid of my suitcase and stuck his hands on either side of it, digging in deep. Oh my God, I thought, I hope he does not find the Playboy Calendar, and sure enough, the inspector pulled out the one thing that I should not have brought with me to Russia, the Playboy Calendar 1978.

The customs inspector looked at the calendar. I could see his eyes lighting up in an otherwise expressionless face. He leafed through the calendar slowly, page by page.

By this time, he was joined by another customs inspector, who said something to him in Russian. The other inspector then leafed through the calendar. Then they were joined by another customs official, who again leafed through the calendar. Later, the three customs officers were joined by their superior officer. I could make out the inspectors' seniority by the number of stripes on their sleeves, and this last guy seemed to be the most senior.

All this time I was standing upright in my lightweight suit and tie, trying to remain calm. I remember ripping off my bag tag from behind my boarding pass and crunching it in my hands. It looked like the entire Russian customs service was standing in front of me, glaring at me.

The senior inspector took the calendar and looked at each playmate carefully, as if studying her. Midway through the calendar inspection, he asked me in perfect English, "Is this your personal property?"

"Yes, Sir, it is my personal property."

"Is it for sale?"

"No, Sir, it is my personal property, it is not for sale. As you can see, the pages for the months of January and February have been ripped off. Even if I wanted to sell it, it would not be possible."

He looked up at me. "Okay," he said flippantly, "you are free to go."

With that the customs inspector just walked away, leaving me to put my belongings together.

I threw the calendar into the bag, shut it and hurriedly went to the exit. The guard on duty asked for my bag tag. "Billet billet," he kept saying.

For the last 30 minutes, I was the only person in the customs hall. The guard must have seen me, as I was in full view; yet, he insisted on me giving him the bag tag. I looked around for the customs inspectors. I could see them in the far distance talking amongst themselves; one of them was looking at me.

Just then I remembered I had thrown the bag tag into the dustbin adjacent to the customs table where I was standing. I pointed to the dustbin, and half walked, half ran to the bin. I could not find the bag tag. So, I upturned the dustbin; it was more or less empty. The guard came running after me and started bellowing in Russian, literally shoving his bayonet against my back. Just in the nick of time, I found my bag tag, totally crumpled, but I had it. I showed the bag tag to the guard, put all the rubbish back into the trash can and walked out of the customs hall.

By this time, it was going to be six pm, so I went straight to the money changer as I needed rubles. I changed a couple of hundred dollars into rubles and asked the lady where I needed to go to buy a train ticket. She told me that I should go to the Hotel Metropole, City Center, but I should hurry as the ticket office closed at 6:30 p.m.

"If the city office is closed you must go to the Moscow Oktiabrskaia railway station and tell them you want to go to St. Petersburg. From the City Center, take a metro, as that's the only way you will make it. The ticket office at Moscow Oktiabrskaia station closes at 7 p.m., so you must hurry," she explained.

I asked the lady, who was very helpful, to write the address of the Moscow Oktiabrskaia railway station and the City Center in Russian and hurriedly left the terminal building looking for a taxi.

I found a taxi right outside. I told the driver to go to the Metropole Hotel railway booking office; he said he knew where it was. The driver asked me where I was from and when I said India, he started saying, "Gandhi, Nehru, wonderful."

"Yes," I responded, "wonderful. Please drive fast."

Then he started on Raj Kapoor and began to croon a song from one of Raj Kapoor's films. Please drive fast was all I could think about.

When we got to the railway reservation center at Hotel Metropole, shortly after 6:30 p.m., it was closed. I asked the railway reservation clerk, behind the closed counter, where the closest metro station was; he pointed right across the large square. So, I set off, half running, half walking with my suitcase and briefcase in tow. I entered the metro building and saw people just rushing past me; they would drop something into a box and continue. There was a Russian man sitting in a tiny room with a dimly lit bulb. I tried to tell him that I wanted to go inside, and he kept gesticulating for me to go. I, in turn, kept asking him for a ticket.

"Billet, billet," I kept saying.

Not making much headway, I pulled out the rubles and small change I had from my pocket and shoved it under the steel grill. He took the smallest possible coin, equivalent to five cents or five kopeks and pointed for me to drop it in the box and continue. I did just that.

I had now entered the metro. I was standing at a fork: one tunnel was going to my left and another to the right; I did not know which one to take. I pulled out the railway station address written in Russian from my pocket and tried to stop a couple of people, but no one did; they just brushed me aside and continued walking.

I saw a young couple walking, holding hands. I stepped in front of the man and pushed the slip of paper in front of his face; he merely brushed my hand aside, side-stepped me and continued walking. I stood there looking helpless. I saw the couple stop, the girl was talking to the man, and they kept looking at me. The girl let go of the boy's hand, came toward me and said something in Russian. I replied in English and showed her the piece of paper I had in my hands. By this time her friend had also joined us. They briefly spoke to each other and indicated I follow them. With my suitcase and briefcase once again in tow, I hurriedly ran after them and got into the train.

I kept telling them that I had to be at the railway station at 7 p.m.

We changed trains twice and arrived at Moscow Oktiabrskaia railway station at 7:10 p.m. Now, the boy took charge; he took me by the hand to the ticket counter; it was still open. He had a conversation with the person behind the counter, but they said a railway ticket was not possible as the counter was closed. We went to the officer's room, where the boy tried to reason with the officer. I took out my passport and gesticulated repeatedly that if I did not get a train ticket that day, I was finished. I indicated this by running my hands across my throat.

The girl tried to pacify me, but I was quite agitated and did not know what to do.

"You Hindi?" the boy asked me.

"Yes, I am Hindi," I replied.

When I finally understood that a ticket was not possible that day, I told the girl, "Please take me to a hotel. I will pay for the taxi," and pulled out the money I had; she just smiled at me and put the money back in my pocket.

We took a taxi and arrived back at Hotel Metropole, where I was earlier that evening. I noticed a long line of people trying to enter the side entrance of the hotel. The young couple and I entered the lobby and I approached the reception desk. I asked them if they spoke English, they said they did. I breathed a sigh of relief and asked them if they had a single room available.

"Yes, we do. May I see your passport?" I gave them my passport, but the receptionist looked at it and said, "I am sorry. I cannot help you."

"Why?" I asked, confused. "You said you had rooms available."

"You do not have a reservation; you must have a reservation prior to arrival."

"But you have rooms available. I am here now, so please give me a room!"

"I am sorry, Sir, we cannot do that."

The couple came up to me, looking very sorry for me. I must have looked totally flustered and dejected. By this time my tie and shirt were in total disarray, and I am sure I looked a complete mess.

"You Hindi?" the boy asked again.

"Yes, I am Hindi," I replied, unable to think of what to do next. We got into a taxi and off we went somewhere. We entered a good locality. I could make out by the smart buildings and walkways.

Suddenly, the taxi stopped in front of a building with iron spikes on the walls and I saw the Indian tricolor flag; we were standing in front of the Indian embassy. The young Russian couple, bless their souls, had brought me to the Indian embassy.

I got out of the taxi, spoke to the guard in Hindi and asked him if I could go inside. He said the embassy was closed, but I insisted it was important for me to go inside and he allowed me. Once inside, I found a couple of the clerical staff drinking milky tea. They told me the embassy was closed and that I should come back the next day. "No, I have to meet the consul," I said. "It's very important."

I suddenly remembered the Russian couple in the cab. I went outside to thank them for bringing me to the embassy, only to find they had quietly left the taxi and gone away. The taxi driver said that as soon as I went inside the embassy they had walked away. I had not even thanked them. I ran to the top of the road, but I could not see them anywhere. In a way, the young couple, I do not even know their names, had saved my life, that of a total stranger. I still remember the young girl's pretty face, curly long hair and blue eyes and her handsome boyfriend.

I walked back to the embassy with my suitcase and briefcase and again requested that I meet the consul. The drivers offered me a cup of tea, which I had. I asked them to connect me with an officer, which they did. I explained my position, that I had arrived in Moscow without prior hotel reservations and without a connecting train ticket to Helsinki and that my visa was due to expire at midnight. The person asked me to come back to the embassy the next day.

"Where will I sleep?" I asked. "I do not have a hotel. Can I sleep in the embassy on the sofa?"

"No, that is not possible. It is against the law," he said.

"So where do I go, then? If you will not allow me to sleep on the sofa and I do not have a hotel, where should I go? Sleep on a park bench?" I asked.

"You cannot do that," said the drivers and the guards.

"The Russian police will pick you up." I told the officer that I would not leave the embassy till they had made alternative arrangements. The drivers by this time had brought me a blanket; it was beginning to get cold. I had also not eaten anything since I had left Tehran. I was famished.

At 10 p.m., someone called Mr. Sharma, who was the embassy's Russian translator, spoke to me on the phone. I again retold my full story. He said he would see what he could do. 45 minutes later, he called to say that the embassy had found a room for me at a hotel.

He said I should go to the hotel and come back to the embassy in the morning. A taxi was called, and I was taken to the hotel, which I was told was the single largest hotel complex in the world; it certainly went on forever. Block F was found, where a mother and daughter were managing the front office and were expecting me.

I paid for my room in full and was taken up in an old rickety lift. The room was large and comfortable, but the toilet was down the corridor. But, hey, at least I had a room for the night. Oh boy, I thought, what a night!

I was both emotionally drained and physically very tired and hungry. I slept uneasily, really worried what would happen the next day.

I got up early, got ready and left the hotel around 7 a.m., bag and baggage. The young girl was at the desk. I inquired where I could get a taxi, and she told me to go to the bus stand, which was a ten-minute walk from the hotel.

I carried my suitcase (it did not have any wheels) to the bus stand, and within a few minutes, I got a taxi and showed the driver the address of the railway station I had to go to. Fortunately, I had kept the address in my pocket. I purposely chose not to return to the Indian embassy.

I arrived at the railway station at the top of a huge square, which seemed deserted. The square in front of the railway station had a few cars on the road. I paid the taxi and went to the railway ticket reservation counter where I was approximately 12 hours ago, the intent being to be the first in line. I got there to find several people had the same idea; there were at least 12 people standing ahead of me.

Fortunately for me, immediately ahead of me was a young boy from Madras named Venkat, who had come to Moscow to study medicine.

He was on his way to Stockholm, on a three-day holiday. I told him I was going to Helsinki.

I told Venkat my full story of how I had arrived in Moscow, what I did the previous evening, and how the young Russian couple had helped me. I don't think he quite believed me at first, but finally, as the story unfolded and reached the stage where I arrived at the Indian embassy, he looked at me and said, "Goodness, you are telling the truth."

Venkat told me that he was due to sit for his final MBBS exams in a few months. He spoke fluent Russian, had a beautiful Russian girlfriend and loved being in Moscow.

It was 9:30 a.m. by now; time had flown, and the ticket counter opened. Venkat asked me if I had filled out the reservation form. I replied that I had not.

"Go and do that," he said.

"I hope they will accept US dollars," I said.

"Gosh, no," said Venkat, "absolutely not, only rubles."

"What, they will not accept US dollars? What about Deutsche marks or British pounds?"

"No, and please keep your voice down. Why are you saying US dollars in a loud voice? Someone may hear you."

"Okay," I said, "I will go to a bank and change US dollars to rubles and come back. Is there a bank close by?"

"There is no bank here; you will have to go to the city, close to Metropole Hotel. That's a 90-minute round trip and the ticket counter may close for lunch; worse, there may not be any train tickets left for tonight."

"What do I do then?" I pulled out all the Russian currency I had left and counted about 75 rubles. "How much does a ticket cost?"

"I don't know," Venkat said.

"Can you please lend me some money?" I asked Venkat.

"After we purchase the tickets, we will go by taxi to Metropole Hotel, and I will change some money and return it to you immediately."

"I don't know if I will have enough money left to make up the shortfall for your ticket," said Venkat.

I was in a quandary. I went to the Russians standing in front of me and asked them if they could give me rubles in exchange for US dollars. They just looked at me silently and turned away. I then noticed a middle-aged Russian man wearing a blue coat sitting at the entrance of the ticket lounge. I went up to him, pulled out a hundred-dollar bill from my pocket, stuck it under his nose, and said, "Please give me rubles." Seeing the hundred dollars under his nose, the man turned white and he actually looked frightened.

Venkat, all this while, was looking at some papers. Suddenly, he appeared out of nowhere and pulled me away, saying loudly, "Have you totally lost your mind? They are not allowed to accept dollars. If someone sees you doing this, you will be in a lot of trouble." Now I had everyone in the room looking at me. I just shrugged my shoulders and quietly looked at the ground.

"Can you give me the money in dollars when we cross the border?" asked Venkat.

"Yes," I said, "no problem, I can definitely do that."

"You must not tell anyone you are paying me dollars; even if they ask you, please do not say anything. But I do not know whether I have enough rubles. If I do, then you must pay me in dollars in Finland."

I breathed a sigh of relief.

At 12:30 p.m., it was Venkat's turn. First, he purchased his ticket to Stockholm, then my ticket to Helsinki. It turned out that I was 20 rubles short, which fortunately Venkat paid. I asked Venkat to lend me another 30 rubles as I wanted something to eat. I was ravenous.

After we purchased the tickets, Venkat told me to meet him at platform number three at 9:45 p.m. "Your ticket, I will keep," he said, "since you owe me money."

"Fine," I said, "please just show up as I have to leave Russia tonight."

"Yes, I will definitely be there; you will meet my girlfriend as well."

I spent the entire afternoon at the railway station restaurant, sitting in one corner, watching people, thinking about what I needed to tell Russian immigration, why I had overstayed my visa by one day. I remember having read somewhere that an overstay by 24 hours is allowed by most countries and is generally not acted upon. The question was, would the grand USSR consider it that way?

I was at platform number three at 9:30 p.m., waiting for Venkat outside bogie number six. He showed up on time, as he said he would, with his girlfriend in tow. She was a pleasant young girl who only spoke Russian. She had come to see Venkat off.

The train left on time at 10:10 p.m.

Venkat and I were both in the same second-class four-berth compartment. It was like an Indian AC first-class compartment. It had bed sheets, blankets, pillows; the beds had been laid out for the night. I was quite impressed. The first-class compartment had an attached en-suite toilet!

Venkat was traveling to Stockholm; he would change trains at Helsinki and continue to Sweden. There was only one other person in the compartment, a Russian, who was traveling somewhere close to the Finnish border; he kept to himself and did not say much.

Venkat had brought some food with him which he proceeded to eat, taking mighty swigs of Stolichnaya vodka. "Why are you drinking it neat?" I asked, but the more I queried him, the more he drank.

"This is the way it's drunk here," he said.

I did not drink anything as I wanted a clear head when Russian immigration came for the inspection. I went over the story again with Venkat.

"Please speak to the immigration person on my behalf," I said, "as they may not understand English."

"Okay, I will handle it," he said. "I know how to speak to these guys. I also had a lot of trouble with the authorities in college, but now I am okay. I even have a Russian girlfriend."

The Russian person in our compartment and I were on the lower bunk. Venkat was on the top bunk. Shortly after dinner, he said he wanted to read his book and went on top. I was very tired from the whole Russian episode and fell asleep.

I woke up around 5:30 in the morning. The entire compartment was smelling; I couldn't make out the smell, but it was decidedly coming from somewhere close to where Venkat was sitting. I went to the loo and washed my face and cleaned myself up.

Shortly thereafter, the Russian person, who I learned from Venkat was an engineer, got off the train. That indicated to me we were very close to the Finnish border. Some 15 minutes later, the train slowly ground to a halt. A few minutes later, a policeman came into the compartment and asked us to remain seated and to stay put.

The immigration inspector arrived, a very smart young man, wearing a clean, neatly pressed, blue uniform with a cap. He first asked Venkat for his passport, looked at it briefly and then he asked for my passport. I indicated to Venkat, and he started speaking to the inspector in Russian. I am not quite sure what he said, but the inspector interrupted Venkat's slightly slurry speech and said, "I did not ask you anything, did I? Keep quiet." With that, he turned around and disappeared with both our passports.

"Are you drunk?" I asked Venkat.

"No, I am not."

"Did you finish the entire bottle of Stoli?" I asked.

"Yes. So what?" said Venkat.

Oh my God. Now I had to contend with a semi-drunk passenger whom I had relied upon to plead my case with Russian immigration.

"Please do not say anything when the inspector comes back," I said. "I will handle it on my own."

"Don't worry," said Venkat. "I will not let you down."

After 15 minutes, an interval that seemed to stretch interminably, the inspector returned. He first returned Venkat's passport, then asked him to open his bag, went through his papers, and pulled out a piece of paper. He then lifted the blanket on Venkat's bunk and shouted something in Russian; the smell of vomit and vodka was pervasive. Venkat had puked all over his blanket on his bunk at night. To hide it, he had covered the mess with his blanket and pillow.

Oh my gosh, that's all I need, I thought to myself. Then the inspector started grilling Venkat. I could see him counting Venkat's money; he kept asking Venkat if he had any more money on him.

All this while, I was sitting quietly on my bunk with my Samsonite briefcase next to me. The inspector looked at me and said something in Russian. Venkat tried to interject, as I said, "I do not speak Russian."

"Do you have anything to declare?" the inspector asked me in perfect English.

"No," I said, "nothing." I did remember the Playboy calendar but decided not to say anything.

"Can you give me your currency declaration please?" he said. I opened my briefcase and gave him the currency declaration.

"How much money are you carrying?" the inspector asked. I proceeded to take out all the money I had. "Wait, wait," he said.

"Give it to me; I will count it." The inspector counted all the money I had: US Dollars, Deutsch Marks, Swiss Francs, British Pounds, some Iranian Rials, and two or three Russian Rubles. I gave him my hotel bill at Moscow. I also took the three or four taxi receipts I had and the receipts for the meals I had eaten. The inspector counted the money once and asked me, "Where did you buy your train ticket?"

"At Moscow," I said.

"Really?" he said. "How did you pay for it?"

"In cash," I replied.

I immediately knew what this was all about: by adding up all my money he was deducing that I had more money than I should have had. Of course, I had not paid for my train ticket in full as Venkat had helped me out.

The inspector said, "This is not correct."

"Please count it again," I said.

So, the money was recounted. This time around the total sum was different than the first time. The inspector counted the money a third time. The total sum was again different. He looked at me, and I asked him,

"Should I count the money for you?" He looked at me and said it was okay, took my currency declaration, wrote something on it and gave it back to me, with my passport.

"Thank you," I said. The inspector just nodded, looked at Venkat in disgust, and went away. "What was he talking to you about, Venkat?" I asked. "What was that piece of paper?"

"My girlfriend had written all the things she wanted me to bring for her from Sweden. The inspector was asking me how I could buy all those things with the little money I had."

"What did you say?" I asked. "I told him, 'You know how women are. They always want everything, but a man cannot give everything, can he? He can only give certain things. I will only buy one or two things, whatever I can.'"

A good answer, I thought to myself.

A few minutes later, the train chugged on, and we entered Finland.

Glorious Scandinavia

On arrival in Helsinki, I gave Venkat the equivalent of 50 rubles in USD. He went off quite chuffed.

I inquired around, changed some money and took a bus to the international youth hostel. The season was over, and the hostel was fairly empty, so I easily got a bed. The lady at the reception desk asked me if I needed sheets. I said yes, and she gave me pink floral sheets made entirely of paper. Even the pillowcase was made of paper. I had never seen bed sheets made of paper before!

When I left Helsinki, I took the paper sheets with me. I was so thrilled with them, and they stood me well all over Europe.

I was so ecstatic and happy to put Russia behind me. I could not believe what I had gone through. It had only been two days, but already Tehran seemed so far away.

Helsinki is a pristine city, neat and clean, nicely laid out. The girls I had come all this way to see did not disappoint; they were tall and drop-dead gorgeous. It had been a while since I had last seen women not covered by a *burkha* (long flowing black covering which all women in Iran and Saudi Arabia have to drape over their clothes, head to foot, compulsorily)!

I was in Helsinki for just two days, during which I visited art museums, saw the sights, and headed to Stockholm.

I took the overnight ferry from Helsinki to Stockholm. I had never been on a ferry before, and it was a novel experience. It had several decks, with food and drink bars all over the place. The lower deck had a Disc Jockey and dancing. A popular song from the movie Saturday Night Fever was playing, and everyone was "line dancing" and singing, with their right hands in the air like Travolta in the movie. I had not seen the movie and was wondering what the heck everyone was doing and how they knew the steps. It was a very pleasing sight, though. You must remember I had veritably come out of jail; seeing so many scantily clad girls was too much for me to take in all at once.

Stockholm was great fun. I walked the cobbled streets of the old city. I saw the crown jewels. However, Stockholm was quite expensive and a bigger city than Helsinki. I only stayed there for one night, at the youth hostel. Walking through the cobbled streets of Stockholm reminded me of the book *Desiree* by Annemarie Selinko. In the book, Ms. Bernardine Eugenie Desiree Clary was represented as the first love and, for a short while, the fiancé of General Napoleon Bonaparte. However, Desiree married General Bernadotte of France, who was later adopted by the King of Sweden and went on to become King Charles XIV of Sweden and Norway. Desiree became Queen Desideria. I had read this book many years ago. It came vividly to mind.

I took the overnight train from Stockholm to Copenhagen; with its hard, wooden seats, it was not nearly as comfortable as the Russian train! The bunks were padded, but that's about it. It was much like an old Indian train.

In the morning around 8 a.m., the ticket conductor came and told us that the train would get onto a ferry, and that we must not leave the train. He said the ferry ride was very short and he again warned us not to get off the train when it was on the ferry.

As the train rolled onto the ferry, the conductor came and locked the door from the outside. A bearded American guy in his early 20s who seemed to look like he was high on something said, "Man, I need to get out."

The door was locked from the outside. So, he climbed on a chair, opened the top ventilator above the window, which was quite large, clambered on top of the window, and jumped out, head first. I don't quite know how he did not land on his head. The next thing we saw was him jumping up and down. We shouted to him to open the door, and all of us trooped out.

The train was right at the bottom of the ferry. There were steel steps going up, so up we went one deck at a time right to the top. The day was clear, the sky a gorgeous blue. The ferry was crossing a small lake; we could see Denmark in the distance. There was a nice coffee bar in the corner. I ordered a cappuccino and a chicken puff. The lady took a couple of minutes to make the coffee and heat the chicken puff in the oven. By this time the ferry was fast approaching the Danish shore.

I gulped down the piping hot coffee, literally stuffed my mouth with the chicken puff and went running down the steps to the bottom of the ferry. The problem with the ferry steps was that it was only possible for someone to go either up or down; it was not possible for two people to pass each other. Someone was coming up, so we had to wait for them to pass.

By the time we reached the bottom where the train was, the ferry had docked, and the train was gently pulling out of the ferry onto land.

We jumped across the steel drawbridge of the ferry onto Danish territory and ran after the train. Suddenly, out of nowhere, a Danish guard, dressed in a long greenish coat with a rifle, started shouting, "Halt, Halt, Halt, or I will shoot!"

There were four of us, all boys; we told him that we needed to get back on the train. The guard was having nothing of it. "Halt, or I will shoot!"

I stopped dead on the train tracks, as did the other three boys. "Please, let us go," I said. "My passport and money are on the train."

"No," said the guard.

Hearing the commotion, the conductor of the train blew the whistle and, thankfully, the train ground to a halt, some 50 meters from where we were standing.

The conductor stepped down; he was livid. "I told you boys not to get off the train. How did you manage to open the door?"

"I don't know, the door was open," I said.

"What nonsense. I closed the door myself. You know where you are standing? This is Denmark, and you do not even have any papers. The guard was right, he could have shot you."

"Please take us. We are so sorry about this," I pleaded. The conductor finally relented, and we all jumped onboard the train.

In about 30 minutes, the train arrived in Copenhagen. I spent four days in Copenhagen, at the youth hostel; it was a bit out of the way, but the buses were very efficient and hassle-free.

Tivoli Gardens or Tivoli is a famous children's amusement park or pleasure garden, bang in the middle of the city. It is the second-oldest amusement park in the world. I spent a lot of time there, wandering around, looking at the sights, just soaking up the gorgeous Danish atmosphere.

Close to Tivoli is the Ripley's Believe It or Not museum, which I found incredibly fascinating. Then there is the Lego store in Copenhagen. What a treat it was. In 1978, from what I can recall, the Lego store was big, but it was not as super gigantic as it is today.

I visited museums, the bronze statue of the little mermaid sitting on a rock, Copenhagen's most famous landmark. Across the river, one can see Malmo, Sweden. These days one can drive across a bridge to Malmo, but in

1978, there was no bridge. One could, however, see the twinkling lights of Malmo on the other side of the Oresund Strait. Each evening I would return to the youth hostel for dinner and plan which countries I wanted to visit and where I could go. The thing was I could only go to those countries that did not require a visa for Indian passport holders.

Freddie Lake or Sir Frederick Alfred Laker was an English airline entrepreneur, best known for establishing Laker Airways in 1966, which went bankrupt in 1982. He was one of the founders of the "no-frills" airline business model that is so popular today.

I thought to myself, USA is where I should go, as I probably would not get another opportunity, to visit multiple countries, freewheeling as I was. In 1978, it was possible for Indian passport holders to get a visit visa for UK, on arrival. I decided to go to the USA embassy in Copenhagen to apply for a USA visa, the idea being to fly to New York, from London.

I arrived at the US embassy in Copenhagen; it was quite deserted. I asked for a visa application form and began to fill it out. I noticed a person who looked like an Indian man wearing a suit in the far corner. He came up to me and asked me if I were from India. I said I was. "So am I," he said in Hindi. "So nice to meet you."

So, we had a conversation, all in Hindi; he told me that he was from New Delhi, his name was Surinder Singh, and he lived in Subzi Mandi, which is the biggest and oldest vegetable wholesale market in Delhi.

"What are you doing here?" I asked.

"I want to go to the USA," he told me and asked me if I could help him fill out his visa application form, which I did. Having duly completed both Surinder's and my visa applications, I dropped them in the visa box, and we waited our turn to be called for an interview.

"Mr. Singh and Mr. Lall," our names were announced. I got up and told Surinder to come with me. We were shown into the visa officer's room and were asked to sit down.

The visa officer, an American gentleman, started asking Surinder questions.

"Mr. Singh, when did you arrive in Copenhagen?"

"I came one week ago," he replied in halting, hesitant English.

"Did you arrive by plane or boat? Where did you arrive?" the visa officer asked.

Surinder could not quite understand the questions; he looked a bit perplexed. I asked the visa officer if I could interpret for Surinder.

"Yes, of course, please do."

I put the questions to Surinder, and he responded in Hindi, and I answered in English on his behalf. The interview was at best basic and perfunctory.

Now, it was my turn. I was asked why I wanted to go to the USA. I said I was on holiday. I noticed that Sky Train was operating low fare flights from London, and it was a good opportunity for me to go to the USA. I told the visa officer that I had come from Finland and was just traveling around. After a few questions, the officer turned around and said, "I am sorry. I have to reject both your visa applications."

"Why?" I asked.

"Well, I am rejecting Mr. Singh's application, and since you are with him, I have to reject yours as well."

"I do not know this guy," I said. "I am not with him. I do not know him at all. I just met him at the embassy."

But the visa officer insisted, "You filled in the visa application forms together."

"Yes, we filled the forms together because Surinder could not fill out his visa application form and asked me to help him, which is what I did. I have come from Tehran. I was there for one year. I was working for an American container shipping company called Sea Land; you might have heard of it," I went on to explain.

"No, I have not," said the visa officer.

I showed him my Iranian exit visa stamp and said, "See, I was in Tehran for over one year."

I tried my level best to convince the officer that I did not know Surinder from a bar of soap; but it did not wash. At the end of it, the visa officer had made his decision. In his mind, Surinder and I were together, our applications were both rejected, and as they do in such cases, the last page of the passports were stamped Den/1978 and given back to us.

I was furious with Surinder. He was walking nervously beside me. "Can we go and have coffee? I will buy you something to eat," he said.

"No," I said, "I do not want anything. You have got me into enough trouble as it is. Please let me be."

My American dream was short-circuited, courtesy Mr. Surinder Singh.

CHAPTER NINE

The Alzey Wine Festival

Since I had already made up my mind to go to London, I decided to stick to my plan. I purchased a one-way ticket from Copenhagen to Luton, England, on 13th September 1978.

I landed at Luton just after lunch and got a visa on arrival. A coach was leaving the airport for the city. Someone suggested I take that, as the youth hostel was not too far from where the bus would terminate its journey.

The hostel was full, but there were some rooms available at a higher rate at the University of London in Camden Town. The university accommodation was far superior compared to the youth hostel in Copenhagen, which was basic at best, though clean.

I did not know anyone in London, not a soul. I was feeling a bit weary but being in London livened me up.

England was easy, not that Scandinavia was difficult, it's just that sometimes one got stuck with someone who did not speak English. I felt totally at home in London. I felt secure and comfortable moving around. The public transportation was wonderful and compared to Scandinavia, London was much cheaper. I could drop in at a pub and have a beer and a sandwich, which in Scandinavia was rather expensive.

I was told that I could stay at the university for one week. It was secure accommodation, so I did not have to worry about where I'd be staying for the next few days. Being in London meant walking and walking and more walking, up Oxford Street, down Regent Street, and so on. I visited the Museum of Natural History which I found interesting but rather monotonous.

I purchased a 30-day Eurorail pass. The problem was that I could not go everywhere in Europe on an Indian passport without a prior visa, much to my chagrin.

To get into Europe, I bought an air ticket from London to Schiphol, Amsterdam, Holland, on 16th September. Amsterdam was good fun; it felt like a lively city the moment I landed at Schiphol, which was efficiency personified.

I found the youth hostel in Amsterdam to be extremely crowded, and I daresay, a tad dirty, but I had little choice. I think I was about the only Indian at the hostel.

The next day I spent the whole day wandering around the city. I was awestruck by the roads, the canals, the bridges, and the flowers everywhere. What can I say about the tulips with their wonderful radiant colors. I had never seen anything so beautiful.

Over the next two days, I took short drives outside Amsterdam, where I saw vast fields of tulips and the famous windmills. Quite extraordinary; the vastness and the kaleidoscope of colors was breathtaking.

I went to the red-light district in Amsterdam; it's exactly as you see it in the movies. Big glass windows with scantily clad girls giving you the come-hither look.

I was walking past a building with a sign that said, "Live Show." I really did not know for sure what a live show was. I dare say I suspected but was not certain. So, I went inside. There were small cubicles with curtains. In front was a ship's porthole. A girl emerged, and the lights came on. The girl started gyrating to soft music, slowly doing a striptease. She saw my eyes going bigger and bigger, so she opened the porthole and asked me, "Would you like some more?"

"Yes," I said, "I want some more."

By this time, I had stuck my head right inside the porthole.

Just as the girl completed the striptease act with great gusto, my three minutes of joy came to an abrupt end. The lights went off, and the girl disappeared. I disentangled myself from the porthole and came back to reality. That was the end of that!

Now that I had a Eurorail pass, I could go anywhere. All I had to do was to get my pass stamped at the ticket counter, and I could board any train other than the nonstop intercity express trains. I jumped onto a train going to Antwerp, Belgium.

Antwerp is a quaint old city with an interesting history. I enjoyed walking around the main city square, admiring the old stone buildings. I had heard that Belgium is known for its chocolates and beer, so I stopped at a café and had the famous Belgian chocolate waffles with ice cream.

Delicious. They lived up to their reputation!

There is something else Belgium is very famous for and that is handguns. Belgium makes the famous Browning pistols. As I was walking, slowly soaking in the sights, I came across a gun shop quite by accident. The shop window displayed several kinds of handguns. I stood there for a while, looking at the guns. I do not know why, but I thought of a book I had read a few years ago called the *Day of the Jackal*. I went inside the shop and asked the shop assistant if I could see some inexpensive handguns.

The shop assistant proceeded to bring out a few handguns from the glass case.

"What are those small pistols?" I asked.

"They are not real," he said.

"Really?" I said. "May I have a look?"

The assistant showed them to me and said, "This is a copy of the Browning No. 2 pistol."

It looked as if it was made of gleaming gunmetal. The real Browning No. 2 comes with six bullets. This look-alike came with small copper pellets, which, when fired, made a bang with blank rounds. It weighed about 600 grams in my hands and had a very solid feel to it. Boy, did it look real?

"What's the price?" I asked.

"USD 15 only." I was so fascinated by the handgun that I immediately purchased it with three boxes of copper blank pellets.

I was utterly thrilled by my purchase. I immediately went to the youth hostel, packed the handgun away in my suitcase and took the train to the ancient town of Ghent.

I walked around Saint Bavo's Cathedral at Ghent, which is a short ride from Antwerp. The cathedral is over 1,000 years old and has long been a place of prayer and worship. I was told that the Cathedral is famous for its concerts and organ recitals, which, unfortunately, I did not have the time to attend and hear.

I spent the afternoon in Ghent and went back to Antwerp. The same day, I caught a train to Rotterdam.

When I was at Sea Land in Tehran, an Indian accountant from Sea Land, Rotterdam, frequently visited Tehran. Anil was Gujarati, had lived most of his adult life overseas, and had been living in Rotterdam for the last five years.

On his last visit to Tehran, I had jokingly told him that if ever I were in Europe, I would meet him. Little did I know then that it would turn out to be true. Before leaving Tehran, I had taken Anil's number from Kar.

Rotterdam was the regional headquarters of Sea Land. I really wanted to see what the city was like as I had heard so much about it. Rotterdam was then the world's largest container port; it was massive, and Sea Land was the largest containerized shipping company in the world. It was quite a sight to behold.

Hans, my boss in Tehran, had also given me someone's reference in Rotterdam. I gave him a call, and he asked me to meet him. I was toying with the idea of getting a job in Rotterdam if possible.

So, off I went to the Sea Land office to meet the person introduced by Hans. He had been to Tehran and knew the operations there. He told me the Tehran base was small in comparison to Rotterdam. Looking through the big glass windows, I could see the port and the huge container ships being loaded and unloaded with containers. The container park was massive, and they had containers stacked one upon another. A few hundred containers were on chassis. The difference between Tehran and Rotterdam was that the Tehran operations being small, almost all the containers in Tehran were on 20 feet chassis, whereas, in Rotterdam, the containers were scattered all over the place.

"How can I help you?" the Dutchman asked me.

"Well, I was wondering whether I might be able to get some kind of a job in Rotterdam."

"Do you speak Dutch?" he asked.

"No," I said.

"Well then, I will have to be frank, it will be impossible for you to get a job in Holland."

That evening, Anil had invited me to his house for a drink, which was very sweet of him, as he hardly knew me. Anil's parents were staying with him. I spent a little time with Anil and told him what I had been told about working in Holland. He explained to me why it would be impossible to work in Holland without knowing the language, especially if I were to work in the terminal, in dispatch, where I would have to deal with truck drivers, etc. Upon hearing this, I could see that it made sense

After dinner, Anil very kindly dropped me back to the youth hostel as it was getting a bit late and I did not know my way around the city.

Now that I knew working in Rotterdam was not happening, I could breathe a bit easier.

The next day, on 22nd September, I turned 23 years old. I took the train to Den Haag or The Hague, which is a short drive from Amsterdam and home to the International Court of Justice. I was on my way to the international youth hostel.

The bus dropped me off at an intersection, and the driver pointed down the road. "Where," I asked, as I could not see any signs.

"There, go there. It's a bit of a walk."

I walked down a broad tree-lined avenue; it was a fairly long walk. I was not sure I was walking in the right direction until I saw some young boys and girls with rucksacks walking past me, and then I knew I was going in the right direction. I found that the youth hostel was set in the middle of a forest; it had very large grounds. At that time of the year, the hostel was surprisingly full. The lady at the reception told me that a large group of schoolgirls had come from Germany.

I settled myself in, and was given a bed in a dormitory, a bit like Sanawar, but the bed was not as poky! I had a quick shower and went down to the lounge, where I was told happy hour was from 6:30 p.m. to 7:30 p.m. I bought myself a bottle of beer and sat down in a corner, looking at everyone in the room. The bunch of schoolgirls was sitting to my far right, playing some kind of an indoor game.

I went up to the bar to get myself another beer and noticed a girl sitting at the bar, reading what I made out to be *The Prophet* by Kahlil Gibran. This immediately caught my attention, as I knew that Kahlil Gibran was serious reading.

"You've got a very serious book there," I said.

"Yes," said the girl, who was very pretty and young, with blonde hair and blue eyes. "I am enjoying it."

"Don't you find it serious?" I asked.

"No, not really, I like it."

I was quite fascinated how a young girl, amid a bevy of bubbling noisy girls, could be reading Kahlil Gibran. I remembered something: "*One day you will ask me, which is more important, my life or yours. I will say mine, and you will walk away not knowing that you are my life.*"

"Are you from around here?" I asked.

"No, I am with all these girls," she said, pointing to the group of German girls in the corner. "I don't like playing silly games," she said. "I wanted to read, so I am sitting here."

"Can I buy you a glass of wine?" I asked.

"No, thank you," she replied.

"Go on, please have one. It's my birthday today."

She looked at me and said, "Excuse me, it's your birthday today?"

"Yes, it is," I said. "I am 23 today."

She started laughing, "It's my birthday today as well, and I am 17 years old today."

"Wow, then you must have a drink," I said.

"Yes, that would be very nice," she replied.

"My name is Sanjiv," I said, introducing myself.

"I am Merle Helmute," she said.

I asked Merle to come and sit with me at my table, next to the window. The girls saw her talking to me and started exchanging snide remarks. She just turned to me and said, "Don't listen to them; that's why I don't like their girly company."

Such wisdom coming from a girl so young.

"If I don't get lost, how will I find my way?" Kahlil Gibran.

Merle and I chatted the evening away; her friends went to their dormitory. The lounge closed, and we were told to go outside. So, Merle and I went for a walk outside. It was a moonlit night. We were sitting on a bench, overlooking the forest; it was a beautiful, serene evening. Merle and I were holding hands talking about all kinds of things, when she said, "I must go inside, or they will wonder what has happened to me." And off she went.

I spent the next day walking around Den Haag. I had told Merle that I would meet her in the evening over "happy hour". I was walking back to the youth hostel from the city, down the tree-lined street, when I noticed a batch of about eight to ten girls from Merle's class walking toward me. When they saw me, they burst into a German song, skipping along hand in hand, mischievously looking at me and laughing.

When I passed them, one of them said, "Merle is waiting for you."

"Really?" I said smiling. I had bought some chocolates for Merle for her birthday from a specialist chocolate shop in Den Haag, wrapped in pink tissue paper; I was carrying them in my hand.

"This is for your 17th birthday," I said.

"But I do not have anything to give you," said Merle. "I cannot take your present."

"It's only chocolates; we will eat them together," I said, "just you and me."

"I live in Alzey," said Merle, "it's close to Mainz in Germany."

I did not know the first thing about Germany, and yet I said, "I will come and meet you."

"Really?" asked Merle. "You are just joking."

"No, I will come and meet you," I said.

"When will you come?" she asked.

"I will come exactly one week from our birthday, next Friday, 29th September."

She looked at me and counted on her fingers. "Yes, that's fine. I will be in Alzey that day."

We agreed to meet at 3 p.m. at the Alzey railway station, next Friday.

"I must go now," Merle said, "but I really want to meet you after dinner. So, if you like, I will come out of the dormitory when the girls have gone to sleep."

"Really?" I said.

"Yes, I will come; you wait for me outside the girls' section at 10:30 p.m. I will come," said Merle.

Merle was a big girl, five feet six inches tall, and she spoke perfect English, which definitely helped! I tried to recollect if I knew any girls back in India, six years younger than me, whom I could talk with as I was talking with Merle. Almost on the dot at 10:30 p.m., Merle emerged from the girls' section.

"How will you get back?" I asked.

"Don't worry; I will manage." Merle and I set off toward the forest area under a full moon.

"I have never been kissed like this before," Merle said. "Please kiss me again," and I did.

The fact that we shared a birthday brought Merle and me even closer. All along, I kept wondering if I were doing the right thing here, kissing Merle, half expecting the hostel matron to come bearing down on me.

Around 11:30 p.m., Merle said she had to go, as they were leaving very early the next day for Germany. "I will wait for you at Alzey, Sanjiv," she said, and off she disappeared into the girls' hostel section.

In Den Haag, I went to an art museum and saw the world's largest painting. It stretched right across the wall. I also went to the Madurodom, where you see snippets of the typical Dutch lifestyle in miniature form. Very intriguing and informative.

Sunday, I took the train to Hamburg.

Hamburg looked considerably boring compared to Amsterdam when I got off the train and checked into the youth hostel. That evening, along with a young Swedish boy, Johaan, who was also staying at the youth hostel, we made our way to the Reeperbahn, a street in the St. Pauli district of Hamburg, the center of the city's pulsating nightlife, and also the main red-light district.

I had just arrived from Amsterdam; the red-light district there was controlled, sedate, and in fairly good taste. The Reeperbahn, on the other hand, was sex in your face, as much as anything could be. It was all there to be had, the only consideration being how much you were willing to spend.

"I don't want to see any of this," young Johaan told me. "You can go on your own; I will go back to the youth hostel."

"Okay," I said, "let's go someplace quiet and have a beer and something to eat, and we will go back."

So, we found a place that was quiet; not much was happening there. A man was standing outside trying to pull people inside. Most of the tables were empty, and it was not pitch dark as were a lot of the other places we had peeked into. It was a rather sedate club. I ordered a beer for myself and a Coke for Johaan.

When our drinks arrived, the lights suddenly dimmed, and the music started.

"Oh dear, what's this?" Johaan asked.

"I don't know. Let's see."

The curtains lifted, and behold, there was a man and a woman; a total full-blown live sex show literally a few feet from our table. There was no porthole this time to look through: it was clear as daylight. The man proceeded to disrobe the girl and then himself and then calmly started making love to the girl. This was definitely a first for me!

Johaan was getting more and more agitated by the minute. "I am not going to see this garbage. I am going home."

It was hard trying to pacify Johaan and see what was happening on the stage at the same time.

I do believe I was the only dark-skinned person in the entire room at that time. When the act was over, the lights came on. Johaan said, "For goodness sake, do people really watch this kind of thing?"

"I guess they do, Johaan," I said.

Just then the manager of the club came to our table and said, "Would you like to come to the stage and perform with the girl you just saw? We are looking for a black and white combination."

Before I could even digest what the man was saying, Johaan said, "Please, for goodness sake, you cannot...No, I am leaving."

With that, Johaan almost ran out of the club. I thanked the maître d' for his invite and ran out looking for Johaan.

"I was not sure you would come out, you know," Johaan said, much to my annoyance. What did he take me for, I thought!

We took the bus back to the youth hostel after quite an eventful night.

On Tuesday morning, I took the train to Dusseldorf. I spent the afternoon there and took the train to Cologne, a short distance away. Cologne, or Koln, is quite imposing; the train station itself is quite breathtaking, as it is situated right next to the Koln Cathedral.

Wednesday morning, I went to Frankfurt, another short train ride away. I was just whiling away time as I wanted to be at Alzey on Friday. I spent the whole day strolling around Frankfurt, which is a big buzzing city. I spent the night there, too.

Thursday, late morning, I went to Mainz, which is very close to Frankfurt. Mainz is on the Rhine, one of the great rivers of Europe. The other side of the river is Wiesbaden. I never got to Wiesbaden, just saw it from a distance.

Alzey is on a non-electrified line route and could not be traveled to with a Eurorail pass. I had to purchase a separate ticket.

I had checked the train timetable; it took about one hour 45 minutes to get from Mainz to Alzey. There was a train departing from Mainz at 1 p.m. I wanted to be on that. I left my suitcase at the Mainz luggage counter and just took my briefcase with a change of clothes with me to Alzey.

In 1978, there were no mobiles phones. Merle had promised to meet me at Alzey. I took her word for it, as she took mine. I did not even call her before I left Mainz; she did not want me to call her in case her parents stopped her from meeting me.

The train slowly chugged into Alzey at 2:45 p.m. I looked out of the train window; I could not see Merle anywhere. I thought to myself there were still 15 minutes to go and she might show up, when suddenly I saw Merle standing there in her school uniform, which is why I had not recognized her initially. I waved to her as the train came to a halt; she immediately recognized me.

We met, warmly shaking hands.

"Everyone knows me at the station," she said.

"How did you come to the railway station?" I asked.

"I came by bicycle," she said.

That I truly believe was the first and only time a girl had come to meet me on a bicycle. I thought Merle was awfully cute.

"I was not sure you would come," Merle said.

"Why? I did tell you I would come, didn't I?"

"Yes, you did, but I was not sure. I decided to come to the station anyway to check."

"We had better go and check into a hotel first," she said.

"Today is the first day of the annual Alzey wine-drinking festival. I don't know whether we will get a room."

"Oh, but I will need a room to stay the night," I said.

We went to the biggest hotel in Alzey, but there was no vacancy. I noticed a lot of small pensions in Alzey as we were walking along from the railway station; most of them had a "No Vacancy" sign displayed.

"The thing is most of these people know me; they will wonder why I am with you," Merle said.

So, I would go in and inquire for a room by myself while Merle waited outside. I did this about six times - no room, no room, no room. By this time, it was 5:30 p.m. We stopped by a café for a cup of coffee.

"The owner here also knows me," Merle said, and sure enough, the owner said, "Hello, Merle, how are you?" in German.

"This is my friend from India."

So here I was in Alzey, to meet Merle, a 17-year-old German girl in high school, and had no room to stay the night. Merle and I went to several hotels, pensions and guesthouses looking for a room. Merle, poor thing, was getting most embarrassed by the whole thing. I did not know what to do.

There was just about only one thing to do: to go to the Alzey wine-drinking festival which was showcasing Alzey's 1978 wine.

I purchased a small glass tied on a glass thong, with Alzey written on it, strung it around my neck, and off we went. The idea was to go from stall to stall, sampling wine from various local vineyards, which was poured into the wine glass around your neck!

There were also stalls serving grilled sausages and other kinds of snacks. Merle and I had some delicious sausages.

Merle's elder sister and her boyfriend were also at the fair.

"I told my sister I met you in Holland. You happened to be in Alzey, and I asked you to come for the wine fair," Merle said. So that was my story to all and sundry.

Merle remained by my side for most of the evening, in her school uniform. For about 30 minutes, she disappeared, saying that it would look funny if she didn't spend at least some time with her family. Everywhere I went with Merle, I was introduced as her friend from India.

"Hello. *Guten tag.* What are you doing here?" and so it went on. Around 10:30 p.m., Merle said, "My sister wants me to go back home with her, so I have to leave with her."

"Please go home," I said. "But where will you stay? I wish I could be with you. I am so sorry you could not get a hotel."

The fact was that the entire evening, Merle and I could barely hold hands. I did, however, hold her fingertips below the table in the coffee shop. Merle was very excited, nervous, and very talkative the entire time she was with me.

"I would like to meet you tomorrow at Mainz," Merle said.

"Where can we meet?"

"I know a hotel where my father stayed; it is quite close to the railway station. Tomorrow is Saturday. It's a holiday for me. I will come to Mainz, to the hotel, at 12:30 p.m. Please wait for me."

At 10:45 p.m., Merle left Alzey with her sister, leaving me standing alone outside the wine festival, which was now beginning to shut down. The only place that was open was the pub, which had a bonfire outside. I got myself a pint of beer and sat down close to the bonfire. It reminded me of the bonfire in Peacestead, at Sanawar, during Diwali.

It was cold, and I, fortunately, was wearing my light blue ski jacket, which Amarjit had given me in Tehran. I zipped it up and was quite warm. The problem was I was feeling rather sleepy and had no place to go.

I thought I would go to the railway platform, but the Alzey railway platform was an open uncovered platform; there was only a little covered potion, mainly the underpass or the tunnel that connected the two platforms. I thought I could sit there, at least it was covered. I did sit there for about 10 minutes; it was well lit and totally empty. But the underpass was like a wind tunnel; it had huge gusts of wind bellowing through it, which made it impossible for me to sit or sleep there.

I went back to the road and sat down on the park bench opposite the pub. I saw the last few stragglers leave the pub around 12:30 a.m. I dozed off sitting on the park bench. I got up around 2:30 a.m. and found myself covered in frost. The bench around me, where I was sitting, was completely wet; my jeans were damp and my hair was damp. The grass below my feet was completely wet. I thought to myself I better get the heck out of there, but where could I go?

I walked down to the main Alzey square, where the earlymorning bus departed from. I thought of sitting on the steps of a building, but they, too, were wet. To keep awake and dry, the only thing to do was to keep walking, so I walked right down the square to the far end of the street and back, and back again for another round. I was all by myself walking up and down to keep warm.

The first bus for Mainz left Alzey at 6 a.m. I had to wait it out till then. The lights in the main square were on; it was fully safe, it was just a bit uncomfortable, especially lugging my Samsonite briefcase with me all over the place. As I visited each country, I stuck their respective national flags on my briefcase. By this time, it had quite a few colorful stickers on it.

I thought about Merle, spending time with her at the hotel. It brought a smile to my lips thinking about sweet Merle. By now, it was 4:30 a.m. A few other people had joined me at the square. I had no idea where they came from. I continued my slow walk up and down the square.

At about 5:15 a.m., a young girl with red hair came to the square. She was also walking up and down to keep warm. We got talking. She told me she was not from Alzey, was just visiting, and was from Wiesbaden, across the river from Mainz.

"What do you do?" I asked.

"I am a designer," she said. "

What do you design?" I asked.

"I design brassieres," she replied.

I was quite stunned when I heard this. I stopped for a moment and looked at her.

"Yes, that's right, I design bras," she repeated, looking quizzically at me. We spent the next hour chatting and walking up and down the square to keep warm until I took the 6 a.m. bus to Mainz, less than an hour's drive away.

I went to the railway station and collected my bags and came to the hotel Merle had recommended. Fortunately, there was a room available. I had a shower and went to sleep.

I got up by 11:30 a.m., shaved, showered and waited for Merle to show up, which she did, promptly at 12:30 p.m. She was not in her school uniform and looked older than the previous day. She came to my room and immediately started telling me how sorry she felt for the previous night; she was most eager to know what I did after she went away. I told her it was okay, these things happen. Had it not been for the wine festival, I most definitely would have found a room for the night. I was not at all upset with what had happened.

Merle and I had lunch together and talked the afternoon away. I told Merle how I had passed the night at Alzey, walking up and down, waiting for the early morning bus to Mainz.

Merle was with me till 6:30 p.m. She took the last bus to Alzey.

"I wish I could spend the night with you. I would like to, but you do know I have to go back home; my father will wonder where I am," she said.

After Merle left, I had an early dinner and went back to the hotel to sleep.

I saw Merle again 20 years later, when I happened to be on a business trip and was staying in a hotel in a vineyard in the Black Forest, close to Heidelberg. I was intrigued enough to meet Merle but did not have her number, so I looked up Helmute in Alzey and spoke to her father, who gave me the number. Merle came along to meet me with her baby daughter, and we spent a pleasant afternoon remembering the time we had met, 20 years earlier, first in Den Haag, and then in Alzey.

CHAPTER TEN

Wonderful Madrid

The next morning, on 1st October 1978, I left for Munich for the Oktoberfest. The famous Oktoberfest, with literally hundreds of people under one roof, drinking beer as if it's going out of fashion, and the Bavarian waitresses carrying six pints of beer in each hand. I tried carrying three pints of beer in one hand and gave up almost immediately. Here the Bavarian waitresses would carry six pints of beer in each hand, for literally hours on end. Impressive! What can I say about the Oktoberfest? It was sheer revelry. In all the years to date, I have never had the occasion to participate in such a lively event.

Munich or Munchen, itself, is a fun city. I spent three days in Munich, staying at the youth hostel and exploring the city. I found Bavaria to be fun and lively with its buzzy atmosphere, historic buildings, bars and restaurants. From Munich I went to Konstanz, situated on Lake Konstanz. The youth hostel in Konstanz was in an ancient fort, quite imposing and impressive. I took the ferry across Lake Konstanz and back to the mainland, just to see the view from the ferry. It was quite breathtaking.

The next day, I took the train from Konstanz to Zurich, Switzerland, on 4th October. My Eurorail pass was due to run out on 14th October. I had to be in Madrid before the Eurorail expired, that was the master plan.

I did not stay in Zurich but took a train to Bern, where I stayed the night. I remember going to the zoo that night, something I had never associated with Bern. From Bern I went to Fribourg, where again I only stayed for the day and continued to Lausanne.

In Hamburg, I had met a young man from Lausanne who had asked me to please look him up in Lausanne if I ever came to Switzerland. So, here I was in Lausanne. I gave him a call, and he insisted I stay with him for the night. Henri was a professor at Lausanne University and he lived in a tiny, matchbox-size apartment. He insisted I sleep in his bedroom; all my protests were to no avail. He even took me out to dinner and insisted on paying for the full fare. He said he knew what traveling was like and what it meant to have a good square meal.

I felt so bad about causing an upheaval in Henri's apartment and life, I left Lausanne the next day, though I had planned on staying two days.

My stepfather had been in a tuberculosis sanatorium in the mid-50s in Davos, so I would have liked to have gone to Davos; however, it was not on the Eurorail map and I was running short of time. Moreover, I found Switzerland to be expensive.

On 6th October 1978, I arrived in Geneva. I had a few days to spare, so I decided to spend a couple of days in Geneva. I thought I might make a short trip to Neuchatel for the day. On Saturday, the 7th of October, I happened to be sitting opposite the French embassy in Geneva and idly wondered whether an Indian passport holder i.e. me, would need a transit visa for France en route to Spain. However, being a Saturday, the embassy was closed, and I could not factually verify the need for a transit visa. The other place I wanted to visit was Andorra, the principality tucked away between France and Spain. I had heard a lot about Andorra from Kar and Charles, who would talk incessantly about it. It was their dream to retire in Andorra and they had been thinking of buying a house there.

I spent the weekend in Geneva. On Monday, 9th October, I went to the French embassy and was rather abruptly informed that I did need a tourist visa and that I should apply for that from my country of origin.

Here I was in Geneva, close to the French border and they were telling me to go to India to get my visa. I asked to meet the French consul, who was also in charge of visas. The visa lady was not keen on allowing me to meet the French consul, but since I persisted, I was allowed into the consulate office. The secretary told me that the consul was away for a meeting and would come back around noon. She also said that there was no way I could get a visa in Geneva, and that I should not waste my time trying to meet the consul.

I had to get to Madrid, and I did not want to fly there when I could just as easily get there by train. I told the consul's secretary that I would wait for the consul's return. I waited and waited, and he finally arrived at 12:30 p.m. His secretary spoke to him about me and he told her to tell me that a visa was not possible. I insisted that I had to meet the consul and that I would not leave the office until I had met him.

I finally met the consul at 2:30 p.m., on his return from lunch. I just sat there reading some magazines and looking at his secretary. I think she felt a bit bad for me. She told me he had just come back to the office and that she would speak to him and see what she could do. The secretary came out of the consul's room in a couple of minutes and told me that he would meet me now and wished me good luck. I thanked her and walked in to meet the consul.

"My staff have already told you that you have to apply for a visa in your home country," he told me bluntly. I looked at him and said, "Sir, I am a student, I have been traveling all over Asia and Europe for the last year; my Eurorail pass will expire in one week's time. I cannot go in reverse, I can only go forward, which means, from Geneva, I can go either to France or Spain. I cannot get to Spain without going through France. Please help me. All I need is a transit visa. I have no intention of staying in France."

The consul heard my monologue and said, "Okay, I will grant you your visa, but it will take three days."

"Three days, sir?"

"Yes. If you want your visa, you can collect it on Thursday, 12th October."

I deposited my passport and left fuming. I waited in Geneva for another three days, which meant, in total, I had spent six days in Geneva, the longest I had spent anywhere since leaving Tehran. I was very sore about that and not at all happy.

I collected my visa on 12th October and went to the railway station early. Since I was two hours early, I went to the supermarket to get something to eat on the train. At the supermarket, I purchased my standard food fare that I would buy whilst traveling, some ham, cheese, a French loaf, and a carton of milk. I got talking to a boy from the Philippines, who was also going on the same train to Paris. I told him I was going to Paris and would change there to continue to Spain. He asked me how long I had spent in Geneva and I immediately let the expletives fly about the French and what I thought of them. I told the young Filipino how the French consul had strung me upside down. By this time, it was time to board the train.

At the Geneva railway station, which is an integral part of Switzerland, when you board the train to Paris, you have to clear French immigration and customs before boarding.

We were standing in line to clear French immigration. I was carrying on about the French and their warped superior ways when the Filipino asked me to keep quiet as my turn was next. The French immigration officer looked at my passport and visa and said, "Welcome to France."

With that, I had cleared immigration.

"See, I told you it would be easy," said the Filipino. I just grunted and smiled. Now all we had to do was to clear the French customs and board the train. We were slowly walking forward in a queue to board the train. I think I must have been sticking out like a sore thumb as I was about the only person traveling with a leather suitcase and a briefcase. Almost all the other passengers, including my new-found friend from the Philippines, were traveling with rucksacks.

"You," the customs officer shouted, indicating to me, "please step here."

I was the only person on the entire train to be pulled aside for questioning. I stood to one side, with my bag on the trestle table, waiting for the customs official, watching the passengers boarding the train. The customs gendarme arrived and proceeded to open my suitcase.

"Do you have anything to declare?"

"No," I said.

Just like the time in Moscow, the inspector put his hands on either side of the suitcase, digging deep, and lo and behold, pulled out the pistol I had recently purchased in Antwerp. The year was 1978 and there had been some trouble brewing in the Middle East. The gendarme could not believe what he had found; his hands were literally trembling holding the pistol. By now, everyone standing in line to board the train, including the Filipino, had seen the pistol being fished out of my bag and were wondering what the heck was going on.

"It's a toy pistol," I said, but the gendarme could not speak English. He was most frightened, and I realized there was little point in speaking to him. I opened my briefcase and thought to myself it was all I needed. I took out my gold-rimmed glasses and put them on, thinking it would be a good time to look a bit bookish.

Another gendarme was sent with a rifle and a bayonet to guard me; just like in Russia, I had to communicate in sign language for permission to open my briefcase.

Fifteen minutes later, a very smart, young customs officer, wearing a brown tweed jacket with a scarf, came and asked me, "Is this your pistol?"

"Yes, it is," I said.

"Where did you get it?"

"Antwerp," I said.

"How much did you pay for it?"

"Fifteen US dollars," I said.

"No, tell me the real price."

"That's what I paid for it. It's a toy pistol, the barrel has been blocked. As you can see, the pellets only fire blanks."

"Yes, I can see that; it took us a while to figure this out. I had to scratch the barrel to see if it was real," the customs officer said. "It certainly looks very real."

He gave me back the pistol and pellets and said I was free to go. My passport, which had been sent for photocopying of all the pages, was also returned to me.

I was the last one to board the train. I went looking for an empty berth. The first coach was entirely full. In the third coach, I found the Filipino sitting by himself in a four-berth compartment. I entered the compartment, and before I could say anything, he said, "Look, I do not know where you have come from or where you are going, and I really do not want to know. Everyone on the train thinks I am with you and no one is allowing me to share the compartment with them." With that, he lifted his rucksack and said, "Please don't come with me. I have had enough for one night," and he left.

I thought to myself if he had had enough for one night, what about me? The silver lining was that I had the four-berth compartment to myself for a while at least. In Paris, I changed to another train going down the French Riviera. We stopped in Nice for a few hours, which gave me the opportunity to see the Marc Chagall museum. It was a lovely town.

From Nice, the train went to the French border and stopped. We had to physically cross over into Spain and get onto a Spanish train to Madrid. This was unlike the other countries where I had been traveling in Europe, where the border crossings were seamless.

I arrived in Madrid on the last day of my Eurorail pass. I had used it to its fullest possible extent; from that perspective, I was quite happy with the way things had worked out, the only wrinkle being the six-day forced halt and stopover at Geneva.

When I checked in to the youth hostel in Madrid, the first thing I did was my laundry. I had been carting around dirty clothes for far too long. I cleaned myself up in anticipation of meeting Matt Quartel. I did not have his number and had not spoken to him. I thought I would just swing by his office and meet him.

CHAPTER ELEVEN

Sea Land Spain

On Monday, 16th October, I set off for Sea Land, Madrid, to meet Matt Quartel. I arrived at 10:15 a.m., and asked for Matt. When his secretary asked me why I wanted to see him, and if I had a prior appointment, I replied that I did not, that I just wanted to meet him as I was in Madrid and that Matt was my former boss in Tehran.

I was standing outside Matt's office. His secretary went inside and told him there was a young man outside who says he worked for Sea Land, Tehran, and wanted to meet him.

"Tehran," said Matt. "Who is that?"

His Secretary replied, "Sanjive," totally mispronouncing my name.

I could see Matt looking a bit nonplussed, unable to place the name immediately; however, he got up and came outside his office to find me standing there.

"Sanjiv," he said. "Hey, what a surprise! What are you doing in Madrid?"

"I am in Europe on holiday," I said, "and you did tell me to look you up if I were in Madrid, so here I am." I smiled at Matt, and he smiled back at me.

"Come inside, have a coffee, and tell me where you are coming from."

I told Matt that I left Tehran shortly after he did and came to Spain via Russia, Scandinavia, UK, Germany, and France.

"How do you like it here?" I asked him. "How are your daughters?"

"They are fine in school here, in Madrid," Matt replied.

He looked at me and added, "You must be broke from all the traveling you have done."

"Yes," I said, and smiled back at him, "I am a bit."

"Do you want a job?" he asked.

"Yes, I would very much like that," I replied.

"So, let's get you fixed up," he responded, and just like that, just as he had promised me, he gave me a job, and once again I was employed by Sea Land, albeit in another country.

Matt personally took me around the Sea Land office; it was much bigger than the Tehran office. He walked with me, introducing me to the accounts manager, finance controller, shipping clerks, etc. Some of the people Matt did not know himself, having assumed charge as the country manager just a few weeks earlier.

The accounts manager and the shipping team were not quite sure who I was or what I was doing there. They were just told to give me a desk.

"Come back tomorrow," Matt said, "and start."

I went back to the youth hostel and found a nice pension close to the metro station. The pension was cheerful, and the room was nice, with breakfast thrown in; the only problem was that there was no toilet in the room, I had to go down the hall.

The next morning, I had breakfast and left early to arrive at Sea Land on time. I went and met Matt's secretary who took me to my desk and asked Juan, a young man in the shipping section, to help me out. Juan was very helpful and attentive; he even showed me where the coffee bar was. The first day, I pretty much did nothing. Juan and Pedro took me out for lunch to a sandwich bar. Juan was quite keen to know where I had come from.

At my second day at work, a whole heap of shipping consignment notes was put on my table, and Juan asked me to categorize them, which I did. He would then enter the details on a worksheet and courier them via DHL to Rotterdam. This was effectively what I had done for Matt in Tehran. It was easy work, no pressure, with no deadlines to keep.

I just lightened the workload off Juan and Pedro. As the days went by, more and more shipping consignment notes were placed on my table.

Juan was particularly sweet; he invited me to his home, which was walking distance from the office. He introduced me to his wife, who only spoke Spanish, and his very cute young daughter. I also met his wife's friend Anna, a spunky Spanish lady.

Every weekend, Juan would ask me if I wanted to go out with his family for a meal or shopping. One such weekend, he suggested that we go to the bullring. I had never been to a bullfight before.

Juan, his wife, and Anna and I went together to see my first bullfight. I had always assumed that a bullfight was an even contest between man and bull. I was wrong. First came the two horsemen with spears. They literally speared the bull with two to four spears, deeply embedding them in the bull's back or neck. Then came the men on foot with spears; their job was to again spear the already-injured and weakened bull. The matador came on last with great flourish, with his cape, hat and sword.

By the time the matador came on, the bull had about five spears sticking all over it, mostly on its back and one on its hump. It had lost a lot of blood and had difficulty moving. The matador came with his red cape or *muleta*, the idea being to irritate and instigate the bull to charge at the matador. Bulls are color-blind, so it is not the color of the cape but the movement of the cape that makes the bull charge.

The red cape is brought out last, just before the final kill, to hide the blood splatters. I was quite pleased to know that even in its terribly weakened condition, at times, the bull did manage to get the matador off guard. The horsemen and footmen were always ready in the event the bull upstaged the matador, in which case, the bull was immediately subdued.

There was no chance for the bull; it was certainly not an even contest. I could not understand why everyone was screaming their guts out. I did notice Anna cringing a bit; that made me warm up to her. She told me that she did not want to come to the bullfight, but Juan had forced her to come, saying Sanjiv would also be there.

After the bullfight, we went dancing. Juan, his wife, Anna and I. Juan taught me the Spanish word for dance, *bailar*. He taught me the correct pronunciation and I said, "I want to *bailar* with Anna."

Most evenings, after work, I would walk down to a street that was lined with lively bars and restaurants. Some of them were festooned with strings of garlic, hanging from the ceiling and doorways. It was always fun to be there. I was sitting in a bar one evening, in my light blue ski jacket, having a drink by myself when I noticed three girls sitting diagonally to my left, looking at me occasionally.

The waiter came over and signaled to me that the girls wanted to talk to me. I looked at the waiter and pointed to my chest, asking whether they wanted to talk to me; he nodded and smiled and walked away. I looked at the girls; one girl with jet-black short crinkly hair smiled at me and gestured with her hand to join them. I again pointed to my chest, wondering whether it was really me they wanted. I initially thought it was the Spanish guy on my right whom they really wanted. But now that I was sure, I got up and walked to their table and sat down.

Barely had I settled down, when the Spanish guy who was sitting on my right and had been observing the sign language all this while, came and asked the girls in Spanish if he could join them as well. The girl with dark hair just said, "No," and told him to go away.

So, here I was, invited to sit at the table with three young girls. The girl wearing tight black jeans with black hair was from Honduras; she spoke absolutely no English, not even "hello". The girl doing the Spanish translation was a slim-built girl with light brown shoulder-length hair from Panama. She was not fluent in English, but far better than her friend from Honduras. The third girl was a beautiful Spanish girl from Madrid, who spoke no English at all.

From what I could figure out, the girl from Honduras took a shine to me, and wanted me, as was relayed to me by the girl from Panama. The Spanish girl just laughed all the time. The girls suggested we go out dancing somewhere.

They took me to a discotheque, which was very dark. We could barely see each other. It was also warm inside the disco, and I had removed my jacket. The girl from Honduras pulled me to the dance floor and held me close, very close.

She was looking at me longingly, the problem being that I could not talk to her. A couple of dances later we returned to the table. Next, it was my turn to dance with the slim girl from Panama.

She again held me up close, but not too close, and said, "My friend really likes you."

"I cannot understand her," I said.

"Yes, I know, but she is a very good friend of mine. I like you and would like to be with you. I do not have a boyfriend, but now you are hers," she said sadly and matter-of-factly. "I have not been with a man for a long time, but my friend really wants you now; let's go back."

The music changed, the lights became a bit brighter, and she moved away.

It was one of those moments in life that come and go. Here I was with two appealing women, both of whom wanted me that night. The Panamanian girl gave me up for her friend from Honduras. The fact is that I ended up with neither, as I had no place to take either of them!

Never has this experience ever been repeated in my life. In retrospect, I could have gone with the Honduras girl; they did ask me to come home with them, but I really did not want to take the risk of getting into a sticky situation. I just had one more dance with the beautiful, spunky Spanish girl; she simply laughed all the while.

I stayed at the pension for one month, in the same room, with the bathroom down the hallway. Almost every night, between 1 a.m. and 3 a.m., I would hear a woman moaning in sexual passion. "Miguel, Miguel," she would scream. This lady was one noisy lover. Her passionate screams would rent the air for about five minutes; nothing was really said other than, "Miguel, Miguel..." Her moans and screams got louder and louder and then would suddenly peter out when she was done. Oh yes, that I could hear, loud and clear.

I visited the Prado Art Museum in Madrid. It has one of the finest collections of European art. For someone who does not particularly like museums, I thoroughly enjoyed my visit to the Prado. I remember seeing a lot of work by Francisco de Goya.

Goya painted with oils directly onto the walls of his house in Madrid in the early 18th century. Goya never did put up all his paintings for sale. He did a series of intensely haunting paintings called the Black Paintings. It was only after Goya died that the paintings were transferred from the walls of his house to canvas, and they can now be seen at the Prado Museum. Goya's statue adorns the entrance of the Prado museum.

One day, I went to see flamenco dancing. It is a great, invigorating dance sequence, which I thoroughly enjoyed. The girl doing the flamenco dance was a dusky, beautiful Spanish lady with long black hair.

I did not have a work permit to work in Spain. Matt had allowed me to work as long as I had a valid visa for Spain, which was for 30 days from my arrival. Into my third week at Sea Land, Madrid, the accounts manager called me into his office one day and said, "Would you like to continue at Sea Land, Madrid? I am checking to see where I can fit you in. We have an opening coming up for a financial analyst. Would you like to do that?"

I looked at the accounts manager and said, "Finance is not my best subject, maybe I should let it go."

"Are you sure?" he asked.

"Yes, I am sure. If it were in Operations or Shipping, I would have loved to take you up on it," I said.

"Where will you go now? Will you return to Rotterdam?" he asked.

For some reason, many in Sea Land, Madrid, thought I had come on deputation from Sea Land, Rotterdam, in some quality assessment role.

"No." I looked at him, a bit surprised. "I will probably return to India."

I went to meet Matt and told him that I had passed up the financial analyst job.

"Why did you do that?" he asked.

"Because I cannot add two and two. Each time I do, I get five!" I said.

"What nonsense, all Indians are good at Math. You did a great job for me in Tehran, and that was a lot of Math, you did that quite easily," he said. "There is, unfortunately, no other opening at this time, that's why I had told the accounts manager to offer you the financial analyst role. You are welcome to stay at Sea Land, Madrid, as long as your visa permits you."

That decided, I knew my time in Spain was soon coming to an end. I had all of one week left. In all honesty, I had not expected Matt to offer me a job at Sea Land, Madrid. Knowing the visa situation, especially after I had been to Rotterdam, where they did not even give me a try, I was bowled over by his graciousness and generosity in offering me an opportunity to recoup some of the money I had spent on my travels in Europe.

Matt was always a bit of a maverick. On an Easter Sunday in Tehran, on the Resurrection of Jesus, Matt had sent a fax to all his colleagues that read: "Happy Jesus fly-up day." He had an innate sense of humor.

To this day, I think of what Matt did for me. In later life, too, I found that it was always total strangers, and in my case, my overseas bosses who helped me out - Kar, Charles, Hans, and Matt. My story would be totally incomplete without Matt and what he did for me.

So, finally, I purchased a one-way train ticket from Madrid to London and decided to leave Madrid on the last day of my Spanish visa, 14th November. I was going to go back the same way I had come, via France, but this time I had unequivocally decided not to apply for a French visa. I was thoroughly disgusted by the French and did not want to give them another opportunity to upset me. If they did not allow me to enter France, so be it, I would fly to London. My last week in Madrid was fun. I visited El Escorial, the traditional home of the King of Spain, which is a short distance from Madrid. El Escorial is like a monastery. I also visited Valle de los Caidos (Valley of the Fallen), the final resting place of Francisco Franco, the former Fascist dictator of Spain. Franco lies entombed under a 150-meter-high stone cross, which can be seen from afar, rising as it does from a rocky outcrop.

On my last day at Sea Land, Madrid, I wished everyone goodbye, especially Juan and Pedro. I profusely thanked Matt for everything he had done for me and left the company smiling with a bunch of lovely memories.

On my last evening, I was strolling around my pension. I was walking past the metro station when I saw the beautiful Spanish girl whom I had met with the two girls from Honduras and Panama. She instantly recognized me, and we got talking or rather started gesticulating! She introduced herself to me: "My name is Elena Moreno, or Helen Brown in English."

I invited Elena out to coffee and she instantly accepted.

Elena could barely speak English nor could she understand any English. She was so beautiful, so effervescent, so charming, with a knockout smile. Why must I meet this woman on my last night in Madrid, I thought to myself. Elena and I had a cup of coffee together and some muffins, and off she went, very happy with herself. A rather beautiful end to my Spanish story I thought.

The train from Madrid left midmorning for London.

Jumping the French Border

I arrived at the railway station and found myself in a fourberth empty compartment. I was tired, and all I wanted to do was sleep. I just could not get Elena out of my head; I could not stop thinking of her.

A few minutes later, a rather bedraggled English girl in her late 20s entered the compartment and sat down opposite me. Her name was Kay. She told me she had just arrived from Morocco, North Africa, via Gibraltar, the day before, that all her money had run out and that she had not had a bath for a week, which I could quite easily smell.

Kay lay down on the berth opposite me and passed out. The train chugged out of Madrid. As it made its way north to the French border, the scenery turned rural and rustic. The train would stop often; some people came with their hens in a basket, one guy came with his sheep. I was quite amused; this was like India.

When Kay got up, I told her that I might not get a French visa. She said not to be stupid, that I would surely get one as I was going to London. Around ten o'clock at night, the train came to a stop at the last point in Spain. We were all told to get off.

The platform where we disembarked was narrow and very dimly lit; I wondered where the heck I was. In a single line, we made our way to the French immigration counter which was manned by an immigration officer in a tweed jacket with a gendarme, all in blue, at his side. What's with these tweed coats? I thought. This was the second time I had come across them.

The immigration officer looked at my passport and said, "India, how nice, where are you going?"

I said "London" and kept quiet.

He flicked through my passport, looked at my onward ticket to London, smiled, and gave my passport back to me saying, "Welcome to France."

I was so surprised that he did not ask any other questions. "Are you not going to stamp my passport?" I asked.

"No," he said, "you are going to London, you are not going to break your journey in France, are you?" "No," I said, "I am not going to do that. I have a plane to catch from London in three days."

I entered France without much ado. Kay looked at me and said, "I told you; it was easy, wasn't it?"

I did not know what to say. Oh well, this time it worked. The train left for Paris a little later. Kay and I found another fourberth compartment to ourselves and went to sleep for the night.

The next day, the train reached Paris. We had a four-hour wait before we caught the train to Calais. I asked Kay if she would like to come and check out Paris with me. We wandered up and down the Left Bank, had a coffee and something to eat and got back to the railway station to catch the train to Calais.

The train to Calais is a chair car; it's about a four-hour ride to the Calais-Folkestone Ferry. About halfway to Calais, the train conductor started doing the immigration formalities. He came and checked everyone's passport and gave them a pink-colored card which denoted that they had cleared French immigration.

I could see the conductor doing this from the far end of the coach. Kay was sitting next to me on the adjacent seat, reading a magazine. The conductor came to me, looked at my passport, flipped through it, said something in French and returned my passport to me without the pink card. Kay was given her pink immigration card without much ado.

I asked the conductor why he was not giving me an immigration card; his English was limited, so he could not tell me what the issue was. He took my passport, saying he would check and left.

For the next 20 minutes, I was on tenterhooks, wondering what could be going on, why I was not being given my immigration card. When the conductor returned, he gave me back my passport and said something in French which I could not understand.

I got up from my seat and turned around and said, "Can someone please translate for me what this man is saying?"

One man volunteered and spoke to the conductor in French and said, "He says he checked with his superior officer and the thing is you need a visa for France."

I told him that I was going to London and that I was traveling along with this lady, indicating Kay, from Madrid.

The man turned around and explained the situation to the conductor, who had a long conversation in French. They turned to me and the man explained: "The conductor says that you do not have a French arrival stamp on your passport. Without an arrival stamp, they cannot give you an exit stamp. He says that you should go to Paris to get your visa sorted out." With that said, the conductor left.

I sat down in my seat, wondering what the heck I was going to do now. Going back to Paris was not an option. They might inquire what I was doing there in the first place. I had specifically asked the French immigration officer to stamp my passport, to which he had summarily said it was not required.

At the next station, I saw the conductor get off the train. I thought to myself, I was cooked for real and good this time. Kay had gone to the toilet. Suddenly, an idea struck me.

When Kay came back, I said to her, "There is one option."

"Which is?" she said looking at me. I looked into her eyes and said, "Can you give me your immigration pink card?"

"What will happen to me?" she asked.

"Nothing will happen to you," I said, "you have a British passport."

"The train conductor did not even check your passport; he looked at the color of your passport, and immediately gave you your immigration card. I have an Indian passport, that's the problem. If you give me your immigration card, all you have to tell the guys at the ferry boarding gangway is that when the conductor came around to the coach giving the immigration cards, you were in the toilet. That is all you have to tell them. I am sure they will believe you. Please Kay, please do this for me. With my Indian passport, they will give me the run-around in Paris. I will probably miss my flight from London to Bombay. Please help me. I told you about the trouble I went through the last time in France. This time it will be much worse." I went on, pleading, "Kay, if you give me your immigration card, I will buy you anything you want from duty-free. I mean, I will buy you any one single item that you want."

Kay looked at me squarely and said, "Will you buy me a carton of Kent cigarettes?"

"Yes," I said, breathing a sigh of relief, "I will buy you a carton of Kent cigarettes, and if they do not have that in stock, you can tell me what you would like instead."

Kay and I had struck a deal.

The train slowly pulled into Calais and came to a stop, close to the where the ferry was docked.

We disembarked from the train. I was walking hunched, keeping my suitcase on my right, trying to be as invisible as I could. I did not want to get noticed by either the train conductor or even some of the passengers in my coach, who by now would have known that I was not supposed to be there.

I was praying silently that I would not get picked by French customs for an inspection of my suitcase as had happened in Geneva.

I approached the ferry and handed over my immigration card to the Frenchman standing there, who waved me through. I crossed the gangplank and entered the ferry. I stopped at the corner, waiting to see what became of Kay.

Kay was the third person behind me; when her turn came, she handed over her ferry crossing ticket to the Frenchman who said, "Billet?" Kay proffered him her ferry ticket. "Billet," said the Frenchman, and again Kay extended her ferry ticket. "Billet," said the Frenchman and yet again Kay pushed her ferry ticket forward.

"I want your pink slip," said the Frenchman.

"I don't have one," said Kay. "I was in the toilet." He looked at Kay, looked at her British passport, and muttered "Brits!" under his breath and pointed for her to proceed.

I met Kay at the ferry entrance, profusely thanked her, and kissed her on the cheek.

"It's okay, it's okay, it was nothing," she said.

Kay and I immediately went right to the lower deck, carting my suitcase with me. I told Kay that once the ferry sails, I would buy her the cigarettes.

The ferry did not set sail for another 30 minutes. I was beginning to fret that maybe they had counted that they had one person too many on board. I was half expecting someone to come and check all the passengers.

Nothing of the sort happened. The ferry foghorn sounded, one long beep, and the ferry moved forward. As it moved away from Calais harbor, I heaved a sigh of relief. "These bloody French," I muttered.

I found Kay and went with her to the duty-free shop. They had Kent cigarettes in stock, and I got her a carton and again thanked her for what she had just done for me. The enormity of what I had just done began to sink in, crashing the French border, poetic justice I thought, but it could have gone horribly wrong.

From Folkestone, Kay and I took the train to Victoria Station, London. At Victoria, I thanked Kay yet again. By the time I arrived at the youth hostel in London, I was dead tired.

I had a couple of days in London, so I went shopping and got myself some new clothes. In Spain, I had purchased a pair of very trendy tan colored boots and wanted some clothes to match. Kitted out with a new wardrobe, I left for India.

CHAPTER THIRTEEN

Back to India

On the 17th of November, I took the Air India flight from London to Bombay. I wanted to check out some employment options in Bombay.

Sitting next to me on the flight was a large American, Mr. Adams, who was very full of himself. He told me that he frequently traveled to Bombay, selling celluloid chemicals for the film industry. He went on to say that he was fed up of his agent in Bombay and was looking to employ someone. He asked me whether I might be interested.

"You can come with me to some production houses, see what happens there and let me know if you would like to work for me."

It all sounded pretty good to me. We landed at Bombay and Mr. Adams and I shared a taxi together. He got off at the Taj Mahal Hotel. The taxi driver recommended I stay at Hotel Green, on Marine Drive, a few minutes' walk from Churchgate.

The next day, Mr. Adams, his local man at Bombay, Mr. Atul Shah, and I set off in a taxi, going from one production house to another. The taxi was not air-conditioned; it was very hot and got very tiring, and Mr. Adams kept falling asleep. Mr. Shah did not take a shine to me at all; he was actually quite hostile.

"I will call you and let you know whether you are on board or not," said Mr. Adams. I got no call from Mr. Adams. Since I was not really doing very much the next day, I took a taxi and arrived at the Taj Mahal Hotel. I was beginning to have second thoughts about whether Mr. Adams was for real.

I took the lift and went to his room and knocked on his door.

"Why did you come without calling me? You cannot do that. Suppose I had someone in the room with me?" And that was the end of Mr. Adams.

Having put the Adams chemical opportunity to bed, I took the flight to Delhi. It was great to be back in Delhi. I knew a lot of people there, had a stack of relatives and was very much at home there. It's also where my journey to Iran had started.

While I was traveling in Europe, the rumblings in Iran against the Shah had started. By December 1978, most of the expats in Iran had begun leaving due to the perceived instability. Amarjit left Tehran in early December. I am not sure what became of some of the other people I knew there. Amarjit said he could take out all his money from his bank account and convert it to hard currency. Many people who did not mobilize their finances in time were caught on the wrong foot when the Shah decreed that all foreign bank accounts be frozen. I was lucky to get out when I did, unscathed. Had I left at this point, in December 1978, minus a work visa, I might not have been so lucky. In January 1979, the Shah of Iran was evicted and replaced with the Islamic fundamentalist, Ayatollah Khomeini, who returned from France following the overthrow of the Shah.

As I reached Delhi, I mused about my time in Tehran; how lucky I had been to find such nice people who gave me a job and literally took me into their homes. I particularly thought a lot about Kar Sakhuja. I do not know what happened to Kar and Charles, whether they managed to get to Andorra or not.

My great friend from Sanawar, Sonny Chhatwal, who was with me in Siwalik House, was also in Delhi when I returned from my travels. For the next month, I just chilled doing nothing; it was great to be back. I had brought some money back with me from London, and a bag full of happy memories.

In January, my first cousin, Gokul Tandan, who was working for his brother-in-law, Mr. Shiv Nadar, at HCL Limited was toying with the idea of opening a manufacturing line for dictating machines, or Dictaphones as they were called. The issue was that Gokul did not want to quit his job at HCL and start working on a start-up, because of the long gestation or lead time involved in setting up a manufacturing unit with imported Dictaphones in kit form.

Gokul offered me a position at Genesis India Private Limited. My job was to set up the production line for his company. This meant liaising with government officials, dealing with the small-scale Industries Board, the Reserve Bank of India, and other regulatory bodies. This appealed to me as I was the sole person pushing this and could do it my way.

Initially, I found it difficult; however, as I came to grips with the bureaucratic system, it became very easy to do. While I was working for Gokul, I also shifted in and lived with Gokul and his parents for a year in

1979.

Gokul's mother, Aunty Mohini, was most keen that I get a "proper job". She set up an interview for me with Mr. Dalbir Kapur, director of Duncan Brothers, the tea company. I arrived at Mr. Kapur's office at Kasturba Gandhi Marg and was shown into his rather small office.

The interview commenced, and routine questions like what did I study, what had I been doing the last year, etc. followed. I looked at Mr. Kapur and said, "Well, I was in Tehran for the last year and got back to Delhi very recently."

"What were you doing in Iran?" Mr. Kapur asked.

"I was working in a containerized shipping company."

"What does that mean?"

I explained the concept of container shipping. Suddenly it was I who was controlling the interview, as the next question was based on my last answer. I had kind of intrigued Mr. Kapur.

"I understand from your aunt that you want a job at the tea gardens," he said.

"Yes," I said, "that's correct."

"Would you like a job with Duncan Exports in Calcutta? That is directly under me. We can fit you in there."

"No, Sir, I would like to go to the tea gardens."

"How did the interview go?" Aunty Mohini asked.

"I think it went quite well," I said and left it at that.

Three days later, Aunty Mohini said, "Dalbir got back to me today."

"Oh? How did I fare in the interview?"

"Very well," said Aunty Mohini.

"Did I get the job?" I asked.

"No, you did not. Dalbir said you did well in the interview, but that he had to interview the other candidates as well for the same job; that is why it took him three days to get back to me. The thing is, you did so much better than the other candidates that Dalbir is not sure whether the tea garden job will suit you."

"Is that why I was not offered a job, because I did brilliantly in the interview?" I asked incredulously.

"Yes, apparently that's the reason," she replied.

A few years later, I bumped into Mr. Kapur at the Gymkhana Club. The tea gardens were taking a beating commercially; it was all over the papers.

"Would you like a job at the tea gardens?" he asked.

"No, Sir, that time has passed," I said and smiled.

By October 1979, I had procured the import license to import Dictaphone kits from Taiwan. My mandate was more or less over; Gokul had quit HCL by this time and had taken charge of his company.

In December 1979, I formally quit Genesis India Private Limited. I was looking for more challenging opportunities.

Trador Inc

In January 1980, I joined my Uncle Kenny and his business partner, HH Maharaja of Jaipur, Lt Col Sawai Bhawani Singh (Retired), in their company, Trador Inc, as an export manager. A few years later, after he had retired, Lt Col Sawai Bhawani Singh, Maharaja of Jaipur, was accorded the rank of Brigadier, a rare honour, by the Prime Minister of India, Mr. Rajiv Gandhi.

Trador was established as a merchant export company with its head office at the Taj Man Singh Hotel, Suite 1026/1027.

This meant that each day I would go to the Taj Man Singh Hotel for work and come back in the evening to Billy Masi's (my mother's sister) house, where I was staying in Delhi at the time.

Life was easy, and it was good. What could be better than working from the Taj Hotel, in salubrious surroundings, and eating at their fabulous restaurants? In 1980, the Taj had the Captain's Cabin; Machan, the coffee shop; House of Ming, the Chinese restaurant, managed by Frankie; and, an Italian restaurant on the rooftop.

HH Jaipur or Uncle Bubbles, as we called him, was always very polite and effusive. He was very particular in maintaining his latest contact list of phone numbers. In those days, there were no electronic phone diaries, and everything had to be typed or written by longhand. Uncle Bubbles had a private secretary, Shyam, whose job was just to maintain a typed list of Uncle Bubbles' contacts on Rolodex cards.

Trador was essentially a contact-based company; there was literally no one we did not know, or could not get to know. Those were party days as well. Whenever I had a date or wanted to impress a girl, I would borrow Gokul's Fiat or his mother's Ambassador.

Around September 1980, Uncle Bubbles' driver, Prahladh Singh, who was an ex-Army man from the Guards, told me that there was a low bonnet, left-hand jeep for sale in Jaipur. I spoke to the Thakur, the current owner of the jeep in Jaipur, who said he was willing to sell it for INR 8,000.

So, off I went to Jaipur. I stayed with Uncle Joey, Uncle Bubbles' gregarious younger brother. The Thakur brought the jeep to the house, a left-hand-drive Willy's MB. I looked at it and instantly purchased it. All it needed was a new 6-volt battery and it was ready to go. A battery was purchased, and straight after a late lunch, I set off for Delhi, which I made in five hours.

The next day, I handed the jeep over to Billu, the mechanic, to spruce it up. The vehicle used to originally belong to HH Maharaja Sawai Man Singh of Jaipur, who later presented it to the Thakur, who used to look after the HH's polo ponies. The jeep had broad seats, with side armrests that could be folded back. At the center was a box equipped to carry bottles, which I assume at some time would have been mostly alcohol, and to a lesser extent soda and water.

The jeep's body, which was in a rather good condition, was repaired; it needed some denting work and was painted dead white in color, with jet-black seats. It looked quite regal and spectacular. I would park the jeep at the Taj Hotel porch where the former 'President's Body Guards', working at the Taj Hotel as doormen and valets, would always bring the vehicle to me with a flourish.

Life was good; I had a sexy jeep to drive (my first vehicle), a great office to work out of and I got to meet all kinds of people with Uncle Bubbles.

Uncle Joey, in those days, was establishing a farm to rear goats for export to the Middle East. He had a manager from Australia called Frank who had retired from a large farm doing precisely the same thing in Australia. "Young Frank," as Uncle Joey called him, would sit and drink gallons of whiskey each day with Uncle Joey. Young Frank was actually in his late 60s but would keep Uncle Joey drinking company day in and day out.

But, but, but that's the way the motorboat goes. Why was I born so beautiful, why was I born at all?

These were some of Uncle Joey's favorite drinking ditties.

Gokul got married in 1980, and I had a bachelor party for him at Sundar Nagar. To spice it up, I organized a *Mujra* or dancing girls for Gokul; it was hilarious and went down very well with everyone.

In late September 1980, I was sent to London for a meeting with Guinness Peat and Co., the firm represented by us in India, to discuss a large transaction. To save money, I decided to crash for a couple of nights with my friend Vivek Kohli who lived in a working persons hostel called London

House in Russell Square. Vivek was studying to be a chartered accountant.

Vivek had a tiny bedroom in London House, with a toilet down the corridor. Guests, as such, were not allowed, and Vivek, being very proper, said that during work hours I should not be in the room, or else the management might catch on that someone other than the actual tenant was staying in the room.

I would leave London House in the morning, shortly after Vivek, for a round of meetings with Guinness Peat and return in the evenings and have dinner and the odd beer with him. I would sleep on the floor on a mattress that Vivek had borrowed from one of his friends in the hostel. One day, the cleaner, who had recently joined the housekeeping crew, came to Vivek's room and found him getting ready to go to work. Normally, the cleaner always saw me in the room at that time. The cleaner asked Vivek why he was getting ready in the room. She had assumed that I was the actual tenant and Vivek the guest!

A couple of days later, Uncle Bubbles arrived in London, along with his personal valet from Jaipur, Mr. Bhanwar Singh. Uncle Bubbles was staying in a three-bedroom villa in Knightsbridge. Having a spare bedroom, he invited me to move across, which I was very happy to do. From London House on a mattress on the floor to a luxury villa in Knightsbridge, opposite Harrods, it was a most welcome change indeed.

One day, I had arranged to meet Uncle Bubbles at Guinness Peat, in the city, at 3 p.m., for an important meeting. Uncle Bubbles was late, which was a bit unlike him; when he did arrive, he seemed a bit flustered. I could tell that something was wrong.

I quickly finished the meeting, promising to return the next day and asked Uncle Bubbles, "Is anything the matter?"

"It's Bhanwar Singh. He got himself arrested for shoplifting at Harrods," he said.

"Goodness, what do we do now?" I said.

"I have spoken to a very good friend of mine, an ex-SAS senior officer, who has contacted a lawyer in the city. We are trying to get Bhanwar out on bail," said Uncle Bubbles.

By the time Uncle Bubbles and I got to Knightsbridge, Bhanwar Singh had been released on bail and was hiding in his room, petrified at what his boss might say. I asked Bhanwar Singh what had happened; he said he had gone to Harrods as he always did for his daily grocery shopping and was just leaving when he spotted a ballpoint pen on the shelf close to the exit.

Bhanwar Singh said he picked up the pen, holding it up to the light for a closer look. Just then, a lady with several shopping bags arrived, trying to leave the store. Since Bhanwar was standing right by the door, he took one step back, allowing the lady to pass him, and found he had actually stepped outside the store as the alarm went off.

I told him to tell Uncle Bubbles exactly what he had told me, but he was petrified, literally shivering in fright. Finally, he confessed to Uncle Bubbles that he had made a mistake by stepping outside the store and that he would never do that again. Instead of shouting at him, Uncle Bubbles gave him a £ 50 tip! Bhanwar Singh was most relieved, and so was I.

A short while later, a translator arrived from the court to take Bhanwar Singh's deposition. Until then, the translator, an Indian lady in a sari, did not know that Bhanwar Singh was HH Jaipur's personal valet; when she came to know this, her demeanor completely changed. Bhanwar Singh gave his deposition, just as he had told me. Uncle Bubbles added that Bhanwar Singh had been working for him for the last eight years and that never had a single item gone missing. He went on to say that Bhanwar Singh had access to valuable things such as gold lighters, cufflinks and the like. So why would he choose to steal a five-pound ballpoint pen when there were other far more expensive items to steal right in front of him? It simply did not make sense.

The lawyer from the city had also arrived by this time and it was decided the best course of action would be for Bhanwar Singh to plead guilty, pay the fine and be done with it. To plead innocence could mean another court date, wherein the whole thing would get dragged for a longer period. Uncle Bubbles was also rather concerned about the media getting wind of this.

Bhanwar Singh, on the other hand, said, "I did not steal, why should I plead guilty? I cannot say I have done something which I have not. I am a Rajput. I will not lie."

I tried to explain to Bhanwar Singh this was the best option, one which would yield the fastest result. Bhanwar Singh finally relented, but when he was giving his formal deposition to the court translator, he said: "But I did not do so."

I asked the court translator to please say guilty when the judge asked Bhanwar Singh, "Guilty or not guilty?" and I coached Bhanwar Singh to just nod his head and not actually say anything. "That way," I told Bhanwar Singh, "you would have not told a lie."

The next day, Bhanwar Singh was to appear at the magistrate's court on Horse Ferry Road. I was under strict instructions from Uncle Bubbles to get

Bhanwar Singh home in one piece, unscathed.

Bhanwar Singh's name was announced, and with that he stood up, wearing a suit. I was sitting at the back of the visitor's gallery. "Is there anyone to represent Mr. Singh?" the magistrate cursorily asked to which the lawyer responded that he was there to represent him. The magistrate got a bit confused as to why a Queen's Counsel, a very senior lawyer, would be engaged in something so petty. The lawyer wriggled himself out of this by saying he was just there to introduce Bhanwar Singh, and that Mr. Sanjiv T. Lall, sitting in the gallery, would actually represent him in court.

The magistrate thought about it for a moment and asked, "Guilty or not guilty?"

Bhanwar Singh, by this stage, was getting increasingly perturbed. He mumbled something. The translator leaned towards Bhanwar Singh and said, "Guilty."

Now it was my turn. The judge asked me to guarantee to get Bhanwar Singh out of the country before the expiration of his visa and ensure he never returned to the UK.

"Yes, I would," I said. A penalty of £120 was imposed. Case closed.

I immediately went and paid £120 fine, gave the receipt to the court clerk, and Bhanwar Singh was released. I went to Bhanwar Singh who was sitting in the court's holding area. I waved the piece of paper at him, and he stepped out with a big smile. Bhanwar Singh returned to India with HH Jaipur ten days later.

Trador Inc. had secured a very large export order for frozen pomfret fish to Kuwait, and I was sent to Bombay to ensure the shipment left on time. That done, I took the evening flight to Delhi in time for the New Year's Eve festivities. My friend Deepak Chhatwal was in town from Los Angeles, as was my school buddy, Sonny Chhatwal, both friends unrelated to each other.

I took a taxi from the airport directly to Deepak's house in Defence Colony, arriving there around 11:30 p.m. to find the guys well on their way with a few whiskeys under their belt. I was on my second drink when the clock struck midnight. Sonny came up to me and wished me a happy New Year, gave me a bear hug, and proceeded to lift me up in his arms. The next moment, Sonny went for a toss, falling backward, his foot having slipped on a cube of ice lying on the floor. Both my arms were locked, as Sonny had his arms around me. I was wearing gold-rimmed glasses and hit my head slap bang into the wall. The glasses broke, and I landed on the floor on top of

Sonny, with blood gushing out of my right eyebrow.

I don't know whether it was plain party exuberance or whether Sonny had slipped as he said he did, the fact was my face was cut up. I took myself to a hospital in Kailash Colony. The guard would not open the gate. Being 31st December, he had been instructed not to allow anyone to enter at night, especially single boys. I spoke to the doctor, a young lady doctor on duty, told her that I had met with an accident, that I had not been drinking, and needed a few stitches. The young doctor looked at me, and said, "Yes, you do need a few stitches."

She was very pretty, so I tried talking to her lying on the gurney as I was.

"Don't talk to me," she said, and put gauze over my entire face. She cut out a small patch over my right eyebrow so that she could stitch. Squinting through my good eye, I could make out her neatly plucked eyebrows.

"You are very pretty," I said.

"Will you shut up please and let me work," she said.

Duly mended and stitched up, Sonny and I went back to the party. It was 1 January 1981.

I thoroughly enjoyed working at Trador; it was a breeze and great fun. Working as I was in a five-star hotel made it even more fun. I even got to travel a bit to Singapore and UK on work.

CHAPTER FIFTEEN

Sakshi

Time rolled on. It was mid-1982. Suheil introduced me to DC, who used to live in Calcutta. DC and Suheil had been together in school in Gwalior. DC was a huge drinker and loved his food and booze. When DC came to Delhi to meet his parents, I met him and got very friendly with him; we began to meet almost every day.

One day, when I got to DC's house, he told me, "Meet my younger sister, Sakshi, from Bombay." I thought Sakshi was the most beautiful girl in the world. She was going through a divorce and had come to Delhi to ease the stress. It was almost Diwali, and the card parties had just begun

Whenever I dropped by at DC's house, we would all sit around drinking. Sakshi would often come and sit with us. One evening, the whiskey ran out, and I said to DC, "Why don't you come home with me? I have half a bottle of Chivas Regal, and we can have a few drinks and go out to the Machan for dinner."

DC came home with me. It was beginning to get cold, and we had a couple of drinks each.

Around 2 a.m., adequately fortified by whiskey, we decided to go out to the Taj Hotel for dinner. We set off in my opentop jeep. I am not quite sure what it was, whether it was the whiskey or the cold or perhaps a combination of the two; I had barely driven two kilometers when, taking a right turn, I totally blanked out. The jeep went over a steep curb; I woke up at that point and remember seeing the jeep turning turtle on its left side. Involuntarily, I stuck out my left hand to break the fall, and lo and behold, my left hand got squashed below my own body.

DC fell on me, fast asleep in an alcoholic stupor. "Wake up DC, wake up," I said.

"Why am I lying in this strange position?" mumbled DC.

"You are lying on top of me, get the heck up," I kept saying.

Fortunately, the jeep had overturned very close to a Sikh taxi stand. They came running and pulled DC out like a sack of potatoes, and then gently pulled me out, with my left hand twisted behind me. They pushed the vehicle upright, and I discovered that the jeep's brake pipe had burst, and all the brake fluid had leaked out. I turned the ignition, and fortunately, the engine started immediately. I drove the jeep slowly without brakes, with DC besides me, back to the Sundar Nagar taxi stand. I jumped into a cab and went to the hospital to get my hand looked at. DC was put into another taxi and sent home.

I came back home by 7 a.m. with my left hand in soft plaster and made arrangements for the mechanic to fix the brake pipe of the jeep. That was a relatively easy thing to fix. That evening, I went to DC's house with my hand in a sling, looking for sympathy, which I daresay I got plenty of from Sakshi. Diwali that year was lucky for me. Sakshi and I would play as a team in the card games. All the money we made would be stuffed into my sling and on we would go. It was good, clean fun.

The Taj Hotel had a disco called the Number One. One day, I took DC, Sakshi, and Suheil to it, and all of us had a drink too many. I remember I was dancing with Sakshi, and she looked at me and asked, "Is DC going to be with us all the time or are you going to invite me out alone? Or, are you going to chicken out?"

Two days later, I took Sakshi out to the Number One, alone. I had gone across to her house and was having a drink with her, DC and his parents. As dinner progressed, around 11 p.m., Sakshi and I announced that we were going out for a bit. "You are going out alone with Sakshi?" DC asked.

"Yes," I said, "we are."

"Okay, I will wait for you both," he said

Sakshi and I went to the disco in my jeep. She was looking absolutely gorgeous in a sari. It would have been around midnight. I was on the floor, having a slow dance with Sakshi, when she said, "When are you going to make love to me?"

I looked at her a bit startled; that was exactly what I had been thinking. With Sakshi saying so, it made it that much easier.

I took Sakshi to my room, and we immediately jumped into bed. Sakshi was a very experienced lover. I knew just about nothing about pleasing a woman. Early in the morning, it became a huge struggle to get Sakshi back into her sari. By the time we got back to Sakshi's house, DC was fast asleep; apparently, he had waited till 4 a.m. for us.

The next evening, as soon as I walked in, DC asked me, "Where did you take my sister last night? I waited until four in the morning."

"We went out for dinner, and then we went for a drive to India Gate for ice cream," I replied.

"Do you expect me to believe that?"

"What, Dada?" Sakshi said. "What's the big deal? So, we went out."

I had never met a woman like Sakshi before; she took me where I had never been before. She was a fabulous cook, a woman extraordinaire. Sakshi was a party girl; she loved throwing parties and cooking.

In late 1982, I shifted to Kaka Nagar, to my grandmother's house. I took my white jeep with me. Living in Kaka Nagar was much more relaxed than living in Sundar Nagar, and then there was Narain Singh, my grandmother's excellent cook. He rustled up some of the most unusual meat dishes I have ever had.

My grandmother, Smt. Naina Devi, whom I have mentioned earlier, was a very famous *ghazal* and *thumri* singer. She ran a music society called Raag Rang, which often hosted Indian classical music evenings, frequented by all the great Indian classical artists of India. Here I routinely met several renowned and acclaimed Indian Classical *ustads* and maestros, who would regularly come to visit my grandmother.

I soon became very friendly with a local astrologer, Mr. J. N. Sharma. We would meet almost every day and have a drink or two. Yes, J.N. was a bit of a hep tantric guru and astrologer.

Sakshi and I continued to see each other. I think I had her parent's approval, and I daresay, her brother's approval as well, though he never did tell me. After his tenth whiskey late at night, he would say, "I hope you have honest intentions towards my sister. Where did you take her last night?"

Sakshi wanted love; she was yearning for love. Maybe it was her bitter divorce, and the young son that she had. She would tell me that her husband would beat her up, literally beat her, till she had scars on her body. She suffered the marriage, maybe because when she got married, her parents did not approve of her husband, and perhaps she wanted to prove her parents wrong. Instead of the marriage getting better, it steadily got worse until it totally broke down.

One night, around 11:30 p.m., I heard a knock on my bedroom window; I looked out and saw Sakshi outside. It was winter; she was standing in her cotton kaftan, shivering. I pulled Sakshi inside the bedroom through the toilet which had a door leading out to the rear garden. "What are you doing here?" I asked. "It's almost midnight; my grandmother is sleeping next door."

"I was lonely and wanted to see you."

We talked the night away and a few hours later, I walked Sakshi to the Oberoi Hotel taxi stand and saw her home.

Sakshi coming to Kaka Nagar late at night became a regular feature. On the third occasion, in the morning, my grandmother asked me, "Bablu, is there someone with you?" We all had morning tea together. My grandmother at that time was secretly quite happy because Sakshi was a Bengali, and she was pleased I had a Bengali girlfriend.

Suheil got married in Jaipur, in early 1983. Alex, Udit, Sakshi, and I drove down to Jaipur for his wedding. Suheil had advertised for a bride in the matrimonial column of the newspaper and had selected his wife himself.

A month later, I went to Manila to meet Sonny, who was doing a two-year MBA program at the Asian Institute of Management. Sonny had just finished his final papers.

Some of the girls I saw in Manila were stunning. I was told it was the mix of the Spanish and Filipino blood or Mestizo, as it was called, that created these staggeringly beautiful women. Tall, long-legged, fine features, great complexion - all made for gorgeous-looking elegant women.

In Manila, sex was in your face, just like it was in the Reeperbahn area of Frankfurt. You saw it wherever you turned. As an impressionable young man, I was shocked at what I saw. Anyone wanting sex could just get into a taxi and tell the cabbie to take them to the nearest motel where the rooms were available for hire by the hour or by the night. The motel rooms were often adorned with mirrors on the walls, and even on the ceiling. Sleaze everywhere. Sonny was very amused at my reaction and laughed at the expressions on my face. Sightseeing was fun with Sonny. The highlight was the Pagsanjan River, the location where the movie *Apocalypse* Now was shot. Manila was also as cheap as chips; it was simply just great fun to be there.

After a few days break, I was back in Delhi and back to Sakshi.

One day, she had gone to attend a wedding, and just as she returned home, I showed up and asked her if she would like to come out for dinner. She readily agreed. She came out in her heavy, Bengali green silk sari and looked gorgeous in it. We set off in my jeep for Pandara Road. I was taking a wide turn into the small lane of Pandara Road, and Sakshi was sitting without a seat belt and not holding the handrails. The next thing I noticed was that she was sliding off the seat. I tried to grab her sari to prevent her from falling, but all I got was a bit of the sari in my hand. It tore off as Sakshi hit the road. I immediately stopped, ran around, lifted Sakshi off the road, and put her back in the jeep. Thank goodness, she wasn't hurt!

By now Sakshi's divorce had come through, and we were spending a considerable amount of time together. When Sakshi was nice, she was very nice. I was totally smitten by her, and in love with her. To be honest, I had never met anyone remotely like Sakshi. Her passion, her food, her verve for life; she had totally bowled me over.

I was also totally amazed that a girl like Sakshi, with her looks, her sensuality, her connections, would want to go out with me. Here I was an ordinary guy, doing ordinary things. In a way, I was flattered that I had Sakshi. Each day with her was a refreshing new experience. I was totally consumed by her. There are no other words to express what we felt for each other. It was almost as if the intense love that we felt for each other burned both of us out of existence.

However, Sakshi's brother seemed to have different plans. He had been talking to Suheil who informed me, "I have to tell you something. I was drinking with DC last night, along with Udit. DC kept asking me your intentions for Sakshi. I kept changing the subject as the bottle of whiskey depleted fast. I decided to leave at midnight. I had left the house when DC yelled from the first floor, 'Will Sanjiv marry Sakshi? What do you think?' I just held my hands up and said we would talk later and left."

Unknown to Suheil, inebriated as DC was, he mistook Suheil raising his hands as an acknowledgment that, yes, Sanjiv would marry Sakshi.

The following week of October 1983, I had to go to London for work.

I stayed with my friend Bony in Sussex, UK. Sakshi would call me every day, sometimes twice a day. One day, Sakshi called, all excited. "I just heard something today from DC," she said.

"What did you hear?" I asked.

"Well," said Sakshi, "I heard you are going to marry me."

"No," I said. "Who said that? I did not say anything of the kind."

No, Sakshi and I did not get married. Things were never the same between us after that; we gradually drifted apart.

CHAPTER SIXTEEN

Tusks and an Elephant Gun

I n 1984, I went to collect my father's elephant gun from his regiment, the Central India Horse or CIH.

My father had been posted in the Congo in the early 1960s as a part of the UN peacekeeping force, in his official capacity, as the French interpreter of the Indian Army. There were two rogue elephants in the local vicinity; my father was one of the two *shikaris* who shot the two elephants. One was a huge fullgrown tusker; the other was not that big. The two *shikaris* divided the tusks amongst themselves. My father wrote to my mother and asked her whether she wanted some ivory from the Congo. My mother replied in the negative. When my father returned to India, all he had with him was an eight-inch piece of ivory, which, even today, is used as a paperweight at my home!

The regiment, the Central India Horse, was posted at Ambala at that time. When my mother went to the officers' mess, my father casually turned around and said, "Those tusks are the ones I was referring to in the Congo."

My mother looked around and saw a huge six-feet-long tusk, encased in brass at either end, on a wooden stand on the main dining table. The other smaller one was a three and a half feet tusk, again with brass studs on either end, hanging on a brass chain over the bar.

My mother was surprised. "You never told me you were talking about such big tusks," she told my father.

"When you said you did not particularly want any ivory, I gifted both the tusks to the regiment. Here they are," my father said, pointing to the tusks.

The rifle that been used to shoot the elephant, a point 404 Jeffries elephant gun, had been left with the regimental armory or *kot*. After my father died in 1966, the elephant gun and the two tusks remained with the regiment.

Years went by, I could not get the tusks back, but I was always looking for ways to retrieve the elephant gun, for sentimental reasons. Around 1982, I did manage to contact the regiment; they told me I could collect the weapon as long as I had a valid point 404 elephant gun license.

My father's first cousin, Mr. Subhash Tandan, had been appointed the commissioner of police at Delhi in 1983. I went to meet Uncle Subhash, or Uncle Tunu, as we knew him. I had not met him in years. I explained the background of the elephant gun lying at the regimental *kot* and asked him to kindly grant me a license for a point 404 elephant gun.

Uncle Tunu was reluctant to issue me a license. I explained that I could not, in any case, get bullets for the point 404 rifle and that I only wanted it for sentimental reasons. "I cannot get the tusks; I might as well try and keep the rifle," I said. Uncle Tunu eventually cleared my application; I was given a license for a point 404 elephant bore rifle.

Early 1984, I went to Gwalior, where the regiment was posted, along with Udit. I recall walking into the officers' mess where the war movie, *Tora Tora Tora,* was being screened. The movie was paused, and I shook hands with all the officers who had been told that I would be coming. They were all wearing blazers and waiting for me.

Army issued Peter Scot whiskey followed, and dinner. The next morning, I was officially handed over the point 404 rifle, which was removed from the regiment's Shikar Club.

Udit and I returned to Delhi. We were escorted to the Gwalior railway station by a JCO or junior commissioned officer from CIH. He told me that he was one of the men who had taken my father to the field hospital when his jeep was blown up by an anti-tank mine on 11th September 1965 at Barki, Lahore sector.

Unfortunately, in mid-1994, my mother had a burglary at Tikratoli. The burglars, luckily, were unable to find the elephant gun, but they stole my briefcase that contained the gun license that Uncle Tunu had given me in 1983. When I discovered that the license had been stolen, I filed a report with the local police and requested that a duplicate license be issued. Years went by, I neither got the duplicate license nor did I pursue the matter further.

My mother was getting a bit tense about keeping a veritably unlicensed weapon at Tikratoli. A retired General had come to visit my mother, and she asked him to take the weapon away from Tikratoli. The weapon was deposited in the General's car and, subsequently, formally handed over to

CIH, as the regiment happened to be stationed at Ranchi at that time.

In 2007, I received a letter from the regiment, asking me to produce my license for the elephant gun or to remove the gun from the regiment. 23 years after Uncle Tunu had issued me the elephant gun license, I went back to him and asked him to help me again. "What were you doing all these years?" he asked.

"I was in New Zealand," I said, which was the simple truth. I went to the gun licensing (police) authorities based in Delhi, where the license had been issued. They tried to help me obtain a duplicate gun license, but when they realized as I had not renewed the license for the last 10 years, they were unable to do anything.

The only option I had was to drive to Bhatinda, Punjab, which is a five-hour drive, and bring the weapon back to Delhi and surrender it to the police headquarters in Delhi. This meant that I would have to take the risk of driving from Punjab via Haryana to Delhi with an unlicensed weapon. This was not advisable by any means.

My driver assured me that it was doable; we would leave Bhatinda at 5 a.m. and arrive by 11 a.m. in Delhi, driving nonstop. The options were limited; if I did not collect the weapon, the regiment was threatening to either destroy it, or worse, to report the matter to the authorities.

I went back to Uncle Tunu, and he said, "Let me see what I can do. There may be something in the Arms Act for obsolete weapons." As luck would have it, a bylaw was uncovered, and I was given leave to officially donate the rifle to the regiment, on the condition the rifle was de-armored and the firing pin removed.

On 15 December 2007, on the 150th Raising Day of the regiment, I officially presented my late father's weapon to the regiment, 41 years after his death.

The elephant gun and the tusks are now proudly displayed side by side. The six-feet-long elephant tusks, I understand, are the single largest animal trophy owned by any regiment in the Indian Army. The first thing I did was to inform Uncle Tunu that all was well and fully legal.

CHAPTER SEVENTEEN

Redec

Around April 1985, I heard on the grapevine that Dr. Ghaith R Pharaon, a Saudi Arabian billionaire, was expected in Jaipur and that a poolside party was being hosted by HH Jaipur, which was to be attended by some of the social, business, and political luminaries of Jaipur and Delhi. I wanted to meet Dr. Ghaith Pharaon but did not think it proper to ask Uncle Bubbles to invite me to the party as he would want to know why. I could not tell him that I was looking for a job.

Instead, I asked Uncle Joey to invite me to the party. "I don't know about any such party, but if there is one, I will definitely be invited, and you can come as my guest. So, sure, come to Jaipur and stay with me," Uncle Joey said.

I went to Jaipur, stayed with Uncle Joey in Civil Lines and went with him to the Rambagh Palace for the poolside party hosted by HH Jaipur in honor of Dr. Ghaith R. Pharaon.

I did not know anything about Dr. Pharaon, other than that he was super rich. I knew that he was very big in the cement business and had his headquarters in Riyadh, Saudi Arabia.

Dr. Pharaon, a short, stocky man with a goatee, was standing alongside his new wife, a pretty French lady. I was at the end of a long line of people to greet Dr. Pharaon and his wife. The greetings, at best, were perfunctory. It was not really possible to have much of a conversation with Dr. Pharaon as there were far too many people with the same idea.

It was a sedate evening; nothing much happened. I never got to have a one-to-one conversation with Dr. Pharaon. The evening ended, I went back with Uncle Joey to his house and returned to Delhi the next day.

10 days later, I went to Singapore on holiday and was staying with my sister and brother-in-law, Kunkun and Ajay. I decided to call Dr. Ghaith Pharaon. In those years, there was no internet, and it was difficult to obtain

basic information. All I knew was that Dr. Pharaon had an office in Riyadh. I asked my friend Sonny Chhatwal, who was then working for the Saudi American Bank, Riyadh, the local affiliate of Citibank, to help me locate Dr. Pharaon's office phone number in Riyadh.

Sonny Chhatwal gave me the name of Dr. Ghaith Pharaon's secretary and her phone number in Riyadh. Sonny also told me that Dr. Pharaon was the world's biggest dealer in cement. He had huge tanker ships that had been converted into floating factories with silos for packing and storing 50kg bags of cement. The bags were loaded straight onto big flat-bed trucks at the port quayside for delivery direct to the end user.

Sonny also informed me that Dr. Pharaon's business in recent years had taken a bit of a hit. Cement was not as much in demand as it used to be. That was all I knew about Dr. Pharaon's business.

I called Dr. Pharaon's secretary, Rosy, and introduced myself, saying that I had met Dr. Pharaon in Jaipur at a dinner hosted by HH Jaipur some 10 days ago and that I wanted to speak to him. Rosy told me that Dr. Pharaon was currently in Washington. So, I asked for his number there. She told me that he was staying at the Pierre Hotel, and gave me his room and phone number.

I found out from telecom inquiry that Washington DC was exactly 12 hours behind Singapore and that late evening in Singapore would be a good time to call as it would be morning in Washington DC.

I called the Pierre, was connected to room 1024 and spoke to Dr. Ghaith Pharaon's wife. I introduced myself and said, "I met you at Jaipur along with Dr. Pharaon at HH Jaipur's dinner; I came with Maharaj Jai Singh."

"Yes," she said. "I remember meeting you. How are you? Dr. Pharaon is away on business but will be back in eight hours. Why don't you leave your number and I will ask my husband to call you when he returns? You can expect a call in eight hours. Would that be okay, or will that be too early for you?" Mrs. Pharaon inquired.

"No, that will be okay, as I am catching an early-morning flight and will be up and about at that time." I was actually going nowhere, but could hardly tell Mrs. Pharaon that I could not take the call at 4:30 a.m.

I put down the phone and wondered if she actually remembered meeting me or was mixing me up with someone else. Eight hours from now meant 4:30 a.m., the next day. Mrs. Pharaon was so categorical and precise that Dr. Pharaon would call me at that time; I needed to be prepared to take his call.

And, indeed, the telephone rang at 4:30 a.m. sharp.

"Is this Mr. Sanjiv Lall? This is Dr. Pharaon speaking. I understand you spoke to my wife this morning. How can I help?"

"Thank you for calling back, Sir," I said. "I wonder if you remember meeting me in Jaipur. I met you along with Maharaj Jai Singh, HH's younger brother."

"Yes, I think I do remember you," Dr. Pharaon said.

"Dr. Pharaon," I said, "I do believe I can make some money for you."

"How's that?" Dr. Pharaon asked. "Well, I could market your cement in the Southeast Asian region. We could look at Bangladesh, which is the biggest importer of cement in the region, with imports coming from Indonesia and Taiwan," I said. "We could also look at other countries in the region."

"What will this cost me?" he asked.

"Not much," I said. "You can pay me a small stipend of around USD 1,500 per month, plus travel expenses. Should the Bangladesh market open up, we can look at how we can proceed thereafter."

At that point, I did not quite know how I would open up the Bangladesh market. What was important was that I convey to Dr. Pharaon that I could utilize his floating silos to sell his cement and make some money for him.

"What kind of quantity are you talking of?" Dr. Pharaon asked.

I countered the question by asking: "What size floating silos ships can you offer for Bangladesh?"

"We have six large floating silos, of which two are under repair," he said and added, "Will you by any chance happen to be in central Europe in about 10 days? We could meet in Paris and discuss the issue further."

"As it so happens, I have a spot of work in Europe next week," I said. "I would be happy to swing by Paris to meet you. I will call Rosy, and she will set up a meeting in Paris in about 10 days."

"Thank you, Mr. Lall," said Dr. Pharaon, and I put down the phone.

So, here I was, my initial gut feel of wanting to meet Dr. Pharaon in Jaipur had proved to be correct; all I had to do was to go to Paris. The first thing I did was to apply for my French visa. I had a new Indian passport and hoped that my name would not pop up because of crashing the border at Calais in late 1978. Nothing of the sort happened. I got my French visa in Singapore in two days.

England, too, had introduced visas for Indian passport holders. I already had a five-year multiple-entry visa for the UK from my visit the previous year.

After a couple of days, I called Rosy. She told me that Dr. Pharaon had spoken to her and asked me when I would like to meet him. We discussed a few dates, and a meeting was arranged for Thursday, 18th April, at 10 a.m. at Dr. Pharaon's office at the corner of Rue Royale and 4 Place de la Concorde. Rosy assumed I knew Paris well. She said, "We are next to the Crillion Hotel, opposite the Champs-Élysées."

I just said, "Yes, of course, no problem," pretending I knew exactly where the office was located.

I checked out the flights, and the cheapest ticket I could get was on Royal Jordanian Airline via Bangkok. On 16th April, I left Singapore for Bangkok and on to Paris via Amman, Jordan. I arrived at Charles de Gaulle Airport, Paris, on the morning of the 17th and took a taxi to the pension I had booked on the Left Bank, close to the River Seine.

I then took a taxi to Place de la Concorde and walked around the area. I did this to familiarize myself with where I had to go the next day. I did not want to get caught up in traffic and be late for my meeting. Place de la Concorde was only 20 minutes or so by taxi from my pension.

I found 4 Place de la Concorde was adjacent to Maxim's of Paris, the famous restaurant. It was an imposing building made of stone with big columns; it had a big brass plaque on it which said that the Treaty of Alliance between France and the United States of America was signed in the very building in February 1778. The famous Hotel Crillion was just to its right.

Having got the general lay of the land, I went back to the pension, had an early dinner, and went to bed. I was up early the next morning. I dressed carefully, took a taxi to Place de la Concorde, and was there by 9:30 a.m. I walked around a bit and entered Dr. Ghaith Pharaon's office at 10 a.m. sharp.

I remember the building had literally floor-to-ceiling doors and a huge marble hallway with a staircase going up with gold handrails. I walked up to the first floor, as I could not see any lift, and came straight to Dr. Pharaon's office. I met his secretary, who was expecting me. She asked me to wait, saying that Dr. Pharaon was on the phone. A cup of coffee was put in front of me when his secretary asked me to go and meet Dr. Pharaon. "Please take your coffee with you," she said.

I walked into Dr. Pharaon's office. The first thing I saw was a wall made with small glass windows, providing a breathtaking view of Place de La Concorde and the Élysée Palace, the official residence of the president of

France.

It was a huge office with a massive ornate desk against the far wall to the right. I had never seen such a large office before. Dr. Pharaon was sitting in the front, close to the windows overlooking Place de la Concorde around a small round table, with a cup of coffee on the table, a cigar in one hand, and worry beads in the other, which he kept twirling.

I felt a bit odd walking into Dr. Pharaon's office with a cup of coffee in my left hand, but I had no choice. The coffee cup was white with the rim of the cup and saucer in gold. The spoon was also gold colored.

Dr. Pharaon greeted me warmly. "How was your flight?" he asked.

"Fine," I said. "I came to Paris via Amman." I had decided to stick to the truth as far as possible. "You have a most beautiful office."

"Yes," said Dr. Pharaon, "I think so, too. It is even more beautiful than the Élysée Palace. Now tell me more about what you have in mind."

"I am looking at selling cement to Bangladesh," I explained.

"Will the ship be able to dock?" Dr. Pharaon asked. "We need a six-meter draught."

"To be quite honest, that is something I do not know for certain. I am told at high tide we can get over the sand bar, which has a six-meter draft. At low tide, the draft is about 5.25 at Chalna Port, where the major cement shipments are discharged."

"How do you know HH Jaipur?" Dr. Pharaon inquired.

"I have been working for him for the last three years. He has known the family as long as I can recall," I said.

"Are you still working for HH Jaipur?" he asked.

"No, Sir, I am not. I am looking for something to do on my own."

"Let me introduce you to Christina. She runs the international business for Redec."

Redec, I discovered was short for Saudi Research and Development Company.

He picked up the phone, spoke in fluent French and soon Christina walked in, a very tall and well-built lady, in a beige skirt with a white blouse. She had long blonde hair, pulled back and tied with a ribbon.

"Hi," said Christina.

"This is Sanjiv," Dr. Pharaon said. "I was talking to you about him the other day; he is looking at getting some cement shipments through to Bangladesh."

"Will our silos be able to go there?" asked Christina.

"That is what I am going to look into," I said.

"We also have the monsoon months to contend with, when the cement delivery will not be possible."

"What will this cost, Sanjiv?" asked Dr. Pharaon.

"Fifteen hundred dollars per month, plus full travel and board." I looked at Christina; that did not faze her one bit.

"Okay. I will leave you with Christina to sort out the details; we will try this for six months and see where we go," said Dr. Pharaon. He got up, we shook hands, I thanked him, and he left the room.

"When would you like to start?" asked Christina.

"I would say next month as the silo ships cannot get into port before August. We can start planning now," I said.

"Yes, I agree with that," said Christina.

With that, I had secured myself a job for the next six months. Commercially, I was to report to Christina in Paris, while all the travel accounts and bills had to be sent to Redec, Riyadh.

I thought to myself, that's neat. Here I was from India, living in Singapore, traveling all over the Southeast Asian market, selling cement for Redec, getting paid for my work from Riyadh, Saudi Arabia, and reporting to Christina at Redec International, Paris!

I returned to the pension and went on a wine and cheese cruise along the Seine. Everyone was in pairs. I was the only single person on board. The next day, I took the train to Calais. I remembered my journey on the same route, seven years ago, with Kay. This journey was without incident. From Calais, I took the hovercraft to Dover, England, and a train from Dover to London.

Sakshi was doing a TV media course in London. I had already informed her I was going to be in Paris.

"Are you coming to meet me while you're in Europe?" she had asked.

As I arrived in London, she was waiting for me at Victoria Station with a bunch of red roses; she looked very pretty in a black skirt and black top, draped over with a bright red shawl. She had cut back her hair over her ears and looked quite beautiful. I must say I was very pleased and happy to see her. I had so much to tell her.

"Where am I going to stay the night?" I asked.

"Well," she said, "you can stay with me in the girls' hostel. I have two other girls in my room, but they know you are coming and would be quite happy to sleep in their friend's room for a night or two."

"No," I said, "I would not want to inconvenience them as they may do the same to you one day."

I thought it better to take a cheap room in one of the lodges in Earl's Court for £15 per night. I was given a tiny room on the third floor with a bed and a cupboard and a toilet down the corridor. On top of the bed was a speaker with two knobs. One was to listen to the radio; I was not sure what the second was for and did not bother to find out.

Sakshi and I went out to dinner to the Muffin Man Café, just down the road. I came back to my room and asked Sakshi if she would like to come up.

"Do you want me to come up?" she asked.

"Okay. Yes, please do," I said.

The next day, as I was leaving the reception desk, the lady asked me, "Tonight will it be single or double?"

"Double," I said.

"Good," she said. "Better that way. Could you please pay five pounds for the double room last night?" I looked at the receptionist, wondering how she could have known that Sakshi was in the room.

She saw the rather perplexed look on my face and asked, "Do you know what this box is?" She pointed to the box I had thought was the radio.

"It's a radio," I said.

"Yes, it is," the lady said, "but do you know what the other knob is for?"

"No," I said, "I do not." "You turn the knob when you want to talk to the receptionist," she said. "Seems last night one of you turned the knob on and everything could be heard. Be careful."

I sheepishly paid the extra five pounds and left feeling rather embarrassed.

I returned to Singapore via Paris, Amman, and Bangkok and waited to start my new job with Redec. My new visiting cards came; Sanjiv Tandan Lall, SE Asian Representative, Redec International, Singapore.

For the next six months, I was in and out of Singapore. In those years, Indian passport holders were only given 14 days stay per visit in Singapore, but I was traveling so much that I would never be in Singapore for more than a week at any time.

I went to Dhaka thrice and once to Sri Lanka, Karachi, East Malaysia, Sabah, Kuching, and Brunei.

The primary issue with Redec was that the silos were huge monster ships. To do justice, the cargo loads had to be 20,000 metric tons upwards.

That, in itself, was not the problem as Bangladesh did import huge volumes of cement per month. The issue was that most of Bangladesh's cement imports were discharged mid-river into smaller dhows and boats, as the ports had too much silt, which prevented big vessels from docking at the ports. The silos were large mother ships, which, at the end of the day, were too big and too sophisticated for Bangladesh to handle.

I almost struck a deal with a large cement importer in Bangladesh, but the logistics of the deal were far too complex; in the end, it was thought best to let it go.

I made lengthy monthly reports which I would send by DHL in hard copy to Christina in Paris. I made some concrete suggestions on how some business might be possible.

My six-month term with Redec came to an end in November 1985. It was great fun working with Redec, and a big learning curve. By now, I was fairly widely traveled in Southeast Asia.

CHAPTER EIGHTEEN

Hong Kong

After my Redec stint, I went to Hong Kong looking for a job. Hong Kong is a bustling city, full of energy and vitality. I took a furnished studio apartment on the side of the river, giving myself one month to find a job.

In the evenings, I would often go to the street close by, full of strip clubs. I would generally frequent one place where I had become friendly with the owner, a Chinese lady in her early 30s.

Seven to eight p.m. was always happy hour. If I got there in time, I would save a heap of money. I would generally sit and chat with the manager at the counter and tell her what I did for the day. One day, she invited me to her home for dinner. It was a tiny Hong Kong style apartment, small but compact, which had everything the lady required. On another occasion on the weekend she drove me to the New Territories, to a sophisticated new shopping complex.

One day, when I was coming down the lift from my seventh-floor apartment, the lift stopped on the fifth floor and a Filipino lady got in. "Hello," she said, "are you from India?"

"Yes," I said, I had my room key in my hand. She saw it and asked, "Are you in room 732?"

"Yes," I said.

"Okay, bye, might see you later," she said, and she was off.

I thought nothing of it and went on with my day. At night, I went to my usual bar, had a couple of drinks, had some dinner and came back. Soon I was fast asleep. I could hear someone knocking on my door. I thought it was a dream. The knocking continued, till I suddenly realized that the knocking was for real.

I got out of bed in my long knee-length kurta that I used to wear to bed and opened the door. I found the same Filipino girl, who had got into the lift with me in the morning, standing at the door. It was 2 a.m. I was half asleep, not quite sure what was going on. "Hello," said the girl, "I am so sorry to wake you up."

"What do you want?" I asked. "It's so late."

"Yes, I know," she said, "and I apologize. I have no other place to go. Can I sleep in your room for the night?"

"Sleep in my room?" I asked, somewhat bewildered. "I only have a double bed, not even a sofa. I only have a chair." I was trying to discourage the girl.

"I know that. I will sleep on the bed in one corner, you will not even know," she said and with that she just walked past me.

I did not quite know what to do, so I just sat on the bed, wondering what I should do. The girl by now had disappeared to the toilet; the first thing I did was to hide my passport and wristwatch below the carpet, behind the dresser, and lock my suitcase. The girl came out, wearing a nightdress; where that came from I do not know, but she claimed that she had it in her handbag. She went to the far corner of the bed and lay down. Within minutes she was fast asleep!

I put the big bolster cushions in the middle of the bed, lay down on my side and went off to sleep. I swear, the whole night I was sleeping with a girl in my bed, I did not touch her. I did not know why she was there. I reasoned something must have happened to make her do what she did. I left it at that.

The next morning, she got up, showered, got ready, and left, as if it was the most natural thing to do in the world. I gave full marks to the girl, she did what she had to and carried it off with aplomb.

I must say I was also rather proud of myself that I did not touch her or make any advances. I never saw the Filipino girl again. Actually, to be quite honest, I was not even certain that she was a Filipino.

CHAPTER NINETEEN

Elephant Walk

Three weeks had passed in Hong Kong and the only possible lead I had was of pursuing a career in stock-broking. I really did not want to do that, and thus lost interest. It was in early December, in 1985, that I decided to return to India, the decision being to go and live in Ranchi with my mother and try and do something at Tikratoli Farm.

I came back to Delhi, collected my things, loaded my white jeep on the goods train bound for Ranchi and took another train, along with my latest acquisition, the point 404-bore Jeffery elephant gun.

The jeep took three weeks to reach Ranchi. I went to the railway station to pick it up. It had arrived completely unscathed. I connected the battery leads, poured some petrol into the carburetor and started the engine; on the third attempt, it started. I drove the jeep back to Tikratoli, quite pleased with myself.

The jeep had no papers. On one of my trips to London and LA, my Uncle Kenny had borrowed the jeep as his car was in the garage for repairs. The jeep's RC book got misplaced in Kenny Uncle's house and was never found. I tried to get a duplicate from Jaipur, but to no avail. The jeep was a late 1940s issue; the authorities in Jaipur could not locate the vehicle file even though it was registered in Jaipur and the vehicle continued to pay regular taxes for the next 30-odd years or so.

The jeep was now in Ranchi; it did not really matter to me if it had no papers, I drove it anyway. I drove it everywhere, still with its original Rajasthan plates, RJL 4021.

In Ranchi, I was introduced to some young Army officers, mostly of the rank of Captain, some from the Artillery and Infantry Corps and a couple of officers from the Armoured Corps.

Living at Tikratoli was enchanting, as if time had come to a standstill. Especially after my endless travel with Redec, I was glad to be in one place and not rushing to catch a plane to some unknown destination.

Life settled down into a pattern. I would drive Uncle Dilu to Ranchi every day in his old Fiat. We would typically go into town after breakfast and return by lunch. In the evenings, I would sometimes go out and meet the boys in the officers' mess, either in my mother's beat-up old Fiat or in my jeep. There were no girls to meet in Ranchi; at least I did not know of any.

Nothing really momentous happened in the first half of 1986. I settled down to country life; there was a lot of staff with very little to do. The pace of life slowed down drastically.

In late 1987, Sakshi returned to India. I was sporadically in touch with her, in the sense I was largely aware of what she was doing, but I was not in daily or regular touch. I began contemplating life with Sakshi and settling down at Tikratoli with her.

On her return to Calcutta, I invited Sakshi to Ranchi. She arrived at the airport, loaded with goodies from London. She brought with her several varieties of herbs, vegetables, and strawberry seeds.

She also brought her TV camera and showed me what all she had been doing in London. She was totally excited about making a life for herself in Ranchi with me.

Sakshi was put in the small bedroom, next to the kitchen; I was in the room next door. My mother was staying upstairs; Ajai and Kunkun, who were visiting Ranchi from Delhi, were in the guest room.

Ajai, Kunkun, Sakshi, and some friends and I drove to Hazaribagh for the night and stayed at the forest guesthouse. Sakshi had her own room but came across to my room to spend the night, as she had spotted a scorpion in her room. It was entirely true, a scorpion was found, which I smashed with my shoe.

A few days later, Sakshi and I drove down to Calcutta with Jayant, a friend from Ranchi, in his jeep. Sakshi and I never did settle down together, I guess it was just not to be.

I spent a lot of time with Uncle Dilu in Ranchi; he taught me what it meant to drink but never ever allow a hangover to get in the way of work. To this day, I have never cribbed about a hangover. Even though I did get hangovers, I did not ever let it show, or let it come between my work and me.

Uncle Dilu used to say, "Drink as much as you like, but show up for breakfast on time as if nothing happened the night before." I have always believed in this, and whenever people proffer the excuse of a hangover, I don't buy it. At the end of the day, if you can't hold your drink then you shouldn't be drinking.

Uncle Dilu had been planning to sell their lovely two-acre property across the road for some time. There were tell-tale signs the sale might happen in 1988; they were very keen to move lock, stock, and barrel to Bangalore to be close to their kids, Viki and Premi.

Eventually, their house did sell in 1988, and the Chaudhuris bid a final adieu to Ranchi and left for Bangalore in the summer of 1988.

In early 1988, I purchased a practically new Maruti 800 in Delhi; it was Air Force blue in color. I decided to drive it down to Ranchi with Diff, a friend of my mother, who was visiting from London. I asked her whether she would like to see a bit of India, and she readily accepted.

I had arranged to pick up Diff from Sundar Nagar at 5:30 a.m. She was ready and packed when I got there. The understanding was that I would bring the car and Diff would bring something to eat, some glasses, and water.

We set off at 5:45 a.m. from Sundar Nagar, drove across the Nizamuddin bridge, cut across to Ghaziabad and turned north towards Aligarh. We hit Aligarh around 10 a.m., filled up the gas, and drove nonstop to Kanpur, which we reached at 1:30 p.m. and stopped for lunch and refreshments. We continued to Allahabad, crossed the Ganges around 5 p.m., and belted down the road to Varanasi, making it a little after sunset, around 7:30 p.m.

Diff was so tired that I had to literally carry her up the stairs to the room. As it so happened, the hotel only had one room left; fortunately, it had two single beds. Not that it made much of a difference. Diff promptly crashed out and slept through the night.

I had a couple of drinks at the bar, came up to the room, had some dinner, and passed out.

The next day, Diff and I went out exploring Varanasi; we hired a boat and went down the Ganges to see the sights. We saw some dead bodies floating in the river and several funeral pyres burning brightly along the banks of the Ganges.

The boatman stopped and took us to one of the famous temples along the river. I was keen to hit the road, so we headed back to the hotel, had a hearty breakfast, and left for Ranchi around 10:30 a.m.

I drove practically nonstop, halting for a few minutes in Aurangabad to pick up some bananas, which was lunch, and continued to Hazaribagh. Diff drove between Barhi and Hazaribagh, a distance of 30 kilometers. I took over the wheel again at Hazaribagh, around 5 p.m., and continued to Ramgarh after a short fuel and tea break.

In 1988, Ramgarh had two bridges. We had crossed one bridge and got caught in a fierce traffic jam; a truck had met with an accident on the second bridge, and there was a huge mess. Traffic was clogged on both sides for quite a distance.

An adventurous small truck decided to weave its way below the bridge, cutting through the adjacent village. Several cars followed suit, including Diff and I in my tiny Maruti 800. I was following a light blue Ambassador; wherever it went, we followed. The Ambassador forded a small dirty creek with about one foot of water and made it safely to the other side. I followed in second gear, going slowly, and also made it safely.

A little ahead, we rejoined the main highway to Ranchi. The Ambassador stopped ahead and flagged us down. The man traveling in the light blue Ambassador car said, "I think it's time to have a drink. I have whisky but no water."

Diff promptly produced crystal glasses and water!

An hour later, we reached Tikratoli.

My mother, who was in Delhi at the time, called me to tell me that someone from England, an Englishman, would come calling at Tikratoli on an elephant. Apparently, he was writing a travelogue, traversing a part of Eastern India with an elephant.

I was sitting in the lawn, having a beer with a friend one morning, when a rather dirty jeep drove up, stuffed with all kinds of things, and a tall, slim bearded man emerged. "I am Aditya," he said.

"Ah, the elephant man," I said.

"No, that is Mr. Mark Shand; he is following a few kilometers behind on his elephant. He should be here within the next hour or two,"

Aditya said. The staff were immediately instructed to make arrangements for Aditya and Mark to stay in the guest suite. The issue was to find a suitable place for the elephant. An appropriate tree was found, which had the girth to hold the elephant, and more importantly, had enough space for the elephant to move around.

I was told that their travel party would include a driver cum cook for the entire support team, a woodcutter to cut foliage for the elephant to eat and a mahout to look after the elephant.

An hour or so later, Mark made his rather dramatic entrance on his elephant called Tara. There was much excitement all round as the young village kids ran around the elephant. The staff, too, were excited to have an elephant, Lord Ganesh, stay in our home!

The next day I noticed some of the staff making offerings of food, rice, and flowers to the elephant. They did so in prayer and obeisance, keeping their faith fully intact; it was, after all, Lord Ganesha, Lord of the Universe.

Mr. Mark Shand, who sadly passed away in 2014, was the brother of Camilla, Duchess of Cornwall. He was a travel writer who is best remembered for his work on the conservation of elephants. He co-founded the Elephant Family, a wildlife foundation for this very purpose in 2002.

Mark had set off on his elephant journey in Bhubaneshwar, traversed the battlefields of Konarak, where the famous Elephant Battle had taken place, and came to Ranchi, en route to Hazaribagh, Gaya, Patna, and finally Sonepur, on the banks of the Ganges.

Mark and Aditya, and Tara the elephant and the team stayed with me at Tikratoli for four days, recharging their batteries, and then continued their journey to Hazaribagh.

I walked a good part of the way from Ranchi to Patna with the elephant party. Each night we would camp at a place close to where there was availability of fresh water and fodder for the elephant.

This was quite an adventure and good fun. Aditya had a great sense of humor with a stack of rugby jokes in store, which kept us going. From Patna, I flew to Delhi to attend my friend Ranjit's wedding.

Mark's visit to Tikratoli continues to be remembered with great fondness by everyone who witnessed it.

CHAPTER TWENTY

Zoee

I had arrived at Delhi straight from the elephant expedition. I did not have any decent clothes to wear for Ranjit's prewedding cocktail party. I borrowed a yellow and blue Argyle sweater from Kenny Uncle and set off for the party. There were lots of people at the party, a few hundred perhaps. I was standing in one corner when a tall girl with long black hair came up to me and said, "Bablu, my name is Nina. I am Sheila's sister and Ranjit's sister-in-law to be."

"Hi," I said.

"Do you see the blonde lady standing there?" Nina asked, pointing out the only foreigner in the room.

"Yes," I said, "I can see her."

"Her name is Zoee. Would you like to meet her?" asked Nina.

"Sure," I said, "I would love to."

I met Zoee; she was very shy, and we exchanged a few pleasantries.

"Would you like to meet Zoee again sometime?" asked Nina.

I looked at Nina a bit amused. "Yes," I said, "that would be nice."

We fixed our next meeting for the day after at Kailash Colony. At that time, I was staying with Kenny Uncle.

Zoee arrived a bit late and I just assumed she had forgotten but it turned out she had lost her way and was not able to find the house.

"Why did you want to meet me?" I asked Zoee.

"Well," she said, "I was at the party with Nina when she asked me if there was anyone in particular I wanted to meet. I looked around and nothing caught my eye except for your blue Argyle sweater. Nina found out who you were and came up to you."

"I see," I said, a little bemused by the turn of events. Zoee was the buyer for an importer of women's garments, jewelry, carpets, and knickknacks from Wellington, New Zealand; she used to visit India often and would stay at the company guesthouse in Malviya Nagar, New Delhi. Nina was her Indian manager and overall major-domo.

Zoee and I had a coffee together; we agreed to meet for dinner that evening at her place at Malviya Nagar. This was the beginning of a relationship that continued for the next 18 years.

Zoee's mother and stepfather were over from New Zealand. I was not aware of that; had I known, I might not have accepted Zoee's dinner invitation, and maybe New Zealand would have remained a dot on the map to me. As it turned out, Zoee and I had a rather relaxed and intimate dinner together that night.

Had I not gone to Zoee's house that night for dinner, I do believe I would have missed out on the best years of my life with Zoee in New Zealand. It was ordained, it had to happen: Zoee became my life.

Thereafter, I began visiting Zoee quite frequently at her Malviya Nagar apartment; a potent physical relationship soon ensued.

A few days later, Zoee and I drove to Kulu-Manali in her Gypsy. We went via Shimla; we stopped for the night at Chapslee, my mother's paternal home, and continued to Kulu the next day, where we stayed at Span Resorts located on the banks of the River Beas and owned by Mr. Kamal Nath.

The last time I had been to Kulu was on a Sanawar excursion, I think, led by Mr. Sinha and Mr. Sikand. We boys had arrived at Kulu Airport in our worn and bedraggled baggy blue shorts and white half-sleeve shirts. I daresay we looked a ragged lot, straight from some government school rather than the exclusive and famous Lawrence School, Sanawar.

I was not to know that years later, in 1988, I would revisit Kulu with Zoee.

Mr. Kamal Nath had an exclusive brand of single-malt whisky, specially distilled for him in Scotland. I also remember having my first swig of Johnny Walker Blue Label at the resort.

From Kulu, we decided to go for a drive. The only thing was that Zoee did not have a good head for heights, so we had to go somewhere more sedate. I chose a road to Manikaran that seemed safer. But what started as a gentle climb suddenly grew steeper, alongside a gorge with a huge drop on a narrow three meter-wide road.

A bus came from the opposite end, and I had to pull over along the gorge side to allow it to pass. I was trying to negotiate the turn when Zoee finally told me to stop and let her out. She just could not take it anymore. She got out of the Gypsy and started walking alongside as I slowly maneuvered past the bus. The passengers were by now all looking at this blonde lady in white shorts, marching on the road, with me following in the Gypsy!

Well, there was only one thing to do, I turned around and drove quietly back to Kulu. Two days later, we drove back from Span Resorts to Delhi, via Chandigarh, in 12 hours; that was quite a drive.

I was always kind of fascinated by blondes, that is one of the primary reasons I had opted to go to Russia from Tehran, so that I could get to Scandinavia. However, much to my disappointment, I did not get friendly with any blondes. Fastforward to 20-odd years later; I was about to visit New Zealand to meet Zoee, I was infatuated with her, yes, my first and only ever true blonde girl friend.

Zoee was a very good-looking girl; in her younger days, she had often modeled for Vogue, New Zealand, and was considered to be the "Twiggy" of New Zealand. Zoee was a women's clothes designer and had learned her craft in the UK, where she had worked for a few years. Her father was a very famous New Zealand architect, perhaps the most famous architect they have ever produced to date.

In September 1989, I visited Zoee in Wellington, New Zealand. It was my first visit to New Zealand. In those years, it was relatively easy to get a visit visa for New Zealand. I landed at Auckland, walked across to the domestic terminal and took the Air New Zealand flight to Wellington. Zoee had a very neat two-bedroom stand-alone house in Wellington.

Zoee and I drove all over South Island in her little Honda City. We took the car in the ferry across Cook Strait, which can be a mean stretch of water. On a good day, the scenery, as the ferry pulls out from the Wellington Harbor, is absolutely stunning. As the ferry approaches South Island, it passes the Marlborough Sounds, which are essentially an extensive network of sea-drowned valleys. As per Maori mythology, the sounds are the prows of the sunken Wakas of Aorak. From Picton, where the ferry docks on South Island, we drove to Christchurch, which is about six hours away. The drive along the coast is quite breathtaking. From Christchurch, we drove across the Southern Alps, past Lake Wanaka to the tourist town of Queenstown, which is, and remains, one of the jewels of New Zealand.

In Queenstown, Zoee and I went on the jet boat, which, essentially, is a flat-bottomed boat that skims across the water at a top speed of 100 kilometers per hour. At full tilt, the boat can do a 360-degree turn, which leaves everyone gasping and open mouthed. The jet boats were invented in New Zealand and were used by Sir Edmund Hillary when he sailed up the Ganges. Yes sailed the Ganges on a jet-boat upriver, a 1,500 mile trek upstream, from the mouth of the Ganges to its Himalayan source.

A jet boat only requires 10 centimeters of water to sail, that is about one glass full of water. It is an amazing and thrilling craft. From Queenstown, we crossed over to the West Coast, to the Franz Josef glacier. You can walk right up to the glacier and even take a helicopter and land on the glacier. From Franz Josef, we motored down to Greymouth, Nelson, Picton, and back to Wellington on the ferry.

In Wellington, I had a fabulous time with Zoee in her lovely wooden villa. Until that time, I thought only houses in the hill stations, such as Shimla, were made of wood, but in a city like Wellington, this was the norm.

I celebrated my 34th birthday in Wellington. By then, I had decided that I wanted to live in New Zealand with Zoee and make my life there. My infatuation with Zoee had matured into love and we planned a life together.

Zoee resigned from her job in Wellington and put her house on the market, the intent being to move to Auckland. I, for my part, returned to Ranchi and told my mother that I was going to go back to New Zealand to live with Zoee.

I like to tell people that I went to New Zealand for a holiday in 1989, for a month (which I did), and ended up staying there for the next 18 years of my life. I read somewhere that if you knock on the door of opportunity, don't be surprised if hard work answers. It certainly did just that for me.

CHAPTER TWENTY-ONE

The Dream Merchants

I had no money to take with me to New Zealand; I took USD 250 with me, all that I had with me in Delhi.

Back in Singapore, my dear friend Maif Rehman would often exhort me to go to New Zealand. "Don't worry. I am there behind you, go and build your life. I will give you the money to start something in New Zealand," he would say.

I arrived in Singapore, en route to Auckland, in April 1990, and stayed with Maif and his wife, Jayanti, in their grand penthouse apartment. The general idea was to borrow the money from Maif, which he had promised he would loan me, and continue to Auckland.

On my first day in Singapore, Maif skirted the subject of loaning me the money; he did eventually say that he would discuss it at length with Jayanti and there was nothing to worry about.

The next day, Jayanti asked me what my business plans were. I told her that there was nothing specific, that I would consider something when I got to New Zealand.

"How much do you have to start a business?" she asked me. I said nothing at all. That was not a good answer and it did not go down well.

"How do you expect me to put down some money on a business when you are not investing anything from your end?" she said. "Giving money is fine, but I am looking at this as an investment."

Zoee had already set up a company in Auckland called Edana Holdings Limited, the general idea being to import ladies wear from Jaipur and Delhi and sell the imported line of clothing across New Zealand.

Eventually, Jayanti took a lien on Edana Holdings Limited, that is, I gave her a chunk of Zoee's company as security for the money they lent me. I arrived in Auckland with NZD 20,000 in my pocket and told Zoee what had happened; she was a bit upset that I had to give a lien on the company, but there was nothing we could do about that.

Zoee sold her lovely wooden cottage in Wellington and invested NZD 40,000 in Edana Holdings Limited; her sister Hannah put in NZD 20,000, her friend Josephine chipped in NZD 20,000, topped up by Maif's NZD 20,000. That made a capital investment of NZD 100k in the bank to start.

Josephine was already importing garments and accessories from Australia and South Korea; she knew the market very well and said that she would do the front-end selling in New Zealand.

We imported a range from Jaipur and then another, and then another. Zoee and I went around North Island with our sample range selling our line of fashion wear; it was a success. Zoee knew her suppliers in India and was an accredited and qualified designer, so things started moving, albeit slowly.

Life in New Zealand was interesting and different. One of the first things that hit me in New Zealand was that the people there had no religion, or at least many people did not. Zoee, for one, did not. There was no caste, no religion; it brought forward a better meaning to the phrase - egalitarian society. It took me a long time to figure out how a person cannot have a religion. Coming from India, this is one thing that is shoved down your throat from the day you are born.

In time, I realized that not having a religion or not being tied to a particular belief is actually great; it frees the mind and opens it out beyond known horizons.

New Zealand is a stunning country. I recall one of our suppliers from Delhi visiting Auckland around 1991–1992. I took Anil around for a drive in Auckland, pointing out the sights, the panoramic views, the beaches, the green meadows and vistas. Anil turned to me and asked, "Why is it that New Zealand has all this beauty, and that too for a large percentage of people who do not even believe in God? This is unfair, truly unfair what God has done. In India, we all pray; some pray to trees, to water, to fire, to stones, to statues, to animals. We are a people of consummate prayer. Many get up early in the morning to pray, perhaps as early as 2 a.m. We are deeply religious, so why does New Zealand get all this, when people there do not even believe in God?"

I listened to Anil's monologue, bemused and smiling as he went on ranting and said, "We do our thing, they do theirs, it's just that. I am not casting aspersions of right or wrong or good or bad, I will, however, say that it must be the cumulative power of a 1.4 billion people's faith that keeps India trundling along; yes, if there is a God, it must surely be in India."

In New Zealand, I also learned that it was not possible to borrow 90% money from a bank by just placing a mere 10% of the business plan amount. It was also not possible to establish a letter of credit without putting forward the entire money up front, yes 100% up front.

The net result of this was that we had to be very careful with our expenses, and we grew slowly, almost brick by brick, carrying zero debt as we went along. Josephine had long since opted out of the business; we had her investment to return, as well as Hannah's and Peter's.

Two years later, Zoee and I purchased a small two-bedroom apartment. That same year, I started putting money away to repay Hannah, Peter, Josephine, and Maif, all of whom we owed NZD 20k each.

By 1993, Josephine, Hannah, and Peter were paid off, and only Maif remained. It took almost three months for Jayanti to cancel the charge she held on Edana; in order to facilitate that, I had to pay Jayanti interest on the amount they had invested. By late 1993, Edana was totally debt free.

Around Diwali that year, I was in Delhi, and I told Ajai, my brother-in-law, that I felt like doing something different. He said, "Why don't you look at body shopping?"

"What's that?" I said.

"Sell IT skills, by way of people," Ajai said.

I went back to Auckland, bounced the idea of selling hot IT skills to New Zealand with Paul, who was selling us an accounting package. I knew nothing about computers, did not know how to use one, and did not have the faintest idea of how to go about body shopping. Paul found it to be a jolly good idea; the germination of a very good idea as it turned out.

I fixed a meeting with Ms. Thiam, IT Manager at IBM, Wellington. That meeting would change the next 20 years of my life. Ms. Thiam asked me whether I knew of any SAP consultants. "Oh, I will find out and get back to you," I said.

I came back to Auckland and contacted Paul, the only person I knew who was somewhat conversant with IT. "Paul, do you know what SAP is?"

"Yes," he said, "standard accounting practice."

"I don't think so, Paul. I am quite sure it's not an accounting package," I said.

For several days, I tried to figure out what SAP might mean; no one I knew had any inkling about SAP. A few days later, I picked up the courage, called Ms. Thiam at IBM, Wellington, and after polite pleasantries, I asked her what exactly SAP was.

"You know, Sanjiv, I do not know myself."

When Ms. Thiam said that, I breathed a sigh of relief. I was not the only ignoramus on the planet after all!

A week later, I found out that SAP was an Enterprise Resource Planning (ERP) software from Germany.

On a visit to Delhi a few weeks later, quite by accident, I came to know that Siemens India Limited had a software consulting company, headquartered in Bombay, called Siemens Information Systems Limited (SISL), headed by Mr. Raman Sethi. I was told that SISL had a bunch of SAP consultants with basic theoretical training but no active real-time SAP work experience.

Now that I knew where to go, I began networking, and as luck would have it, I made contact with Arvind, who was one of the pillars of SISL, and persuaded him to consider coming to New Zealand.

IBM New Zealand's client in Wellington was the New Zealand Defence Force that was considering implementing SAP across the board in Wellington. This was seriously big business, one that IBM was desperate to grab; the problem was that they needed someone who could speak the SAP language to head the NZDF SAP project. Arvind was a godsend; he arrived at the right time.

In order to bring Arvind to New Zealand, I had to sign a contract with IBM, Wellington. I did not wish to push this business to Edana, which centered on ladies' garments. Literally overnight, I had to come up with a company with which to sign the contract with IBM, New Zealand.

That company was Kleinstar Holdings Limited. It was a shelf company, ready to be picked up by someone. Normally shelf companies are called Alpha, Gama, or some such generic name as most people tend to change the name of the company down the line. Kleinstar was a German name, as was SAP, the software I was marketing. I thought it fitted in rather neatly.

Thus, on a cold August day, 1994, Kleinstar Holdings Limited was born. Within a day of its acquisition, I signed the contract with IBM, New Zealand, to provide SAP consulting resources to New Zealand. The first contract was to bring Arvind to New Zealand.

Arvind duly arrived in Wellington and was appointed the NZDF project manager. One month into his assignment, NZDF formally decided to opt for SAP as their program of choice. To kick-start the SAP program in Wellington, additional SAP resources were required. I brought Ashok and Nilesh, both from Bombay, to Wellington in January 1995.

In 1994, SAP was at a very nascent stage in New Zealand. None of the big six consulting companies had any SAP footprint in New Zealand at that time. Kleinstar had the distinction of bringing the first SAP Consultant to New Zealand for the NZDF project in October 1994.

Now that Kleinstar had a few SAP consultants in New Zealand, circa 1995, I began contacting the big seven consulting firms of New Zealand and Australia, namely Andersen Consulting, Coopers and Lybrand, Deloitte Consulting, Ernst and Young, KPMG, Price Waterhouse, and of course, IBM, offering them SAP consultants. I contacted them all, no holds barred.

It was in September 1995, I was on holiday at Rotorua with my Uncle Kenny and his partner, PP Singh, when I got a call from Mr. Dash Ashok, Coopers and Lybrand, Bangalore. Dash had been given my name by the Coopers and Lybrand's partner in Melbourne and was told that he should contact me as I had a few SAP consultants.

Dash was looking for a FICO consultant for Essar, Hazira. Yes, we had a FICO consultant, ready to travel to Bombay; that was Mr. Jim Montgomery who was Kleinstar's first overseas SAP consultant to work in India in early 1996.

I went to visit Jim at Essar in the summer of 1996. He was staying at the Essar guesthouse at Hazira; the accommodation and food were all quite good. I met the overseas SAP consultants as well as the Essar SAP consultants on the team. One particular consultant was Mr. Naresh Gupta, who later worked extensively with Kleinstar and STLCorp.

The problem with Coopers and Lybrand, India, was that our invoices were not being paid. Dash told me that Essar was saying that RBI had not approved their contract and until that happened, Coopers and Lybrand, India, could not get paid.

Fortunately for Kleinstar, our contract was directly inked with Coopers and Lybrand International, Hamburg, Germany. I started putting pressure on Coopers and Lybrand, Hamburg. They told me that they hadn't been paid, and that I should wait.

In late October, I had to go to Los Angeles to meet the attorneys regarding the setting up and incorporation of SAP Corp, LA. I extended my Air New Zealand ticket from Los Angeles to London.

I arrived at the Coopers and Lybrand office in Hamburg and met the two German directors in charge of the Essar India project. I told them that we had not been paid and how were we supposed to carry on providing SAP Consultants without being paid? To cut a long story short, I was assured contritely that we would get paid the following week, which we did.

Had I not gone to Hamburg to meet Coopers and Lybrand directors personally, I do believe our dues would not have been cleared, at least, not that year.

Whist in Germany, I had a meeting lined up with someone who knew the ropes at SAP AG, Walldorf, the headquarters of SAP Worldwide. I took the ICE train to Mannheim and stayed at a hotel resort in the Black Forest within the confines of a vineyard.

Merle came to meet me at the Vineyard Hotel with her baby girl.

It was so nice to meet Merle after some 18 years or so. We spoke about the time I had come to Alzey for the wine-drinking festival. I reminded Merle that I did not have a hotel room and had to walk all night, just to keep warm and alive and she just looked at me soulfully with her beautiful eyes.

We went for a walk in the vineyard, with Merle pushing the pram. Merle was now a mature, married woman with a baby. I was so happy that I had the opportunity to meet her again.

I returned to Hamburg, since I had to catch my flight to Auckland via London. I had a night to spare to relive my Hamburg memories, especially since I had just met Merle after about 18 years. I decided to go to the Reeperbahn. The clock swung back 18 years to 1978.

This time I was better dressed, in a cashmere overcoat, looking more respectable I liked to think. I was sitting in a bar, drinking rum and Coke, talking to the bar owner and to one of the girls at the bar counter. The girl was telling me that she did Reiki. I did not quite know what Reiki was. She said her mother was a Reiki master.

As we were chatting, I felt hungry and wanted to have dinner, but suddenly realized I did not have enough money. I paid for my drinks, took a cab to the hotel, got some money from my room, and in less than 30 minutes was back in the bar in the same taxi.

The next thing I recall was sitting on a bench on the side of the road; it was very cold, and two cops were waking me up.

I was totally dazed, with a raging headache, not quite sure what was going on. I reached for my wallet; it was empty. All the cash had been taken, but for some reason, all my credit cards, driver's license and IDs were all intact. I realized someone had mugged me, taken my money and left me on the bench to sleep it off. I showed my empty wallet to the cops, and they just smiled. Fortunately, I had the name of the hotel where I was staying in my breast pocket. I gave the card to the cops; they took me to the hotel in the squad car.

Maybe it was the girls I was chatting to. I clearly recall not having touched them. I was, in fact, nice to them, talking to them the entire evening. Maybe my wallet got saved on account of that. There was definitely something in my drink, a mickey or whatever, it certainly knocked the lights out of me. Six hours later, in a semi drugged state, I took my flight to London, connecting to Auckland via Los Angeles.

In 1995, I purchased a flaming red Alfa Romeo; Zoee purchased a Peugeot 306. The Honda City was disposed of. The roar of the Alfa Romeo engine is something I will always remember; such a soothing sound.

That same year I turned 40. My mother and my sister Mala visited New Zealand for the first time. I had a huge party for my 40th. I hired the entire Police Club for the evening and got roaring drunk; a great party.

In late 1995, Zoee and I purchased a beautiful villa in Mt. Eden. A carport was added, a deck was built at the rear, and the kitchen was extended. The small guest room was converted to my office, where I could work after office hours.

In late 1996, I heard that a large LPG company at Doha, Qatar, wanted SAP consultants for their ongoing project. I contacted the company in Doha, participated in their SAP tender, and was shortlisted, being one of two companies to provide SAP consultants to the prestigious client at Doha.

I was very nervous about doing this. How would we manage the cash flow and how would we get paid for our services, I wondered uneasily. The client wanted European SAP consultants, so I flew to Aberdeen, Scotland, to meet potential consultants, some of whom we subsequently provided to the client in Qatar.

I knew very few people in Aberdeen; one person I did know was David whom I had spoken with many times but had never met. I called David and a lady answered. I introduced myself and she told me David was in England on work. We chatted for a bit; she told me her name was Cindy and that she and David were due to get married in two weeks.

"What are you doing tonight?" Cindy asked.

"Nothing," I said.

"Would you like to do something?" "Sure," I said. We agreed for Cindy to come to the hotel that evening and go out from there.

I was having a drink with Alex, a SAP consultant; he had fractured his leg, which was in plaster and propped up on a footstool. I was on my first drink of the evening when the door opened and in walked this blonde lady wearing a dress with a flaming red jacket and a red beret, looking fabulous. She looked at me and said, "Sanjiv."

I said, "Cindy." "I thought you said you did not know anyone in Aberdeen," said Alex.

"I don't, Alex. I am meeting Cindy for the first time today."

Cindy asked me if I would like to go out. I said I would love to. I came down with my jacket, and we set off in a taxi. "There is a 14th-century inn about 14 miles from here," said Cindy. "It's a lovely place."

The weather was absolutely ghastly; there was snow, sleet and rain all night, totally awful. The taxi brought us to the inn, which at one time was a stopover for stagecoaches. We were fortunate to get a table. The restaurant had a blazing open fireplace in the center of the room, with tables on either side.

That was first time I ever saw a whisky list; it only had malt whiskies. I did not know 90% of the whiskies on offer. I went down the list, savoring one whisky after the other. Around 11:30 p.m., Cindy asked me, "Do you have hollow legs or what?"

"No," I said, "I am just so happy to be here with you."

Cindy and I chatted on and on. She told me about her impending marriage, how excited she was about her job as a hairdresser, that she loved fishing, standing in cold, chest deep water in waterproof trousers with a fishing rod.

We finally left past midnight; I dropped Cindy home and continued to my hotel, totally sober. I was proud of myself, I had made no advances on Cindy. I never saw Cindy again, but that evening remains etched in my memory.

In mid-1997, my mother told me that my white Willy's jeep was taking up far too much room in the garage and that since I was not coming back to India, I should sell it. I resisted for a while but then thought to myself, why am I making things so difficult for my mother? Moreover, if I needed a jeep later, I would buy one. Little did I realize that one day jeeps would become my passion.

I instructed my mechanic Kallu to sell the jeep.

"It does not have any papers," said Kallu.

"Sell it without papers," I said. Kallu finally sold the jeep for INR 10,000 in 1997.

Around 1998, Alex approached me with a proposal to build a resort at Alleppey in Kerala. The idea grabbed me immediately and I decided to visit

Alex the next time I happened to be going to India or Qatar.

I went to Alleppey and stayed with Alex and his parents in their family home. He took me to have a look at the property in question. It belonged to Mathew, an old friend of Alex's father. The property was 90 decimals or about 3,600 square meters, bang on the banks of Vembanad Lake in the village of Pathiramanal, about 12 kilometers from Alleppey.

The idea was to build a three-star resort, open for business around November 1999, in time for the millennium party. The plan was to construct 23 rooms over two levels, ground and first floor. The very idea excited me.

Alex was someone I had known for the last 25 years and trusted completely. He came from a business family; he was very good with figures and could calculate in his head without a calculator (something I couldn't do).

The project was kick-started in 1998; a company was formed, and I invested INR 20 lakhs, (USD 40,000) in the project, which was about 15% of the project equity.

The building work got off to a rapid start and every two to three months, I visited Alleppey to check out the progress.

The location of the resort was great; it was almost dead opposite the Coconut Lagoon and the Taj Kumarakom Resort, which are adjacent properties. The advantage Pathiramanal had was that the property was easily approachable by boat as well as by road without making wide detours.

It would have been autumn 1998 when I got a call from Maif in Singapore.

"Bablu, I need your help," he said. I wondered what kind of help Maif could be asking for. "I need to borrow some money. I will return it within three to five days. Please give me the money," he said.

Maif was a rich man, lived in a fabulous penthouse in Singapore, had a fancy chauffeur-driven Mercedes; the European and Chinese antiques in his house alone must have been worth well in excess of USD 1 to 3 million. As Maif was talking to me, my mind was turning with these thoughts. But I also thought, Maif did help me when I wanted money. I had repaid the debt in full and I was grateful for what he had done for me when I was down and out. I immediately wired him NZD 25,000.

The money never came back, there was some excuse or the other - business is bad, I will do it next week, and then the following week. One year later, I was in Los Angeles when Maif called me and said, "Bablu, please believe me, we do not even have any money to eat."

By now, Maif and Jayanti had lost their business, their antiques, their house, everything had gone. They had shifted to a small apartment in Singapore. I thought about this long and hard. I put myself in their shoes, tried to see it from their perspective, and thought to myself, I should help Maif. I instructed my office in Auckland to wire Maif NZD 10,000 immediately. I did not tell Zoee, but when she heard, she, of course, hit the roof.

What upset me was that most of the money I gave Maif was sent by them to Sydney for their daughter's university education, who, at that time, was living with Jayanti's younger sister, Nira.

Maif died a few years later. I guess the money I had given him went with him. When I reason with myself, I put this down to karma. Maif was good to me. RIP Maif. I also realized that a lot of what we do in life is simply because we can.

In late 1998, Alex told me that the Alleppey Resort project had gone into an overrun vis-à-vis prices and that he would have to raise additional capital to finish it on time. To avoid borrowing money at exorbitant rates, Alex borrowed the money from his father. His wife and son also chipped in with small contributions.

In 1999, I visited Pathiramanal. Mathew, the previous owner of the land had been very sick, he had developed some kind of a fungus on his skull. The doctors were trying to get to the root of the problem, trying to eliminate the fungus which had gripped Mathew's skull. In the end, the doctors had no choice but to remove Mathew's skull completely. This left Mathew with just a thin layer of skin covering his brain; he had to go everywhere with a steel helmet. Even sitting in his own house, he had to wear the helmet.

Initially, I thought Alex was pulling my leg. Where do you get to hear of someone without their skull? It all seemed a bit eerie. I went to meet Mathew. He came walking gingerly towards me from his bedroom without his helmet. I remember sitting there feeling rather nervous, watching Mathew gently sipping his tea.

The project was delayed; the grand plans of a millennium party were shelved, and the clock had moved on to the year 2000. I was beginning to get a bit worried as I had signed for the loan from Kerala State Financial Corporation (KSFC) in my personal capacity.

To make matters worse, in 1999, when Alex wanted a further cash injection, I persuaded my good friend Glen to invest in the resort. At that time, I had no inkling that the project had already run aground. Glen, like me, had grand visions of the resort coming good and visiting Alleppey to unwind with his family.

It was 2001 when I finally told Alex that there was not much point in holding onto a losing venture, that we should let it go. I approached my good friend Johnny, who also happened to be Alex's first cousin, to study the Pathiramanal accounts with the view of salvaging what we could and getting out as unscathed as possible. My primary concern was that I had given a personal guarantee to KSFC, and that my friend Glen had invested in the project on my recommendation.

Johnny is one of those super brilliant, know-it-all kind of highly intelligent men, who should be on *Kaun Banega Crorepati* (Who Wants to Be a Millionaire?). He is a lawyer, company secretary, cost accountant, and chartered accountant, all rolled into one, a one-man corporate financial machine. A good man to have on your team.

I really wanted an affirmation from Johnny that what we were considering, i.e. closing off the project, was a sound business decision and for him to let me know what we could recover from the waning project. Johnny promised to get back to me soon.

Johnny came back to me a couple of weeks later suggesting that we sell the property and not bother too much about going into the accounts. Johnny is a consultant, his job is to advise, but intrinsically, Johnny loathes doing that. He revels in giving his listeners and clients options, several options. If you ever went to Johnny to get clarity on any one point, two hours later and several whiskies down, you would come out banging your head on the brick wall, feeling far more confused than before you went in.

That said, I did understand a bit of Johnny and his nuances, he knew fully well I detested these never-ending options; I was looking for workable, practical solutions. And a solution is what Johnny did give me. I give him full credit for that. Johnny told me it was time for me to go home, which I did, albeit without a resort in Alleppey. But at least I went home with 30% of what I had initially invested.

CHAPTER TWENTY-TWO

SAPCorp Inc

In January 1997, our SAP Consulting business ensued with Qatar. We positioned a couple of SAP consultants whom I had met at Aberdeen the previous year in Doha from the UK, and we got off to a rocking start.

The client in Qatar would pay us in New Zealand, and we, in turn, would pay the consultants for their time at Qatar; it was a great business model. Subsequently we added a few more consultants in Doha from Australia, New Zealand and South Africa.

In late 1997, I thought it would be a good idea to start an office in Los Angeles (LA). I traveled there and met an immigration attorney who helped me with incorporating a company in Los Angeles. You have to choose a company name, and if the name is available with the Registrar of Companies, then you can book it and pay the fees to incorporate your company, it's that simple.

I had been advised by an American immigration attorney in New Zealand that I should open the company in the USA as a 100% subsidiary of my New Zealand company. The name I selected for the company in LA was SAPCorp Consulting, Inc. Our main business was SAP Consulting. The SAP software itself was owned by SAP AG, Germany, while the principal company in the US was called SAP America.

With SAPCorp Consulting, Inc. now a registered company in Orange County, California, I quickly established SAPCorp, Canada, in Vancouver, British Columbia, London, U.K. and even one in Auckland, New Zealand.

Since SAPCorp, USA, was a subsidiary of Kleinstar Holdings Limited, New Zealand, it became possible for Kleinstar to depute a manager in the US.

I decided to sponsor myself to work in the US. I applied for an L1 visa to work in Orange County, California, which was granted within a relatively short span of time. From January 1998, I could legally work in the USA.

I invited Al Seymour to join SAPCorp as my business partner in America to start operations, providing consultancy to clients in the US. We rented a three-bedroom apartment at an upmarket condominium, Versailles on the Lake, at Santa Ana. This was one street away from Costa Mesa and a short distance from South Coast Plaza, the very upmarket shopping mall with its fancy bars and restaurants.

Al Seymour took the master bedroom for himself and his wife. The second bedroom became the SAPCorp office and the third bedroom was kept ready for my use.

The management did not allow us to hang our company's name outside, but they did permit us to get necessities like additional telephone lines. For a nominal cost, we had a reasonably good functional office up and running within a few days.

Al was based in Orange County whereas I was based in Auckland.

In February 1998, one afternoon, I got call from a friend in Singapore saying that Reliance Industries in Bombay was looking for SAP consultants for their refinery in Jamnagar. My friend told me that the requirement was for a very specific Oil/ Gas domain/business expertise, with prior SAP work experience, to include a full-blown SAP implementation rollout experience at any Shell Company anywhere in the world as a necessary pre-condition.

I told my friend from Singapore that I was aware of this requirement and had been trying without success to speak to SAP India, for at least the last month. The consulting manager at SAP India had an ego the size of a football field; he was just not taking my call. I assumed that SAP India had the resources and did not need any help from any quarter, least of all from New Zealand.

My friend said, "Look, I am from SAP Singapore. I know for a fact SAP India does not have the requisite skills."

That confounded me even more. Why was SAP India refusing to even answer my emails and phone calls? Ego, I assumed.

Doing a mental shuffle of the SAP consultants' résumés I had on file in my head, I told my friend, "As of now, I have at least four to six SAP consultants with Oil/Gas experience and a couple with Shell experience."

"Call Reliance in Bombay. Speak to them and tell them that you have SAP consultants with Shell experience," my friend advised.

"Who do I call?" I asked.

"Speak to the IT manager or his assistant." I was given both the telephone numbers. "Remember," my friend said, "where this tip came from, should it come good."

"Yes," I said, "don't worry. I will keep that in mind."

My friend Viru had just joined Kleinstar Auckland. I think this was his first week in New Zealand, having just migrated from Bombay with his family. Viru and I had known each other from St. Xavier's, Calcutta, where I had done my BA, whereas Viru had done Commerce. On deciding to migrate to New Zealand, he came to see me in Auckland and I started him off, saying, "Let's see where this goes."

When I had come to Auckland in 1990 and had started Edana, and we were looking for office premises, Josephine had introduced me to her landlord, Bob. "He has several properties; check them out," she had said.

I called Bob and he showed me 24 Garfield Street, Parnell, which we eventually rented. Bob did not want a lease; he preferred something more casual or on a monthly basis. Coming from India, I did not want to be tied down to a lease either, so what Bob said suited me down to the ground.

We also rented our first house at Ladies Mile, Remuera, through Bob; the owner was a good friend of his. After three years at Garfield Street, we moved to bigger office premises on Heather Street, Parnell, which was also owned by Bob, and here again we continued renting without a formal lease.

Bob became a good friend and mentor. He would often give me business tips. "Always keep a larger office instead of a smaller one," Bob would tell me. "Sanjiv, there are two ways to go about doing business, one is to test the waters and start slowly at the bottom by calling the line managers and gradually going up the food chain. The second is to go straight to the top. The risk in going straight to the top is higher; should there be a block, or an obstacle, there will be no lifeline, and nowhere to go."

The problem was that while I understood what Bob was saying, I was a man in a hurry. I was trying to build a company with relatively little money and with no access to further funds. I discussed with Viru whether I should call Reliance, Bombay, and if so, whom do I target, what should our strategy be, and would Reliance even look at a miniscule company from New Zealand?

I thought about what my dear friend Suheil used to say: "No risk, no gain." I told Viru, "Heck, let's give it a try. If you do not dip your toe in the water, you will never know how hot it is."

I picked up the phone and called Karam at Reliance, Bombay, and as luck would have it, he picked up the phone. I introduced myself as Sanjiv from Kleinstar, from Auckland, New Zealand. I told him that we had a few SAP consultants with Oil/Gas experience, some of whom also had Shell experience. Karam listened attentively and then asked, "Excuse me, where are you calling from?"

"New Zealand," I said.

"Go on," said Karam. "You've' got my attention. You are saying the things we are looking for, I am listening."

I continued and more or less repeated what I had just said, stressing on the words Oil/Gas and Shell. "I don't know where you have come from," Karam said, "but yes, we do need these skill sets, so please email the SAP résumés to me."

I took Karam's email address, thanked him and put the phone down. Viru was sitting across the table from me. I smiled and said, "So far, so good."

I had barely put the phone down when it rang. It was a call from SAP India, from the consulting manager, Mr. Ego, whom I had been trying to get hold since the past month. Now he suddenly sounded all too friendly. "Hey, Sanjiv, long time no hear. How are you? I understand you have some SAP consultants with Oil/Gas and Shell experience."

I was taken aback by the sudden call. "Yes," I said, "I do have a few SAP Oil/Gas consultants."

"Please send them to me," said Mr. Ego. "When can I expect the résumés?"

"In a day or two," I said.

"No, please send them now as I have to make an urgent presentation."

I immediately shortlisted the best SAP consultants we had with Oil/Gas and Shell background and emailed them to Karam. I kept SAP India on hold for the moment.

The issue was that I could not send the same SAP résumés to Reliance as well as SAP India, who I assumed would forward the résumés to Reliance anyway. That I thought would grossly dilute my advantage.

I discussed the situation with Viru and decided to call the chief financial officer of Reliance, Mr. Manoj Modi, based in Mumbai. I called Mr. Modi's office a few times that day, and again the next morning and in the afternoon. On my fifth or sixth attempt, Mr. Modi's assistant said, "Let me see if I can connect you."

I introduced myself to Mr. Modi, saying that I had sent several SAP résumés with Oil/Gas and Shell backgrounds to Karam, and that SAP India wanted me to send their résumés to them as well. "What should I do?" I asked.

"Send the résumés to SAP India, as it's their software we are implementing. I don't care who does the work, as long as it's done."

"Okay, I will send our résumés, but I must caution you that if I do that, your project cost will increase by at least USD 3 million," I said.

"What did you say?" said Mr. Modi.

"If I send the résumés to SAP India, they will ramp up the charges by at least 50%," I repeated. "Your invoice value will increase by at least USD 3 million."

"Is that how it happens?"

"Yes, Sir. In this instance, the SAP consultants are not employees of SAP India; they are my consultants. SAP India will definitely increase their charges."

"Do not give these résumés to SAP India until I tell you otherwise," said Mr. Modi. "Send them to Karam only." This was exactly what I wanted to hear. I put down the phone and turned to Viru smiling.

To maintain the pretense and play ball with SAP India, I emailed Mr. Ego a few second-string résumés which I had not sent to Reliance. That brought the curtains down as far as SAP India was concerned. They never contacted me again, probably thinking that we had totally useless SAP consultants.

Thereafter, Al took over from LA. He did all the talking with Rajesh, the Reliance IT manager who had been brought in specifically from Houston for the automation of the Jamnagar plant, of which SAP was the most critical component.

Al would give me a daily roundup on what was happening. Raj would have long chats with Al on the phone and by email to discuss the strategy for going forward.

One early morning, around 4 a.m. in Auckland, mid-April 1998, I got a call from Al, all excited. We had been invited to go to Bombay by Reliance for a face-to-face meeting. "Raj has asked me fly to Bombay to meet him," Al corrected himself.

"How long do they want you in Bombay?" I asked.

"I don't know, I guess a couple of days," he replied. I congratulated Al and told him I would call him later as I wanted to think through the dynamics of what had just transpired.

Later, I told Al that he should go to Bombay, provided Reliance sent a business-class ticket for him from LA and another for me from Auckland.

I also said that Al's time in Bombay would be billable at USD 1,450 per day, plus hotel, car, and full board in Bombay for the duration of the entire stay in the city.

"This way," I told Al, "you can stay as long as they want you in Bombay and not sweat."

"Who the heck is Sanjiv from New Zealand?" asked Raj, when Al informed Reliance about providing two business-class tickets from Los Angeles and Auckland.

"Sanjiv is my boss in New Zealand; he is required for the commercials, and I will look after the SAP technical aspect," Al explained.

"No, we cannot do that," said Raj.

"Okay, that's fine then, don't call Sanjiv. I will come to Bombay at my own cost, the daily consulting fee however will be USD 2,000 per day for my time in Bombay, plus full expenses."

The next day Al called to tell me that Reliance had agreed to provide two business-class tickets, including one for me from New Zealand, plus they would put us both up in a hotel!

So, Al flew in from Los Angeles, via London, as he required a visa for India. I flew in from Auckland and we arrived within an hour of each other at Mumbai. A car met me at Bombay Airport, which whisked me away to the Holiday Inn, Juhu, where I met Al.

The next day, Al and I went to Reliance Petroleum, Ballard Estate, to meet Rajesh, our first face-to-face meeting with the Reliance IT manager. I remember sitting in the reception area, waiting to be called in for the meeting. I kept telling myself not to give in, to stick to my guns, that it was great to be here and that to have come this far was fantastic in itself.

We met Rajesh and his assistant, Karam, whom I had first spoken to from Auckland on the proposal which had initiated the whole thing a few weeks ago. Karam was a young man in his early 30s, karate black belt, extremely athletic and fit, with a razor-sharp mind. He was one of those people who did not require a pen and paper; he thought fast on his feet and took quick decisions.

Reliance already had our consultant résumés with them, and they went through each individual skill set with Al, detailing what precisely each consultant could provide. We were asked to come to the Reliance head office at Maker Towers the next day, around 11 a.m.

All we were told was that another company had also provided some good SAP résumés and was in the race for the job along with SAPCorp, and that a joint meeting would be held between Reliance, the other company and ourselves to determine who was getting what chunk of the SAP Consulting pie.

I came back to the hotel in the evening a bit fatigued, more mental tiredness than physical. I guess it must have been the lead-up to meeting Reliance H.O. for the first time that had got me wound up.

The next morning at 11 a.m., Al and I arrived at Maker Tower and were shown to the second floor, the offices of the chairman, Dhirubhai Ambani, and his two sons, Mukesh Ambani and Anil Ambani. We were immediately escorted to the board room.

A few minutes later, Rajesh and Karam joined us; we were told that the second company would be joining us in the boardroom in a few minutes. In walked the second company, led by Mr. Ego himself. I saw him and said to myself, "Oh my God," with a wry smile. Mr. Ego saw me, and for a moment, I do believe he stopped in his stride before continuing to the other side of the boardroom table. SAP India was represented by at least six senior executives; SAPCorp just had Al and me, sitting in one corner close to the projection camera and whiteboard.

SAP India started by saying that they did not wish to discuss everything openly in front of another company (i.e. SAPCorp). Rajesh countered by saying, "All we are trying to establish is which skill set each of you can provide, nothing more. So, what I want you to do is to write on the whiteboard the skills you have, and then SAPCorp will do the same, so that it is all out in the open."

SAP India, went on to say that they had access to a full German team of SAP consultants who had just come off a SAP Oil/Gas project with Shell, Manila, and would be available to start in Mumbai within 15 days. The four Germans included the project manager/IS Oil consultant (PM/IS), the financial accounting consultant (FI), the costing consultant (CO), and shipping consultant (SD).

Well here goes, I thought to myself, SAP India is going to bulldoze their way to the full project. "We can cover the other areas as well," said Mr. Ego.

"Oh great," said Rajesh, "please give me the résumés so that we can detail the skills on the whiteboard."

SAP India were reasonably weak in the areas of logistics, Materials Management (MM), Plant Maintenance (PM), and SAP Integration.

Where SAP India were unable to plug the gaps, SAPCorp ably slipped in. Al gave four CVs, including his own.

Using this tactic, SAP India were effectively stymied; they wanted to crib but could not as Rajesh had shown them to be lacking SAP skills in the non-financial areas, logistics and shipping modules.

The meeting, which lasted a few hours, exceeded my best expectations. Things were beginning to look good and we went back to Juhu to our hotel to celebrate.

The next day, I called Mr. Pradhan, based in Pune, who was spearheading the Tata Technologies (TTIL) SAP requirement for TELCO (Tata Motors) for their Pune and Jamshedpur factories. I had been speaking to Mr. Pradhan from New Zealand and thought it was an opportune time to go and call on him whilst I was in India.

The following day, Al and I were asked to go to the Reliance office in Andheri. This was where we were told it had all started, where Mr. Dhirubhai had started building his empire. I believe this is where Mukesh and Anil grew up.

At Andheri, we were introduced to some of the accounting line managers. I am still not quite sure why we were asked to go there. Was it a trick to break us, to arm twist us into lowering our fees perhaps? The talk swung around to the prospective payment terms in the event we did sign a contract with Reliance.

"You know the reputation Reliance has in the market; we are good paymasters."

I did not want to tell the manager I had no intention of standing at the end of a long line of vendors waiting and pleading to be paid. I just kept quiet and let him go on about how great the company was. "What is the payment schedule?" I asked, finally.

"As per normal, two months after the invoice is made for services rendered."

"Is that normal here?" I asked. "It's not normal to me."

In New Zealand, invoices are paid on the 20th of the following month. An invoice dated the 29th would be paid on the 20th of the following month, after 22 days; an invoice dated 7th would be paid after 43 days. I did a quick calculation and deduced that if the payment was made according to the Reliance payment schedule, we would be out of pocket for a minimum of a 105 days before payment.

To be on the safe side, that would mean we would have to carry the fat for three and a half months before payment from Reliance.

I just shook my head, smiled, and politely told the gentleman that there was no point discussing these matters with him as this conversation was going nowhere. "What do you mean going nowhere?" he asked incredulously.

"We cannot work on these terms," I responded. "Can you give me a letter of credit, guaranteeing payment after 60 days of production of invoice for the preceding 30 days?"

"No, we cannot give you a letter of credit, we have never done so; our reputation in the market is solid," he said.

"Then there is nothing to say, as I cannot agree to 60 days."

I turned to Al. "This is not happening, let's not waste our time here."

"Okay, how many days do you want to be paid in?" the man asked.

I looked at him for a few seconds, "Seven days flat," I said, without batting an eyelid.

"Seven days, impossible," he said, scoffing.

"That's why I have been saying it's no good talking about this now. Please inform Rajesh that we cannot work on your prescribed payment terms." With that, Al and I got up and politely left.

The next day, when we met Rajesh and Karam, they were unfazed and did not react to the meeting the day before. I have no idea what they might have been informed by their line managers whom we had met.

I asked Karam to give me a copy of their standard contract that we could study. "We don't have a standard contract," said Karam.

"You make one and we will get back to you," said Rajesh. I wondered how we would come up with a workable contract. We thanked Rajesh and Karam for their hospitality and left.

The next day, Al and I went to meet Mr. Pradhan in Pune, to introduce ourselves and explain what SAP consulting services we could offer to TELCO on demand. We were very well received by Mr. Pradhan.

I asked TTIL for a copy of their standard contract, as Reliance had refused to give us theirs. Mr. Pradhan pulled out a copy of their standard materials purchase contract. It was not IT-centric at all, far from it.

Al and I returned to LA and Auckland, waiting to be called to Bombay to finalize our contract. No call came. After two weeks, I went to LA on a routine visit and told Al, "Maybe we should have offered 45-day payment terms." Even that would have been stretching it, I felt, far too risky.

It was in late April 1998 that I emailed Johnny, my chartered account friend in Bangalore, a copy of the TTIL contract and asked him to formulate a SAP contract out of that.

"How do you expect me to make sense of this material contract?" Johnny said.

Well, Johnny," I said, "there is nothing else I have. Tear it up and begin from scratch if you have to. I need a contract to put on the table."

One thing that was bothering me was the process of paying overseas consultants working in India. I was trying to model it on my Qatar operation, wherein all the consultants were paid their salaries tax free. Johnny told me that withholding tax would have to be deducted in India, and that it would be better if the client could pay the withholding tax component on our behalf. These complex tax issues were way above my head. I was glad to have palmed them off to Johnny to sort out.

I was in LA for about a week, and after discussing the issue at great length with Al, it was decided the best option would be for me to fly to Bombay, supposedly on a routine business visit and try and elicit some information from Reliance. I decided to take the risk, go for broke and force the issue. Not knowing where we stood, the suspense was killing me.

To be on the safe side, I emailed Karam the copy of the contract that Johnny had rewritten, a very basic contract covering mainly the payment terms. The tax issues were covered in the payments column in fine print, to be paid by the "Company". I called Karam and told him that I expected to be in Mumbai on Monday, 11th May, and asked if it would be possible to meet him to discuss the contract. He agreed. I was pleased as that was what I had been waiting to hear.

My Uncle Kenny happened to be visiting LA, and he stayed with me for the night. In passing I mentioned that I was trying to do business with the Tata Group. "Do you know Mr. Ishaat Hussain?" I asked.

"Yes, I do. We were in the same house together at Doon School," he said.

"Can you speak to Mr. Hussain?" I asked.

"I suppose I could, though I have not seen him for the last 40 odd years or so." My Uncle Kenny called Mr. Ishaat Hussain in Bombay; the secretary took the call and informed Uncle Kenny that Mr. Hussain was in a meeting.

"Please tell Mr. Hussain I called. Tell him we were in the same house, Hyderabad, Oh, yes, tell him Kotte called; he may not remember Karanjit or Kenny. It's been 40 years since we have met," he said." I am not sure what Mr. Hussain's secretary thought about this. I told Kenny Uncle that

Mr. Hussain would definitely call him, because if he remembered him, then surely Mr. Hussain would also remember him. It was just that simple.

Mr. Hussain called within the hour. It's difficult to talk about things when you are speaking to someone you were very friendly with 40 odd years before and then have to ask a favor to help out your nephew. But that's precisely how the conversation went: "Ask him to call me when he is in India."

I landed at Bangalore on Friday, 8th May, checked into the Bangalore Club, and waited to see how Johnny had fashioned the contract. Johnny came, and we discussed the nuances of the contract. He suggested we offer Reliance some incentive for prompt payment.

Johnny deftly wove in a clause offering 0.75% discount for all bills settled and paid within 15 days of submission. Invoicing was to be done monthly, against authorized time sheets.

Johnny and I landed in Mumbai early in the morning on 11th May and checked into the Marine Plaza Hotel on Marine Drive. We met Rajesh and Karam at Reliance and went over the contract with Karam, who did not seem fazed by the payment terms at all. Rajesh spent a while looking at the contract and said that we should come back the following week, as they were busy attending to other critical issues.

The next morning, 12th May, was my much-anticipated meeting with Mr. Ishaat Hussain, director of Tata Sons in Mumbai.

Johnny and I walked into Mr. Hussain's wood-lined office at 11:30 a.m. sharp. Mr. Hussain was sitting at his large desk; he came around and warmly shook my hand, and I introduced him to Johnny.

The meeting that I had anticipated to be about discussing probable IT business and specifically SAP Consulting Services with the Tata Group, starting with TELCO, got totally derailed by the nuclear devices that India set off that very morning at Pokharan, Rajasthan. I had seen the headline on the news in the morning but did not think that it would consume the day as much as it did.

Nothing of any substance was discussed with Mr. Hussain at all. The entire hour that we were with Mr. Hussain, was spent discussing the potential fallout of the nuclear test blast at Pokhran. Mr. Hussain said he could only wish us well; we had an excellent cup of tea with Mr. Hussain, that was it. Johnny and I left almost immediately for Pune to meet Mr. Pradhan at TTIL.

We stayed at Hotel Pride, near the university area of Pune, that's where a lot of visiting TELCO managers and visitors stay when they visit Pune. The next day we met Mr. Pradhan at Pimpri, which is the TELCO factory just outside Pune.

Mr. Pradhan introduced us to C. R. Ramakrishna from TELCO, Finance, who was heading the SAP project for TELCO. Johnny and C.R., both being finance guys, hit it off from day one. They found common ground, having done their articles for the same accounting firm in Chennai years ago.

C.R. introduced us to the TELCO program manager, Dee Hunt, a no-nonsense lady from South Africa. I could see her eyes gleaming when I showed her the résumés of the SAP consultants we proposed to deploy at TELCO. "These are the consultants I want, and I want then now on this project," Dee Hunt said.

Talk about being in the right place at the right time, I said to myself.

With Dee doing our bidding for us, and C.R. acknowledging the requirement and not batting an eyelid at our costing and payment terms, things were moving really fast.

We were asked to return to Pimpri the next day to meet Mr. Pradhan, as we would be working under his aegis. Our SAP consultants were to work in tandem with the TTIL team that would implement the SAP solution for TELCO.

The next morning, Johnny and I met Mr. Pradhan at Pimpri; he had already been briefed by C.R., and after a few minutes of polite talk, he asked me whether it might be possible to sharpen our rates a bit.

"Yes, I will definitely look at the rates," I said, looking at him, "but please understand that there is not much I can do; the rates are quite tight as they are. Kindly give us a few minutes."

Johnny and I went to the far end of Pradhan's office. Johnny had a calculator and I had the contract with the daily rates of all the consultants we were proposing to TTIL. "There is not much to discuss," I told Johnny.

"Yes, I know," he said. "Pretend you are seriously looking at the costing." Johnny and I had already decided what we would drop our rates to if asked.

Ten minutes later we went back to Pradhan's table and gave him the predetermined, revised costing for all the consultants' daily rates. The important issues of withholding tax and payment overseas had already been sorted out.

"Can we meet in Bombay next week at Mr. Kadle's office?" C.R. asked.

"Yes, of course, we can," I said.

"Okay. Please come on Friday, 22nd May, at 4 p.m. to sign the contract," said C.R. I wanted to shout with joy but held back.

The following week, Johnny and I returned to Mumbai and took up the matter with Reliance with renewed vigor, armed with our draft contract. We now had a workable document.

Unfortunately, I had some bad news: one of the SAP consultants we were hoping to deploy at Reliance had opted out at the last minute.

I did not want to draw up a contract with a work order for SAP consultants and then tell Reliance that we could not deploy a certain consultant whom we had committed to earlier. With totally honest and transparent intent I informed Rajesh that we were unable to provide one of the selected and approved SAP resources. Rajesh was quite upset and went off the boil. Karam was a little more philosophical. "These things happen. I am sure you will find someone else. Let's at least finalize the contract. Please come to Maker Towers IV at 7 p.m. today and we will finalize the contract this evening."

On the dot, we arrived at Karam's office. I had never been to a more congested office building. Karam's room was so tiny, you couldn't swing a cat in there, his desk alone took up almost the entire width of the office.

There was only one chair in front of his desk. Karam arranged another chair, which meant that the sliding door of the room could not close easily.

First came the tea, *pakoras* and *bhaji*. After a few minutes, Karam said, "Let's look at the contract." When he got stuck on a particular point, he said, "Let me go and ask Rajesh."

A few minutes later, Rajesh came and took over from Karam. I do not know why Karam allowed this; we knew that Rajesh would put up obstacles. And sure enough, over the next three hours, this good cop/ bad cop scenario played out. Karam's office was so small it was just not possible for both Rajesh and Karam to sit behind the desk together at the same time.

This literally meant that we had to discuss the contract paragraph by paragraph with Karam and Rajesh individually. They would switch seats every 10 to 15 minutes. Concessions given by one would be cancelled by the other. "I do not know why Rajesh said that," Karam would say, and Rajesh would say, "I do not know why Karam allowed this." At no point could we talk to both Karam and Rajesh at the same time. What an interesting negotiation strategy I thought! Each time Karam came, he would print out the amended contract; when Rajesh came, portions of the contract that had been approved by Karam that he did not agree with had to be rewritten.

This was the Reliance art of negotiations, played out to perfection. Wear the opponent down gradually, slowly but surely. I had heard that Reliance had deferred the signing of the master contract with SAP AG (Germany) until the evening of 31st December, a year ago.

SAP AG was keen to conclude the deal with Reliance on the last day of the year to accrue the benefit of booking the contract in the last quarter of the year. For that to happen, the contract had to be signed before midnight.

I understand Reliance kept pushing the ball around and kept SAP AG guessing to the last minute about whether they were signing or not. The idea was to take as many concessions as possible. I believe the contract was finally signed with SAP AG around 11 p.m., an hour before midnight!

I had heard this story but had not given much credence to it; I had filed it away as a business event that had happened. At that time, I did not know that soon thereafter, I would also be in a similar situation.

In the art of negotiation, it is said that you should grudgingly give away things you do not need and fight hard for things you do need.

From our perspective, the payment terms were by far the most important. We fought hard for it, and late in the evening, I said that we would be willing to give 0.75% discount for the prompt settlement of our invoices. This was the ace in our negotiation strategy. We offered this when we knew it would make the most impact and turn the negotiations in our favor.

Reliance and TELCO were both cash-rich companies; they had their coffers full in 1998 and there was no question of raising any funds from anywhere to get the SAP project going. Reliance just negotiated hard and I understood and respected that.

When we offered the 0.75% concession, the whole tide turned our way. Rajesh, who had been playing the proverbial hardball, softened a bit.

The final amended contract was finally printed out around 10 p.m. and was eventually signed between Reliance Industries Limited and SAPCorp Consulting, Inc., around 10:30 p.m. on 21st May, 1998.

After the contract was signed, there was general bonhomie. Rajesh and Karam were both relaxed, while I was totally exhausted, mentally and physically.

The enormity of what had just happened had not hit me until Johnny turned around and said, "Congratulations Mr. Lall, you have pulled it off."

Johnny was a partner in SB Billimoria and Co., Chartered Accountants. He was used to doing big deals involving multiple countries. I had never done one before myself. Four days after arriving from Bangalore, Johnny and I had signed off on the Reliance deal.

We went back to Marine Plaza. The mental tension of the week had got to me and I was down with an attack of gout; my right big toe had swollen up and I was walking with great difficulty.

First thing I did was to email Al and give him the good news. I was worried that Reliance might ask for details on SAPCorp, LA, but they did not. Kleinstar, New Zealand, had a SAP Consulting track record, whereas SAPCorp, LA, was the new kid on the block; but the new kid had won the day.

The next morning, Johnny and I went over the TTIL contract with a fine toothcomb. Learning and benefitting from the Reliance experience made the negotiation with TTIL - TELCO that much easier.

Later that afternoon, we arrived at Mr. Pravin Kadle's office, followed by C.R. and Pradhan. Johnny proceeded to inform the TELCO team that we had just concluded a SAP contract with Reliance the day before.

Kadle looked suitably impressed. He asked me whether I had gone through the TTIL contract. I said we had, and that we were happy. Here again, the payments were critical to the whole thing hanging together. But we managed to pull off the contract.

Johnny was incredulous. "I do not believe this; it just does not happen this way," he said.

"What does not happen, Johnny?"

"You came from New Zealand a week ago, you did not even have a proper contract, and one week later, on two consecutive days, you signed two multimillion-dollar contracts," he said.

I had known Johnny for about fifteen years now, having first met him at Alex's wedding at Alleppey. Alex had told me, "I have more than 100 cousins whom you will meet; seven of them are called Johnny."

After Alex got married, I would meet Johnny regularly in Bangalore, have a drink with him and his cousin George and occasionally join them either at the Catholic Club, The Bangalore Club, or the Bangalore Golf Club.

I daresay that Johnny never took me seriously, even when I called him in April from Delhi saying that I was in India to negotiate a SAP contract with Reliance and that I wanted his input on the tax angle. Johnny was used to working for large pedantic firms where decision-making was slow, where it took forever with endless meetings that eventually got nowhere. Here, within seven days, we had concluded two multimillion-dollar deals. Johnny was truly confounded!

I did not have a footprint in India. I quickly needed to open an office to facilitate the overseas consultants and ensure that the operations ran smoothly. Johnny's mandate was to establish SAPCorp Consulting India (Pvt.) Limited within a week.

SAPCorp India opened in Alex's office at Walton Road, Bangalore. Adjacent to his office was stockbroker George, who was Johnny's younger brother. Alex and Johnny became directors of SAPCorp India.

The idea was for Alex to run the company and for Johnny to provide the financial input, to do the invoicing, and liaising with Reliance and TELCO for the payments. At the end of the day, I have to admit that it was Johnny and not Alex who ran SAPCorp India.

As for me, I remained in Auckland, New Zealand.

I now had SAP Consulting operations in Qatar, USA, and India. I mused to myself that 1978 had been a momentous year for me personally, and now, 20 years later, 1998 was a momentous year for my business.

Reliance and TELCO were both demanding clients; however, their style of doing business was entirely different.

The one distinct feature that was common to both contracts was that there was a dual rate structure for foreign overseas consultants and yet another rate for NRI Indian consultants. The overseas consultants were paid a substantially higher amount, and they were provided better hotels, better amenities, and were looked after better.

The belief was that the consultants should be treated at a level consistent with their standard of living. An Indian, it was assumed, would accept lower wages and lower-grade amenities, based on the belief that they were used to that particular lower standard of living, and thereby, lower rates.

Coming from Auckland, this did shock me at first. I dealt with it, extracting the best possible deal I could from the clients for the expat Indian NRI consultants coming from overseas to work in India.

The Reliance SAP project kick-started almost immediately. SAP India brought the four-man German team from Manila as they had promised they would and put them up at Oberoi Towers. The SAPCorp four-man team was put up at Hotel Marine Plaza, a few minutes walking distance from Oberoi Towers.

The project started at Reliance, Tulsiyani Chambers, Nariman Point, where the SAP server was housed. Month two into the project, I heard rumblings from the German team. As it so happened, the Germans were big beer drinkers, whereas Al and Bob from SAPCorp were a bit partial to Johnny Walker. They would meet every day and gossip.

"We are not getting paid," the Germans would complain.

"Really? But we are being paid by Sanjiv." "SAP India is just not paying us."

Month two, on my next visit to Mumbai, I was told the same thing: the Germans had still not been paid. They had signed their contract in Deutsche mark, whereas SAP India's currency of payment from Reliance was US dollars. The DM had appreciated sharply in value, which was creating payment issues. As these were hearsay accounts, I had no details to go on. All I knew was that as per our contract, we were being paid on time for our consultants actual time worked. Johnny's job was to invoice the clients for the days worked, which was easily substantiated by the respective consultants time sheets.

All we really had to ensure was that the time sheet was signed and returned to the consultant on time for the preceding month.

I began traveling extensively. To keep things at an even pace, I divided my time equally between LA and Auckland and between Mumbai, Delhi, and Bangalore. I spent about 10 days to two weeks in each country. New Zealand was the halfway point between India and LA; that worked out wonderfully. I could return to Auckland to recharge my batteries both from LA and Mumbai.

Al was in Mumbai on the Reliance project. I had to keep the SAPCorp LA end up, which meant I had to spend considerable time there. The payments from India were made to our Bank of America account; the consultants in turn had to be paid from SAPCorp, Santa Ana, California.

The Germans were still cribbing that they had not been paid, that they were going to walk out on the project. This charade would carry on daily once the beer started flowing after office hours at the Oberoi bar.

I landed at Mumbai in late August 1998 and was informed that just the day before, the Germans had carried out their threat; they simply walked off the project, just like that. They had been threatening to do so and one day they did just that.

As luck would have it, I happened to be in Mumbai. I went to meet Karam, which I did routinely every time I came to Mumbai. "Not today," said Karam, "I am very busy." He was cursing the Germans for walking off the project and he was cursing SAP India, as it was their responsibility.

"I don't know what to do," Karam said, tearing his hair out.

"What is the most critical requirement?" I asked.

"Shipping - SD," he said. "The financials we can defer for some time. Project management also I can defer. SD and IS OIL, I cannot."

"I have a solution for you, Karam," I said.

"No, I need to find consultants to replace the Germans right now," he said.

"That's what I am talking about, Karam," I said calmly.

"You have the consultants?" he asked.

"Yes, I do. They are already on the project," I said.

"What do you mean?" "Simon, who is on the integration side, is also an expert SD consultant. Peter Schat can fill in the IS OIL slot," I explained.

"Really?" asked Karam, surprised. "Are you sure?"

"Yes, I am sure. Please try them out." Karam looked at me a little doubtfully and said, "Fine, I will try them out."

I generally stayed in Mumbai for a maximum of two days and three nights as I was conscious of the hotel costs and did not want to run up huge bills.

The next day when I met Karam, he was smiling and looked relaxed. He shook my hand. "Simon and Peter have taken over," he said. "Screw the Germans and SAP India".

"See, I told you that those two could do the job," I said.

SAPCorp saved the day for Reliance; even to this day, Karam gives me credit for saving their fat from the fire. A delay in the project would have been disastrous and costly. As it so happened, there was no delay; if at all, there was only a gentle ripple which was easily contained, courtesy SAPCorp. Again, it was a question of being at the right place at the right time.

At this time, Bombay had become Mumbai, and the change was evident and apparent. All the signage read Mumbai.

From Mumbai, I would go to Pune to check in on the consultants at TELCO. All the Reliance consultants were at Marine Plaza, a great boutique hotel, with a fabulous bar called Geoffrey's. The office was just a few minutes away.

At Pune, the consultants were at Hotel Pride, a four-star property, a far cry from Marine Plaza. Pimpri, where the office was situated, was also quite a distance, about 45 minutes at the very minimum. The SAP project office was on the first floor of an industrial shed; it was, after all, a factory site.

The office was basic; only the managers' cabins were airconditioned. The toilets down the corridor were rudimentary Indian toilets, with no signs of toilet paper.

I diplomatically asked Dee Hunt how she managed. "Not very well," she said.

The senior manager's loo was kept well stocked with toilet paper and other amenities. "Why don't you use that?" I asked.

"Because it's kept locked," she replied. She recounted how on one occasion, when she had gone to the toilet, a large rat ran past her. She said she almost passed out. "Did you report the matter?" I asked.

"You bet I did," she said. The loo was cleaned and fumigated, but that's all that happened. The standard of the loo cleanliness did not change much.

Mr. Ricky Ricardo from Houston came to Pune to join the SAPCorp team on the TELCO project. Ricky was all keyed up about coming to India. He was rather concerned about how many suits he should bring with him. "Can I bring seven suits?" he asked.

"I think seven suits are far too many, but if you like you can bring them with you," I said.

Ricky Ricardo arrived at Pune with his seven suits. On his third day at Pune, Ricky called me. "Sanjiv, my driver uses the wrong side of the road. He is always driving on the other side of the yellow line. Oh yes, and another thing, the restrooms at the office are a total mess. The floor is always wet and dirty. My expensive suit has got ruined. I don't think I can work here. Please send me home."

I tried to cajole Ricky and promised him I would call C.R. to set things straight. I called C.R., and after exchanging pleasantries, I said, "C.R., there is something delicate I have to say." I told him that my consultants had complained about the dirty and unhygienic condition of the washroom facilities.

"I will look into that," C.R. said. I thanked him and told him I would meet him on my next visit to India.

"Are you calling from New Zealand?" C.R. asked me.

"Yes, I am," I said.

"You are calling all the way from New Zealand to talk about the toilet situation at Pimpri?" he asked in astonishment.

"Yes, I am doing just that C.R. The washroom situation was reported to me by our consultants at TELCO."

Well, the toilet situation did not improve. Ricky Ricardo left Pune three days later and returned to America, the first and only consultant to do so on account of poor toilet facilities.

I did find out that apparently, after my call to C.R., the toilets were washed and kept dry thereafter, but no amenities followed, no toilet paper was found. I advised all the SAPCorp consultants to bring their own toilet paper!

I would have to say, at the end of the day, it's the temperament of the consultant that makes a difference. Ricky was not willing to give India a chance; he had all of Pimpri dancing around him, but he wanted more. On the other hand, we had John Addendorf, the MM consultant from South Africa, who had recently migrated to New Zealand. John was a totally relaxed kind of a guy. He was unflappable and things like poor toilet facilities, electricity cuts, the Indian heat and dust did not seem to bother him; he took it all in his stride.

John was posted for a while at Jamshedpur, and even there he remained totally unfazed by it all. In hindsight, I will say that there are some kind of people who can take it and others who cannot. I did try my best to fight hard for my consultants to ensure they had a happy and comfortable stay in India. To a very large extent I was successful; the Ricky episode was never repeated.

Tito Das flew in from LA to join the Reliance project at Jamnagar. Upon arrival at Jamnagar Airport, he was taken to the Reliance compound reception; there he was told that they were expecting him. He signed the register and was told a bus would take him to his accommodation. I had told Tito that the facilities in Jamnagar, the accommodation, the room, the food would all be five-star quality. It was only because of my assurance that he would have a comfortable stay in Jamnagar that he had agreed to come to India.

Tito called me, it was night in Auckland. I immediately suspected something was wrong. "I arrived at Jamnagar today," said Tito. "A rickety bus arrived to pick me up. My room is basic, the whole building is basic and to add insult to injury, the loo is an Indian-style toilet. Sanjiv, I have a major problem with my leg, you know that if I squat down on the toilet, I may not be able to get up."

"I will try and do something," I said. Once again, the Indian SAP consultants had been given lower standard accommodation and treatment.

I immediately called up Mr. Batliwala, an elderly Parsi gentleman who was in charge of the accommodation facilities for all the SAP Consultants in Jamnagar, both for foreigners and Indians. I explained what had happened with Tito. "He is an expat, NRI, from LA, Mr. Batliwala," I explained.

"Oh,'" said Mr. Batliwala, "we assumed he was an Indian and thus gave him a room with an Indian style loo."

"Yes, he is an Indian, but one with a gamy leg, Mr. Batliwala," I said.

"I will set this right," he said. And true to his word, Tito was immediately taken to the foreigner's block where he was given a plush five-star room with a western-style WC.

In 1998, we had a great year in Qatar; we positioned four SAP consultants there. My great friend Glen finally relented and went to Doha. Glen later told me, "I should have listened to you and come sooner."

In the Autumn of 1998, Zoee and I took my mother on a European and America trip. My mother flew to Auckland, where she stayed with us for a few days. Then we all flew to Los Angeles. From LA, we flew to London and stayed with Diff in her magnificent apartment in Vauxhall, London, which had recently been converted from a warehouse. From London, we went to Dublin.

In Dublin, we stayed at a small hotel and set off the next day in a rental car towards Kilkenny. We had barely driven 25 kilometers out of Dublin and were passing what looked like a monastery or a school; it had big steel gates, which were closed. We had just passed the monastery gates when my mother said, "Stop, could you go back please?" So, I went back. "I wonder if Mother Cecelia, who taught me at Tara Hall, Simla, will be here; she was from Ireland."

I looked at my mother and said, "That was more than 50 years ago!"

"Yes," said mother, "but at least let's find out."

"Mother, we are at the Loreto Abbey, at Rathfarnham House," I said, reading from the sign.

"Yes, I know," said mother. "Let's go inside and find out if they know Mother Cecelia."

I rang the bell, and a little while later, a gardener, who had been sweeping the grounds, came out. "The school is closed," he said.

"I know, but would it be possible to speak to Mother Superior?" I asked.

"Let me see," he said and disappeared inside. He came back a few minutes later and opened the gates. My mother, Zoee, and I were walking towards the building when a nun asked us, "Can I help you?"

My mother introduced herself, told her that she was from India, visiting Dublin, and that she was looking for Mother Cecelia, an Irish nun who had taught her at Loreto Convent School, Tara Hall, Simla, India, in the late 1940's. The nun looked a bit nonplussed and surprised; this was not the kind of question you are routinely asked. She asked my mother for a few more details.

"Who were the other nuns from Ireland who taught you?" she asked, and my mother gave her a few more names. Then suddenly the nun said, "Mother Cecelia was here till last week. She had come to stay for a while, and we actually know her by another name."

"Really? Would you have her phone number?" my mother asked.

"No, I am afraid not. We do not have phone numbers, but I could get one for you. It might take a few days. I will have to ask around," she replied.

We stayed there for a while. My mother was chatting away with the nun as if she had known her all her life. We had a cup of tea and left.

"See," my mother said, "I told you they would know Mother Cecelia." I later came to know that in the 1920s, a novice nun, Agnes Bojaxhiu (who became the revered Mother Teresa), came to Loreto Abbey, Rathfarnham House, to learn English. This was the language the sisters of Loreto used to teach the school children in India and perhaps also to my mother, in Tara Hall, in the 1940's in Simla! (Simla was later renamed Shimla.)

I loved Ireland. The countryside was beautiful, a bit like New Zealand, I thought. Kilkenny is an old medieval town, which has one of the oldest Guinness breweries in Ireland. The Irish pubs in Dublin are a fun place to be in. The Irish are very nice, warm and friendly people, with a great sense of humor. Ireland is one of the countries I would like to visit again.

From Dublin, we flew to Rome. In Rome, we stayed at the Society of Mary monastery. The Society of Mary have a home, one kilometer from Tikratoli, called Nirmal Deep. My mother was very friendly with all the foreign priests, "brothers" and "fathers", who would routinely come visiting Nirmal Deep, Ranchi.

The resident head of Nirmal Deep in the mid 90's was Father Frank from St. Louis, Missouri, USA. Father Frank had recently moved to Rome as the overall head of the of the Society of Mary, Worldwide, based in Rome. Father Frank had told my mother that if she ever happened to be in Rome, we must stay at the monastery with them, so that is what we did.

The monastery was a very large sprawling house, enclosed with tall walls. Zoee and I were given a large room and my mother had her own room down the hall, close to the chapel. We would eat all our meals in the dining hall with the priests. The priests had been told that I was fond of whiskey and they had kept a bottle of whiskey especially for me. I was quite touched and also a bit embarrassed!

We visited the Vatican, and Father Frank took my mother to listen to Pope John Paul II speak; she sat in the second or third row, quite close to the Pope and came back glowing and looking happy, having heard him speak. Walking around the Vatican was an extraordinary experience. The highlight was easily the Sistine Chapel and St. Peter's Basilica at the Vatican.

Rome is such a beautiful city, with so many historic sites and a monument around every corner. The Colosseum, the Trevi Fountain, the Pantheon...the list is endless. Of all these, the Trevi Fountain was fabulous; we could sit down, have a coffee, and watch the Trevi at leisure.

One thing I noticed in Rome was that the public vehicle of choice, be it the police or the cabs, was the Alfa Romeo 155 V6, the same car I used to drive in Auckland. I thought that I had better get something else for myself, far too many people had it in Italy!

The one sorrow I had about Rome was that the Irish whiskey I had purchased at the Dublin Airport, Connemara, got left behind in the airport cab, and the cabbie did not come back and give it to me. I felt really bad about losing my bottle of fine Irish whiskey.

From Rome we returned to Delhi, the end of my mother's Europe trip. I continued to Doha the same day on business.

I was in Santa Ana again in the last quarter of 1998. Al was also back in California after his three-month stint with Reliance. The primary issue was that whilst SAPCorp was making money out of the SAP Consultants at Reliance and TELCO, there was no money left in the company for its president after payment of wages and expenses.

I explained to Al that I could not pay him both his monthly wages in the USA and his daily consultancy charges in Mumbai. He could not get both, simply because while he was physically in Mumbai, he could not do any routine SAPCorp work in the USA.

I don't quite know why, but Al never quite understood this principle. He was paid his full daily consulting fee for his time in Bombay, which amounted to considerably more than his monthly wage in LA. On his return to LA, Al wanted his three months' wages to be paid in arrears; I told him that this was simply not possible. I also had to fill in a considerable amount of time in LA while Al was in Mumbai; this was vitally necessary as all the consultants' payments had to be made from the USA, and in those years, Bank of America did not have full e-banking facilities.

For the whole of 1998, I was not paid anything out of SAPCorp, LA. I had secured a lucrative contract for the company and all the consultants were being paid handsomely. Al and the SAPCorp office staff were also being paid well; only the president of the company got zilch, and you guessed it, that was me.

Al and I split amicably. I do not know if there is ever is an amicable split. That said, Al and I did part on speaking terms, there was no real rancor. I was grateful to Al for his valuable inputs at SAPCorp, and for his time at Qatar while he was working for Kleinstar.

With Al's exit, nothing really changed; the billing continued from SAPCorp, Bangalore, on behalf of SAPCorp, LA, courtesy Johnny. The payments from Reliance and TELCO continued to be made to SAPCorp, LA, facilitated again by Johnny.

I hired Roger as our point man in LA, to oversee things, and develop a much more streamlined SAPCorp.

The senior executives at Reliance had told me that they would only use external SAP consultants for a maximum of six months. "In that time, we will learn what there is to learn and run on our own from there. Our guys are very bright; six months is all that it will take us to understand and learn what SAP is."

One of the requirements was that the SAPCorp consultants would train the local user team, be it Reliance or TELCO. In the SAP training sessions, there would be a maximum of 25 to 30 seats per training session. At Reliance and TELCO, the training sessions were bursting at the seams, with many trainees standing for hours on end. It seemed that everyone wanted to attend the SAP training sessions.

As 1998 drew to a close, I thought to myself that it had been a great year. So many new things had happened. Also, we were lucky to have lasted to the end of 1998 with Reliance, I thought.

In August 1999, SAPCorp received a cease and desist letter from the attorneys of SAP America, Inc., saying that we were in breach of the trademark and patent law by using the name SAPCorp to unlawful advantage and gain. The letter went on to say that we must either drop the name SAPCorp or face legal action from SAP America.

I had spent a considerable amount of money in building the SAPCorp brand in America, New Zealand, and India. I had paid a lot of money to an ex Saatchi and Saatchi outfit to build the SAPCorp website, which was receiving several hits and résumés from SAP consultants.

I considered the ominous legal threat and its probable consequences and decided that it made little sense to take on the might of SAP America.

In September 1999, SAPCorp changed its name to STLCorp, which essentially reflected my initials, STL. In essence, I incorporated myself!

The Reliance contract was changed and amended accordingly. Other than the name change to STLCorp, nothing changed. All the SAPCorp offices worldwide changed their names to STLCorp.

The TELCO contract came to a natural end in mid-1999. By this time, the SAPCorp-STLCorp consultants had worked for TELCO in their various operations at Jamshedpur, Pune, Lucknow, and Mumbai.

By 1999, the Reliance SAP project had moved to Phoenix Mills, Lower Parel. I continued to stay at Marine Plaza whenever I visited Mumbai, though I confined myself mostly to the Reliance office in Lower Parel.

Business continued as usual; life remained fast paced.

CHAPTER TWENTY-THREE

The Australian Nullabor

It was January 1999, it had beena long-standing ambition. It was a long-standing ambition of mine to drive from Melbourne to Perth. Before the onset of the summer, Viru and I, along with Mark (Zoee's brother from Melbourne), set off on a nine-day road trek across Australia.

Viru and I landed at Melbourne, where we had booked a Nissan X-Trail four-wheel drive. Mark had purchased three individual tents, a camping gas stove, and some provisions for our epic journey. Mark was the chef and guide; his job was to do everything other than to drive, which was left to Viru and I.

By the time we got all the gear together, it was past midday when we left Melbourne. We headed northwest to Mildura. Just short of Mildura, we stopped for the night at Renmark. It was a reasonably short drive that day. We had stopped adjacent to a stream and Mark taught us how to pitch our tents.

On day two, we set forth towards Port Augusta, arriving there around 2 p.m. Port Augusta is a small, neat little town on the coast. While Mark went shopping, Viru got busy getting himself photographed with little aborigine children and men. The aborigine kids were quite taken by Mark whilst shopping at the local supermarket. Mark prepared lunch, following which, we headed west towards the famous Nullabor.

We stopped for the night at a tourist park near Ceduna, on the edge of the Nullabor, camping on pure sand. It was rather windy when we got there. Viru and I made the mistake of having a drink before we pitched our tents. I could see Mark giving us a knowing look; he knew the pitfalls of drinking before pitching tents. We had a hell of a time trying to stabilize the tents in the gusty winds.

On day three, we drove right across the Nullabor, stopping only for fuel and refreshments. Just short of the Nullabor, the road runs along the majestic Southern Ocean. Seeing this huge expanse of water after a long dusty drive is a spectacular sight. The Southern Ocean is considered to be one of the most treacherous ocean crossings in the world. Even where we were, we could see huge waves crashing into the headland. The temperature was above 45 degrees Celsius and there were big flies everywhere. All the houses had wire netting to keep out the flies and creepy-crawlies.

The Nullabor is a treeless, semi-arid desert. It has the longest and straightest road in Australia called the Ninety Mile Road. We stopped at Norseman, a small town at the end of the Nullabor, for tea, and continued to Esperance where we stopped for the night in a Caravan Park with excellent cooking and washing facilities.

On day four, we hit Perth by lunch time and landed at Mark's cousin's home. We had a lazy lunch and waited for Mark's cousin to return home. Mark's cousin was living with his partner, who wasn't happy with three guys sprawled out in the living room. It was a bit of a delicate situation. The idea was to be in Perth for at least two nights. One of the things we wanted to see was the WACA. Unfortunately, that was not to be, as it was getting a bit awkward staying in the house with Mark's cousin and his partner.

By the time we finally left Perth, it was past 4 p.m. We stopped at a Caravan Park later that night. Mark was great at finding good campsites for our tents. As Mark said, grass was the best; that's what we always looked for. It felt cool to walk on, and great to pitch a tent, compared to hot burning sand.

On day six, we hit Kalgoorlie around noon. This looked like a decent place the moment we drove into the city. There was so much life in the city. We had lunch at a congenial café; then we went gold panning, and I found a tiny flicker of gold, which was given to me stuck on a piece of cello tape!

The open cast gold mine at Kalgoorlie is the richest two square kilometers of real estate in the world, which accounted for the hectic social activity in the town and the general bonhomie we saw everywhere.

After we were done with the gold mine and panning, we went to the visitors' center to inquire what was there to do. The girl looked at the three men facing her and said, "I would recommend the bordello museum tour."

"What is that?" I asked.

"It's a tour of a working bordello and a museum," the girl said. "You will enjoy it."

Mark was turning purple at this stage. "I am not going on a bordello tour," he said. "A working bordello, goodness no. I would rather sit in the coffee shop and read something."

So, Viru and I left Mark at a coffee shop to ruminate over his Presbyterian values and went in search of the bordello. We found Questa Casa, Hay Street, Kalgoorlie, *the house that beckoned the miners with sweet promises of hidden pleasures.*"

Viru and I walked the walk where miners emptied their wallets, and where some men left their hearts. The girls prefer men who are given to drinking, we were told, as after a while, the men would generally fall into a drunken slumber, coaxed, no doubt, by the women and laced with oodles of whisky.

We were shown the rooms where it all happened, mirrors and glasses everywhere. Beds that revolved, lacy sheets and curtains. As Mark in his wisdom commented, "Two Punjabi men; the very thought of sex was a bigger money spinner than sex itself."

Following the Bordello tour, Viru and I collected Mark from the coffee shop and drove to Norseman, the town at the edge of the Nullabor. Mark yet again found some grass for us to pitch our tents. He was a great cook and an acclaimed expert in risotto making, which he could whip up in 30 minutes flat.

On day seven, we headed straight to Adelaide. We did stop at the Western Australian border for checks and almost got fined for not declaring the fruits and vegetables we had in the car. We hit Adelaide by 7 p.m., had a quick shower and off we went to see the sights.

Day eight was spent roaming around Adelaide, a great city with a fabulous public transport system.

On day nine, we drove back straight to Melbourne from Adelaide, taking the quickest route. A hundred kilometers short of Melbourne, I was penalized with a traffic fine for crashing a give-way sign. I felt bad about that, but the cop would have nothing of it, and insisted on fining me. We reached Melbourne by 7 p.m., dropped Viru at his cousin's house, and were back at Mark's place for a late dinner.

The next day, I dropped the rental car at Avis. It was a trip of a lifetime; adventurous, interesting, exciting and grueling, but well worth the time and expense.

CHAPTER TWENTY-FOUR

Orange County and Sunny Sirohi

Mr. Sunny Sirohi was a great guy. I had first met him in 1983 on my first visit to LA when I stayed with Deepak Chhatwal, who was just finishing his MBA program at the Claremont School of Business, California. Deepak had introduced me to Sunny.

Sunny was the 'checker' in the student dining hall, which meant that Deepak could sneak the odd guest to the dining hall for a free meal. So, I walked in with Deepak, who winked at Sunny, who just waved me through, saying, "Have a good time." I thought to myself, this is a good system.

In those days, Sunny did not have any place to stay; he had been kicked out of his apartment as he was unable to pay the rent. As a result, he would move around with all his worldly possessions in his beat-up Datsun.

I had first met Sunny at Deepak's house, where he had come to wash his clothes. I remember Sunny throwing his sneakers into the washing machine, along with his clothes.

"Why are you doing that?" I asked.

"I couldn't be bothered with washing my shoes," he said.

Sunny was boisterous, an extrovert, who reveled in the company of women, and women enjoyed his company. He was just one of those likable guys with a heart of gold.

When I came to LA five years later, Sunny was married with three kids, but his boyish grin was still there. He was impish and cheeky as ever.

By then, I was fed up with driving rental cars and decided to purchase a vehicle in California. On the spur of the moment, one Friday, I told Sunny Sirohi that I wanted to purchase a car that weekend. With that in mind, I went to Bank of America and withdrew USD 20,000 in cash. As I was waiting for the cashier to give me the money, the bank manager came up to me and asked me why I was withdrawing so much cash.

"I want to buy a car," I said.

"Please tell us where you are buying the car from, and we will make out the check to the dealer; it's safer that way," said the manager.

"Could be safer," I said. "The issue is that I do not know which car I am going to buy. All I know is that I want to buy a car this weekend, and the bank will not be open."

"As long as you know," the manager said. "Please be careful with the cash. If someone mugs you, the bank will not be responsible."

I assured the bank manager I knew what I was doing and left the bank with USD 20,000 in my blazer breast pocket.

Sunny and I made our rounds of various dealers. I had identified the new Honda V6 three-liter Sedan. I wanted one in black and was going from dealer to dealer looking to see who could give me immediate delivery. As Sunny drove into the Honda dealer at Irvine, I immediately noticed a black Honda V6 in the yard.

"Is this available?" I asked the salesman.

"Yes, it is," he said.

"What is the price?" I asked.

"USD 27,000," he said. "I will take it if you give it to me for USD 26,500, with mats thrown in."

"Let me check with the manager," he said. A few minutes later, he came and said they could do the deal early next week.

"No, I want it right now," I said.

"Okay, let me get the paperwork."

Sunny and I were standing by idly, waiting for the salesman. He came back with a bunch of papers. I filled in the owner's column, name, and address. The details for finance options I left blank.

"You need to fill in the finance options as well," the salesman said.

"Why do I need to that?" I asked, "I am paying cash."

"Yes, I know, but you have to mention the down payment amount and the loan amount. Today is Saturday; that's why I was saying we could do it early next week," he replied.

"I am paying cash," I said again.

"Yes," he said, "how much?"

"The full amount," I said.

The salesman looked at me and said, "Cash, as in folding."

"Yes," I said, "cash, as in folding, and I want to take delivery of the vehicle right now."

The salesman looked at me disbelievingly. "Do you have the cash with you now?" he asked.

"Yes, I do, right here in my pocket," I replied.

"Please wait a minute, let me speak to my manager," he said. I could see both of them talking, with the manager looking at me. The salesman came back and said that it was okay, and that we did not need to fill in the finance options.

"I am going to pay USD 20,000 in cash; the rest I will pay by Amex," I told him. The salesman again looked at me and said, "I must speak to my manager again." I do not think the salesman had ever done a car sale before that was paid largely in cash with a small amount on credit card.

He returned a few minutes later. "That's all sorted now. Please give me your Social Security Number."

I pulled out my wallet and took out a piece of paper on which I had written my Social Security Number. "Don't want to make a mistake," I told the salesman.

I was taken to the finance manager's room, where she counted USD 20,000 in USD 100 bills and took the balance of USD 6,500 on my Amex. She made me sign a paper as I was paying for the vehicle in cash, a regulatory reporting requirement to the IRS, I was told. That done, I came out and asked the salesman, "Can I have my car please?"

"We need to see your original Social Security Card before we can give you delivery."

"The card is at home at Santa Ana." "I can follow your car in your new Honda, look at your Social Security Card, and hand over the car keys to you."

The salesman followed Sunny in the new Honda V6. He did not allow me to drive the car; I think he was a bit confused seeing two dark-skinned guys buying a reasonably expensive vehicle, veritably in cash.

We drove straight home, and the salesman gingerly stood outside the door. I am not quite sure what he was expecting, but he was, for sure, a bit nervous. He saw my Social Security Card, quickly gave me the keys, and made a hasty exit.

In America, the paperwork to buy a car is painfully slow. It takes a minimum of three hours to comply with all the requirements, which includes the finance options. Sunny and I had done the deal in 45 minutes flat. Now, I had a brand-new, gleaming black Honda V6: it was a powerful car, great to drive.

CHAPTER TWENTY-FIVE

Laguna Beach Misery

It was the last quarter of 1999, and I was back at Santa Ana. I was doing some work on my laptop; it would have been about 6:30 p.m., Roger, the LA Manager, had left for the day, and I was on my own, working on my computer when Al called.

He asked me to meet him for a drink. I thought to myself, why not?

"Let's meet at the Irish bar," said Al.

"Fine," I said, "in half an hour."

Thinking I would have a couple of drinks and be back early, I left my computer on. Unfortunately, as it sometimes happens, events get ahead of you; this was one such occasion. I met Al at the Irish bar at Costa Mesa and had one drink there. "Let's go to some place livelier," said Al. We went to Irvine in my Honda, and there we had single malt. "Let's go to PCH," said Al, "I know a really nice place."

Now, I was okay going for a few drinks, but to take my new Honda? It's okay, I thought, as long as I have just another drink, I reassured myself. As it so happened, the bar we went to was full of people, really lively; things got out of hand, several drinks followed. I ran through all my money. Al insisted on buying the next round.

We left the bar at 1:30 a.m. As the valet was bringing the Honda, I was wondering to myself whether I should drive. I swung the car, turning right on to the Pacific Coast Highway, and immediately stopped the car on the side of the road saying, "I think we should take a taxi. I do not want to drive right now. Let's turn back and park the car at the restaurant's car park. I will come back tomorrow and pick it up."

"I can drive," said Al.

"Are you sure?" I asked.

"Yes, I am sure, no problem," said Al. So, we switched sides with Al getting into the driver's seat.

The next thing I knew I was seeing someone knocking on the window, shining a powerful beam of light at my face. I suddenly realized that it was a policeman holding a flashlight. I shook my head, rolled down the glass. "State your name and address," said the cop. I thought for a few seconds and said,

"Versailles on the Lake, Apt HPH2, Santa Ana."

"Please get out of the vehicle, turn around, put your arms at your back, spread your legs," said the cop as he snapped handcuffs on me.

"Please come with me."

"What about my car?" I asked.

"We will take care of it." The cop put me in a squad car and we drove off.

"Where are you taking me?" I asked.

"To the station," he said.

"Why are you taking me? What have I done?"

"You could not state your address lucidly."

"But I am fully lucid now."

"Yes, you are, but this is for your protection."

So, I was taken to Laguna Beach Police Station. I was fingerprinted and had my mug shot taken, side and front. I was made to remove my shoes, my belt, my wallet, my gold chain. I was then taken to the cell where I found Al looking a bit sheepish.

"What happened?" I asked.

"I started driving," said Al. "You fell asleep almost instantly. I was unsure of where I was, and was going slowly through a traffic light, when a squad car pulled me over."

Al was booked for driving under the influence of alcohol and I was held as a threat to myself! With the car gone, the cops could have put me in a cab and sent me home; they, however, preferred I stayed overnight as their guest in the Laguna Beach lockup.

The next morning, breakfast was served early; they took Al to court straight thereafter; it was all rather disconcerting. I was let off with a warning a few minutes later. I went to the ATM and withdrew some money to pay the towing company to retrieve my Honda, which had been towed away the night before. I got back to the office around 10:30 a.m., quite shattered. Never again, I said to myself!

CHAPTER TWENTY-SIX

Meeting President Clinton

When the new millennium kicked in, the immediate impact was that the Qatar contract had not rolled over. This meant demobilizing the consultants from the Qatar project, which was never an easy task.

Reliance, however, continued to sail in clear waters.

Naresh Gupta was our latest find. He was doing a very good job for STLCorp at Reliance and was being called a trump card. It seems he had hit it off with the senior management of Reliance, which was very reassuring.

I continued to travel extensively. I took Binoy to LA with the hope of resurrecting the SAP practice at LA. However, the writing did seem to be on the wall. Binoy finally wound up the STLCorp, LA, practice in early 2001. I struggled with the decision to close at first, and then moved rapidly to get on with it and wind down the operation once I had decided to do so.

I was in Mumbai around September. Karam had invited me out to dinner. He said the SAP manager who was in charge of the Reliance account was buying dinner. Karam and I set off to meet the host of the evening.

"Meet Sanjiv T. Lall," said Karam. "You must have met him before."

"No," said Amit, "I have not met Sanjiv before." We were all sitting in the bar.

"What does Sanjiv do?" Amit asked.

"Sanjiv provides SAP resources when you guys cannot do so," said Karam. As soon as Karam said that Amit's face fell. I, of course, was thoroughly amused.

Sunny Sirohi was a diehard Democrat. I used to spend a lot of time with him. He had photographs plastered all over his walls taken with various politicians and Hollywood stars. I knew that Sunny was fairly friendly with the top brass Democrat decision makers. He would often regale me with stories about going to the White House and all that went on inside and how he had met President Bill Clinton on a few occasions.

One day, in early 2001, Sunny came to me and said, "Do you want to meet President Clinton?"

"It that possible?" I asked.

President Clinton had just demitted office a few weeks ago and was organizing a high-powered Democratic fund-raiser in LA. The cost was USD 25,000 per plate at his table. The cheapest was USD 1,000 per plate on the tables way back lining the rear wall. "I can get you a USD 1,000 ticket," Sunny said.

"Okay," I said, just to humor Sunny. "Sure, let's go."

We drove to LA together; the dinner was at the Staples Center. There were lots of people milling around. Sunny went to the desk issuing the banquet ticket holders their IDs. These came in the form of a gold paper coin, to be stuck to the lapel of the man's coat. I saw the ladies sticking the gold coins to their handbags. The gold sticker assured entry to the Staples Center. Sunny came back with three to four stickers in his hands and stuck one on my jacket lapel. "Let's go," he said, and off we went. No one stopped us, we just walked right into the Staples Center where the banquet was being held. The room was packed. Each table had the names of people who had been allocated seats. Since we did not have officially paid tickets, we did not have any reserved or paid seating, which meant no dinner either. Sunny found a table for eight with only one couple sitting at it. He kind of just took it over.

"Sit here," he told me.

"What about the person whose paid seat this is?" I asked.

"It doesn't matter," Sunny said.

It was quite hilarious: a table for eight eventually fed 12 people. One person would eat, then get up and be replaced by someone else. This went on throughout the dinner. The American guests who had paid USD 1,000 each were fully aware of what was going on but were not complaining; they were actually a little bemused by what was going on. After all, we all had the gold coins stuck to our coat lapels. It's just that we did not have paid reserved seats for dinner.

President Clinton was sitting at the main table, about 25 meters in front of us. President Gerald Ford was also at the same table. We were the very last table at the back. When the two presidents were greeting each other, I managed to get a great photograph of the two of them.

The desserts were being served when Sunny came to me and said, "Come, let's go and meet President Clinton."

With Sunny leading the way, and I following close behind, we took a wide berth of the Secret Service agents hovering around President Clinton's table. The secret service agents were not allowing anyone to approach President Clinton's table from either the back or from the side. Sunny purposely chose to skirt the President's table and came towards President Clinton's table from the front. We side stepped the tables and walked right down the aisle towards the President's table. I could see President Clinton clearly, sitting next to Elizabeth Taylor, eating his crème brûlée.

Just 15 feet from the table, a Secret Service agent spotted Sunny and stopped him. Sunny, by now, was within speaking distance. "Good evening, Mr. President," he said loudly. The President, who was lifting his spoon of crème brûlée to his mouth, put it down, looked up, saw Sunny, and said, "Hello, Sunny, how are you?"

President Clinton immediately got up and came around the table towards Sunny.

"Come," said Sunny to me, "take your photograph with President Clinton." I walked towards President Clinton, trying to quickly untangle my recently purchased Sony camera. President Clinton was most obliging. He leaned towards me, I was straining, trying to lean towards him but the Secret Service agent was pulling me back, as he did not want me to touch the President. All I wanted was a photograph, and what a great photograph it turned out to be. Sunny had also asked a friend of his to stand by, ready with his camera in case I couldn't use mine.

President Clinton was very polite and asked me, "Did you get the photo?"

"Yes Sir, we did, thank you." I have that much-cherished photo with me even today.

CHAPTER TWENTY-SEVEN

STLCorp

Having literally incorporated myself, Sanjiv T. Lall, as STLCorp, I decided it was once again time to try my hand at something new. One of the things that always bothered me was airline ticketing. More often than not, I would make my own travel itinerary and give it to my travel agent to book the flight tickets. I often thought to myself that it might be fun to have one's own travel company.

In 2001, Zoee and I had invested in the purchase of a commercial building in Parnell, Auckland. Two years later, this was sold for a handsome profit.

From the proceeds of the sale of the building, Zoee invested in a travel agency in June 2003 in Auckland. Viru was transferred to work at the travel agency and continues to work there as the general manager. Around this time, I tried my hand at marketing some high-end technologies in India. This was successful to an extent, but nowhere on the scale of SAP Consulting, and the business petered out.

With STLCorp, LA, having packed up, I found that I had much more time on my hands. I was now only traveling regularly to India, with some limited travel to Qatar. My entrepreneurial side once again started me thinking about new lines of business.

Just north of Auckland is Waiwera. Here the natural spring water has alkaline properties. This water is bottled and sold. I started examining the idea of sending alkaline water to India. Each time I thought about it, the better it sounded to me. I thought, alkaline water in India, what a godsend.

To get this venture up and running, I needed a personality to market the water, someone who would give it credible branding. At that time, the Indian cricket team was touring New Zealand for the 2002–2003 series and India was getting hammered by the Kiwis. Coincidentally, around this time, Mr. Sachin Tendulkar had just opened his restaurant, Tendulkar's, in Colaba,

Mumbai. I thought to myself that Sachin Tendulkar would make the perfect brand ambassador. Why not push this? I got a good copywriter to make a fancy label with a picturesque background of some typical soothing New Zealand scenery, with the word "Tendulkar's", the idea being to get Mr. Tendulkar to market the water in Mumbai through his restaurant.

A fair amount of effort went into making this promotion. The Tendulkar team came across fairly enthusiastic about the idea. In early 2003, I carried the bottle and label samples to Mumbai to show them to the Tendulkar team. When I arrived, I found that the team in Mumbai, who had been quite ecstatic about this idea a few months ago, were now looking downright dejected and were having second thoughts. "What happened?" I asked.

"The Kiwis thrashed India. I don't think it will work selling New Zealand merchandise in India at this point," said the team leader looking unhappy. That was the sudden demise of marketing bottled alkaline Kiwi water in India.

In 2002, I had also started STL Migrate, offering consulting advice and services for people wishing to migrate to New Zealand. I quickly found out that this was a dirty business, and I didn't want to be involved in it.

In October 2002, Sunny Sirohi visited Delhi whilst I was there.

"Can we meet some girls?" he asked.

"I don't know any," I said.

"Okay, can we go and eat shish kebabs?" asked Sunny.

"A friend is throwing a party at Friends Colony," I said. "Let's go there first and check out the action."

So, we hired a taxi and went to my friend Ajay's house at Friends Colony. I was meeting Ajay after many years and had never met his wife or any of his friends who were present at the dinner that day. Sunny did a quick recce. "No girls here; let's go and eat shish kebabs."

We left Ajay's house in search of shish kebabs. The taxi I had hired could not be found anywhere. Sunny started walking down the slip road of Friends Colony, running parallel to Mathura Road, looking for a spot to cross over.

The slip road we were walking on was at least four or five feet below Mathura Road. There were small gaps on the high wall to our right, I imagine, to allow water to drain away from Mathura Road. Sunny was walking ahead of me, looking for a gap wide enough for him to pass through. Suddenly, I saw him diving through a gap on the wall and emerging on the other side, jumping up and down, shouting, "I did it, I did it!"

I looked at the gap in the wall and told Sunny I could not jump through it, as I would get stuck. But he insisted that I would not, as he had made it easily. I stuck my head in, no problem. Hmmm, I thought, if the head can pass through an opening, so can the body. Well, not entirely true, my torso got stuck. So, now, I had a crazy guy shouting shish kebabs trying to pull me out through the gap in the wall by my arms.

I emerged from the gap in the wall and stood up. I was covered from head to toe in mud, dust, and leaves. My spotless blazer, purchased in Los Angeles, hand-stitched specially for me by Tom James, was ruined. The Single Malt Whisky Club insignia on my blazer, which I had got from London, was ripped off. I looked a total mess. To add insult to injury, the gate leading out from Friends Colony to Mathura Road, was only 20 meters away. I could have easily walked out.

We crossed the verge at Mathura Road to the taxi stand on the other side; the driver took one look at me and refused to go. I felt like a Naga sadhu covered fully in dust. Sunny and I walked towards the Ashram crossing and found a taxi that took us to Pandara Road for shish kebabs. There the waiters looked at me, felt sorry for me, and gave me a towel and then another towel. It was only when I went to the bathroom and looked in the mirror that I realized what a sight I looked.

In 2003, Mark did extensive work in putting together a course for marketing and packaging soft skills for the corporate world. It largely fell flat, as most companies in India were not willing or prepared to invest in up-skilling their work force. This still remains a huge need in my view, particularly as the level of English fluency and finesse in India is dropping. The idea was to educate Indians in the way of life in the Western culture in a very short span of time. "Up-skilling oneself is a bit like a stage drama," Mark would say. "To be the part, you have to play the part."

So right, I thought to myself, "Now all we have to do is to educate the masses on what part they are supposed to play while they are living overseas".

Mark and I came to India to test the waters of our, 'overseas communications,' and etiquette skills, business idea. We had a meeting with Ajai, my brother-in-law, in Noida, to discuss the idea. Mark had got up early, brushing up on his subject, we were running late. Mark hurriedly got dressed and we left for Noida. I remember looking at Mark while he was talking to Ajai. Mark was wearing one red sock and one black sock.

"In my eagerness and haste to get ready, I grabbed whatever came to hand," he said. So much for dramatizing the part. Needless to say, this idea fell flat.

In early 2003, I started looking at the possibility of marketing pure packaged Ganga water from the high reaches of the Himalayan mountains. To be very precise, about 25 kilometers short of Gangotri, the very source of the holy Ganges.

My friend Adishwar and I drove up to Harsal together in his Santro. It was early March and we had not taken into account that the mountains would still be frozen solid. We were fortunate to reach Harsal, driving the last two kilometers in darkness. The headlights of the car were totally ineffective, as they were striking solid snow walls. We could hardly see anything.

We stayed in the Garhwal Tourism guesthouse although it was actually closed for the winter. The caretaker very kindly allowed us to stay there, saying that there was no running water as all the pipes were frozen solid. Adishwar and I were given a room with two single beds. It was really cold; the room was like a fridge freezer.

I asked the caretaker if he could arrange for a bottle of rum to warm us up.

"No, no," he said, "this is the land of Ganga mata."

"Please get me some rum," I requested. "It's very cold."

"Not possible," said the caretaker.

"Please get the rum from the Army camp across the road," I persisted.

"How many bottles do you want?" the caretaker asked.

"Just one bottle will do," I said. Literally, within five minutes, a bottle of Contessa rum, Army issue, was produced.

"Wait," said the caretaker, "let me get you some warm water." A few minutes later, the caretaker got a jug of boiling Bhagirathi River Ganga water. "If you drink alcohol with this water, you can drink double the amount," the caretaker said. "It's so pure." That was the first time I ever had rum with boiling hot Ganges water. It tasted darned good.

The next day, we collected Ganga *jal*, and were on our way to Uttarkashi, when we were forced to stop for the night on account of a major landslide. As it so happened, we ended up staying two full nights at Garam Pani, a sulphur spring resort. Fortunately, we found a hotel room. Food and drinks were also close at hand.

We would walk up the road, and then down along the Bhagirathi River, which downstream becomes the Ganges. We met a sadhu at the local tea shop who told us he had come walking across the mountains from Gangotri. "I covered my sneakers in plastic and walked without a problem," he said. I asked him what he thought about my idea of selling bottled Ganges water. "Great," he said. "That way you will spread the goodness of the Holy Ganges all over the world."

We reached Delhi, two days later than planned. As we were passing Meerut, I called Sunny Sirohi who was supposed to be leaving for LA the next day. I had promised him I would meet him on my return from Harsal. To my shock and utter horror, I was told that Sunny had a major coronary in Meerut the night before and had passed away.

I was so stunned with the news of Sunny's passing that the Ganges water project fell by the wayside. I recalled all that Sunny and I had been through over the years and the great friendship that had ensued. He was a mischievous imp, always full of beans. He lived life to the fullest. I thought of all the good times we had enjoyed. He remains someone I continue to remember and miss.

Fortunately for me, all was well at Reliance. The STLCorp consultants were still going strong on the Reliance InfoComm project, now based at the Dhirubhai Ambani Knowledge City, Navi Mumbai.

In December 2003, Mukesh and Anil Ambani had a sudden and unexpected showdown. Unfortunately for me, Anil got control over Reliance InfoComm, where STLCorp had been involved for the last couple of years. As far as STLCorp was concerned, the baby went out with the bathwater. Our project summarily came to an immediate and sudden grinding halt.

After six and a half years at Reliance, we were literally disengaged overnight! In my experience, whenever there is a fall out in big family run business houses, everyone who is involved gets impacted. And we were no different.

CHAPTER TWENTY-EIGHT

A Life to Live

2004 was a year of introspection. My mother fell very sick whilst at Ranchi and had to be evacuated to Delhi by a Medevac plane. Life had become a bit of a roller coaster.

It all happened overnight. I got a call from my sister in New Delhi, saying that Mother had been taken seriously ill. It seemed her gallbladder had burst, and the bile fluid had got infected, which, in turn, had infected all her vital organs inside and outside the stomach cavity and she was grievously ill.

Some dear friends close by took my mother to the Army hospital in Ranchi, where a young Army doctor examined her. The thing was that, the Army hospital did not have an MRI scanner; it only had a basic ultrasound scanner. Major (Dr.) Sandeep Kang, by this time, was getting calls from various people, including the General Officer Commanding, Ranchi, asking after my mother. Major (Dr.) Sandeep Kang had to make his diagnosis literally from gut feeling and experience, as he had no medical test reports to rely upon other than the ultrasound.

Mother could not be sent to the hospital 15 kilometers away that had MRI imaging facilities, as the road to the hospital was in terrible condition. The doctor thought that, if anything, the road trip to the hospital and back could possibly be far too dangerous for her to manage. The doctor put my mother on a very severe and strong medication of liquid antibiotics, which resuscitated her to an extent. The main issue was, most of her major organs in the stomach cavity had been infected by now. She needed urgent treatment. Mother was air-lifted to New Delhi in a Medevac plane and was transferred to a local hospital in the city.

When I reached New Delhi the next day from New Zealand and visited her in the hospital, I found out that the gallbladder, which had burst, had on its own, and rather mysteriously, resealed and repaired itself. The concern was about the bile fluid in the stomach. Slowly but surely my mother started healing, and about 10 days later, she was discharged!

A year later, I recall meeting Major (Dr.) Sandeep Kang in Ranchi. He was giving a medical synopsis of my mother to his commanding officer. He said, "Mrs. Lall had everything conceivably go wrong with her lungs, heart, stomach, brain, etc. She is a walking, talking pathological laboratory. It's a miracle that she survived."

Today, as I write this, my mother is 81 years old, and is hale and hearty!

CHAPTER TWENTY-NINE

Yunca

In May 2005, Terry Young from Yunca, Invercargill, contacted me, asking whether I could advise them on the possibilities of India as a manufacturing hub for their range of machinery products. Yunca was looking to manufacture its goods outside its native shores, as New Zealand was getting far too expensive. The toss-up was between China and India.

Terry had been to China but knew very little of India. I had met him at Invercargill a few years ago and had said that I could perhaps assist them in India.

I checked out various possible manufacturing sites in India and suggested that they should perhaps consider Goa as a possible manufacturing base. Goa stood out above the other states because of its infrastructure, English speaking population and the relaxed life and work styles. Terry did say that after work he would like to sit out and enjoy the sunset and have a cup of coffee or a beer. Goa had all the ingredients to make that and more happen. The only downside was that one would have to import the labor into Goa, to work, or use the transient migrant workforce.

I suggested to Terry and John that they visit Goa with me in September and invited them to my 50th birthday bash at Kathmandu during the same trip.

During the five days that they were in Goa, I introduced them to the Goa State Industrial Development Corporation, Secretary of Industries, Government of Goa, and other senior officers from the Department of Industries who sold them the idea of making Goa their manufacturing base outside New Zealand.

Goa, as a place, generally appealed to Yunca. A disused factory at the Verna Industrial Complex was identified as a possible site to purchase instead of building a factory from scratch, thereby reducing the delays in starting the manufacturing base and saving money.

I guess you could say this was one of those things ordained to happen. Terry and John's visit went off very smoothly. I had also asked Johnny to come from Bangalore to provide the tax inputs as they were an overseas company looking to setup a manufacturing base in Goa.

From Goa, Terry, John, and I continued to Delhi. The next day, we all went to Kathmandu, where we spent a fabulous three days, celebrating my 50th in great style, along with my twin sister, Babli, and several close friends and family.

Yunca, New Zealand, is now manufacturing heaters at Verna, Goa. I thoroughly enjoyed the Yunca project.

What was surprising to everyone, especially Johnny, was that I had never been to Goa before. I had never interacted with any of the bureaucrats we met prior to this visit, and yet, things flowed so smoothly. Quite a feat for an unknown person without any connections at Goa!

CHAPTER THIRTY

Kaleidoscope of Thoughts

Having now lived in Goa for nine years, I can say what transpired in 2005 with Yunca and the smoothness with which the events took place and the way they dovetailed into each other was unreal. As I said earlier, this was something destined to happen.

The biggest event of 2006 was that I managed to sort out the legal quagmire of Similia, our family property in Ranchi, which had been festering for the last 40 years or so.

After my stepfather had died in 1975, the property went into total disrepair. The manager who was supposed to look after the property more or less usurped the unsold part of it, all 17 acres. I did not even know how much property we had, where it started and where it ended.

In the late 1980s, I did try unravelling the mystery, but it took so long that I kind of lost interest halfway, and a bit later, I left for New Zealand. For the next 17 years or so, I did nothing towards solving this problem.

In 2005, I was again in Ranchi. I pulled out the file and started looking for the government officer who had helped me to some extent with unravelling the property predicament way back in 1986. I found this person totally by accident at the Ranchi Club. Having established contact again after close to 20 years, I started pursuing the property case again, determined to put it to bed this time.

I spent the next three months doggedly pursuing the paperwork. I am not sure whether it was my single-minded resoluteness or good old dame luck, perhaps, a bit of both, but I got all the property paperwork sorted by late 2005. The only remaining aspect was the absence of a boundary wall along the 1.5-kilometer perimeter of the 17-acre property. This had to be built fast, really fast.

I hired the entire village. All the men and women were tasked with building a 10-inch-wide, 3-feet high boundary wall with red bricks and mud mortar. I had to build the wall within five days. That was the period specified in the permission that had been given to me by the local authorities. Come what may I had to complete the job within that time.

Against all odds, the boundary wall was completed on the fifth day. The local police and goons tried to prevent me from completing the job, but I did not budge, and the job was done.

Now that we had a boundary wall, it looked altogether a different property. For one, it was visually distinguishable and could be seen from afar. And for another, it was now more secure. The following year, in 2006, the property was sold to a local businessman.

My travels to Doha continued. I rented an apartment in Doha for one year, commencing February 2006, as I was traveling there frequently.

Sonny Kumar and I went to Doha in October 2006. I wanted to show Sonny the Doha operation and introduce him to everyone in Qatar.

After a few days, I continued to London to meet a few SAP consultants. We needed a bank of SAP consultants to draw upon for Qatar; we were looking for cutting-edge skills that would ensure that Kleinstar was well placed to meet the growing demand by our clients in Qatar.

I was visiting London after a gap of about eight years, the last time having been with Zoee and my mother in 1998.

In December 2006, my sister Kunkun and her husband, Ajai, visited Auckland. It was good to have them stay with us. I took them to Rotorua. They thoroughly enjoyed their stay in New Zealand.

During the years 2005 and 2006, I began introspecting about my life, specifically where I would like to live for the next 20 years. I knew at the back of my mind that one day I would have to return to Ranchi. That said, I wanted to go to Ranchi on my own terms, of my own will and volition, and not be coerced into doing so.

I wrestled with this in my mind, tossing the subject around in my head for a while until I finally shelved it, thinking one day it would happen if it were supposed to.

For now, things were cruising along quite nicely. Being with Zoee was the best part of my life. I had come to Auckland with a couple of hundred dollars, and I now had a great life, a terrific woman, and a great business. I had an envious collection of single malt whiskeys, a fabulous home in Mt. Eden, Auckland, which ran like clockwork, courtesy Zoee, and a transit apartment in Delhi that I had purchased in 1998.

Zoee had given my life stability at a time when I had none; she fashioned some purpose and direction into my life. Zoee stood by me through thick and thin, without a murmur, especially during the long periods I was traveling and away from home.

The Foley family were truly fabulous, the way they took me into their *whanau*, or extended family. Zoee's mother, Catherine, and stepfather, Bob, would always come and pick us up from the Auckland Airport for a "dollar" as he always said. There was also Zoee's very warm and generous sister, Tarsisia, who is now a high court judge and Rob, her brother-in-law, an acclaimed architect and avid sailor. In later years, Zoee's younger sister also came from London to live in Auckland, and there is, of course, her brother Mark, the best risotto chef I know, my travel companion in Australia and almost business partner!

What can I say about the Foley family? They treated me like their own. Indians take pride in their families, in their value system and their culture. I would have no hesitation in saying that the Foley family was streets ahead when it came to loving and welcoming new family members joining in than any Indian family I have ever encountered or known, including my own. Without a doubt, I have a lot to thank Zoee and her family for.

2007–2008 was the year I decided to spend a lot more time in India. Zoee was hugely upset, but in time she realized that I needed to be in India and that I had to leave New Zealand, not so much to be away from her, but more so, for other reasons. In the course of my life, the time had come to move on, but New Zealand and Zoee will always have a very special place in my heart.

In 2008, Zoee was diagnosed with a critical illness. The immediate prognosis was not good. Zoee had a surgery in August 2008, and about three months later, she started her treatment.

I went to Auckland to support Zoee whilst she underwent treatment. Slowly but surely the treatment started to work. Nine years later, Zoee is thankfully fit and well. Today, Zoee and I remain good friends.

CHAPTER THIRTY-ONE

Mongolia

When I returned to Delhi, I met Robin, a nice, easygoing guy who was making pashmina shawls in Amritsar. Robin and I hit it off from the start. He asked me whether I could help him in sourcing raw pashmina or cashmere from overseas.

I was pretty much at a loose end at that time, so I said, "Why not?"

We decided to explore the possibility of sourcing pashmina wool from Mongolia!

Robin and I flew to Beijing en route to Ulan Bator, Mongolia. We were met at the Beijing Airport by Peter, the person Robin had set up tentative meetings with in Beijing.

Beijing was a total eye-opener. All my preconceived ideas and assumptions about life under communism went out of the window! We stayed in a hotel close to Tiananmen Square. We visited the Forbidden City, which is at one end of Tiananmen Square, and spent half the day there, walking and soaking in the sights of ancient Chinese history.

That evening we went to Bar Street, the red-light district of Beijing. I was not expecting to see such a thing in Beijing and was totally surprised because it was a bit like Bangkok! We strolled along for a bit, found a nice place to eat and returned to our hotel to prepare for our business meeting.

The next day we took the train to Hubei province, which was a three-hour train ride away. The train was exactly like a crowded Indian AC two-tier train, no difference whatsoever.

Hubei province is the center where cashmere goats are reared. We were the guests of Peter's employers, a local businessman who was highly connected. We had dinner with him that evening; the food kept on coming and coming, and after 25 courses, I gave up counting! The owner did not speak English, all he did was laugh whilst we ate and ate and then ate some more!

A visit to a local bordello is part and parcel of business meetings in Hubei. Much to my surprise, this was extended to our party. When we arrived at the bordello, it was empty. Our host asked us to wait. I saw a long corridor with rooms on either side, each furnished with comfortable sofas and chairs and equipped with their own television and karaoke set. A short while later, a couple of girls trooped in. After a polite interval, Robin and I left and retired for the night, alone in our hotel rooms.

Back in Beijing, Peter continued to host our visit and took us out for a meal after our return from Hubei province. In Beijing, many of the better Chinese restaurants have individual dining rooms. These can be booked for business meetings for greater privacy or for the local Chinese boss to treat his wife or girlfriend or mistress to a cozy, intimate meal. We were having dinner at one such place. I was told the private rooms even had exit doors leading directly out to the side street should a hasty or discreet exit be required. Quite civilized, I thought to myself.

The next morning, Robin and I flew to Ulan Bator, the capital of Mongolia. If Beijing was an eye-opener, Ulan Bator blew my socks off. It was fantastic. Ulan Bator is an ancient city founded in the 17th century. Khan is the most popular name here, be it a drink or a hotel or a bank. If in doubt, just say Khan!

Robin and I finalized the deal after meeting Ronnie. Ronnie would ship out raw Mongolian de-haired cashmere to Delhi. The Mongolian cashmere fiber is substantially longer than what is sourced from the longest Chinese or English cashmere goat. In Mongolia, we also discovered camel hair, which was even longer than Mongolian cashmere fiber.

I was told that every Mongolian boy or girl could ride a horse; they are taught riding when they are very young. The country side of Mongolia is dotted with magnificent treeless steppes and plains, providing fabulous spaces for horse riding. Unfortunately, we didn't see any kids riding.

Whilst in Mongolia, the one thing I noticed was that the food tasted very salty. I was told that salt is used as a natural preservative in very cold weather.

When the time came for us to leave, Robin did not want to leave Ulan Bator; a local girl had fallen in love with him.

"What did you do to her?" I asked him.

"Nothing," he said, "I just gave her a lot of money."

Our cashmere deal inked with Ronnie, Robin and I headed back to Beijing. We stayed in the same hotel, close to Tiananmen Square.

In Beijing, Robin wanted to go shopping. At the shopping center, we were told most shops spoke and understood English. From the road where the taxi dropped us off, the shopping center was about 50 to 75 meters away. We were walking below what I thought was a huge aquarium, but it suddenly dawned on me that it was not an aquarium but the biggest TV screen I had ever seen. It must have been 50 meters long and 25 meters wide. China, what a capitalist communist country, I thought to myself!

After Robin was done shopping, we looked for a place to eat and saw the Golden Jaguar Chinese restaurant. "Let's go there," said Robin, so we headed to the first floor. As we got off the lift, I noticed a line of girls standing outside, all wearing long, light purple, floor-length gowns. They were the restaurant hostesses.

We were welcomed to the restaurant and told the cover charge was USD 39.95 per person, all you can eat.

One of the hostesses took us around. At the beginning was the Japanese table with oysters, crabs, lobsters and shrimps, followed by the Thai counter, and then another, and another. There must have been at least 40 to 50 counters of food, each having about 40 to 50 dishes. In total, there were more than 1,000 dishes available to eat. There was Japanese, Thai, Taiwanese, Korean, Vietnamese, British, American, Singaporean, Malaysian, Laotian, Cambodian...the list just went on.

We found one maître d' from India; he was as excited to see us as we were to see him. "We even have Indian food," he said. "Can I get you some butter chicken?"

"No," I said, "not for me." I was happily digging into oysters. The maître d' looked so dejected that Robin asked him to get him some butter chicken, which arrived with black dal and *tandoori rotis*.

Soft drinks, beer, and wine were thrown in. In all my travels abroad, I had never come across a restaurant like this. When it came to desserts, Robin wanted to eat all the Häagen-Daz ice cream flavors on offer. The maître d' and I were just looking in amusement at Robin gorging on the ice cream.

Robin and I returned to Delhi from quite easily, and by far, the best business cum holiday trip I had ever had. Mongolia, who would have thought.

I began importing de-haired Mongolian cashmere fiber for Robin, which he sent to Amritsar to be spun into yarn and then woven into pure pashmina or cashmere shawls.

I must have imported about eight to ten shipments of cashmere. There was, however, one problem. I was unable to come to grips with the Indian way of doing business. Supply now, get paid later, was just not my style of operating. Robin himself was a bit helpless as he was operating on credit. A cog in the wheel I never was and did not ever wish to be. I wound up the cashmere business in the first quarter of 2008.

On my return from Mongolia, I got a call from Gulu, inviting me to visit him in Pune. "It's great here, you will have a fabulous time," he said.

I was at a loose end at the time, not doing very much, so I took a flight to Pune, and my life changed yet again.

I met Ania in early October 2008 at Gulu's house. At least I can hang my hat on Gulu on this one. I had a great holiday in Pune, one which turned my life on its head yet again.

Once again, the unusual mix of passion and life got me going. Where work is concerned, I am basically a passionate person, in the sense, I bring a lot of commitment with me in everything I take on. In my interpersonal relationships, however, I am very reserved. Ania somehow managed to break through that. Ania and I hit it off from day one. She was totally casual, understated, wore practically no jewelry, was a great cook, and had a wild sense of humor. Perhaps it was the lack of any pressure to do anything that I liked the best of all about her.

My meeting Ania could not have been scripted better. As Ania said, she found her man, sitting on her sofa, in her own living room; what could be better?

CHAPTER THIRTY-TWO

Goa

I was in Pune with Ania in December 2008. I had come to Pune for the New Year's Eve bash, and to spend some time there. Ania and I were looking for possible locations to live. I did not want to live in Mumbai or Pune and Ania was not keen on Delhi or Ranchi.

At that time, we were looking at the possibility of buying a small plot at Mulshi Lake, which was an hour's drive from Pune. Mulshi is a dam on a lake that is used by Tata Power to generate hydropower for Pune.

Mulshi is a very beautiful expanse; it has gentle rolling hills and a beautiful lake, a combination of hills and water, a vista not often seen in India. The only problem with this location was that Mulshi was totally undeveloped, there was nothing there. To get a loaf of bread or eggs, one would have to trek to the village 10 kilometers away. There was not even a tyre shop around.

It was on New Year's Day 2008, during the course of the discussions on Mulshi, that Gulu suggested we look at Goa.

I pulled out my laptop and typed in 'Portuguese Villas for Sale' in Goa, and a villa came up for sale at Moira. The photos looked great; the villa was painted light yellow with white borders, and it had a lawn and a swimming pool. I showed the picture to Ania and Gulu. They both liked it.

I called the owner, Rod, a British gentleman, and told him we would like to come and have a look at the villa. "I have an interested buyer from Gujarat," Rod said.

"I am calling from Pune," I told him. "We will be with you in Goa tomorrow, shortly after lunch."

I don't think Rod took me seriously; in Goan parlance, this could mean, one of *these* days!

The next day, we left Pune at 6 a.m., and at 2 p.m. sharp, we hit Mapusa, where we had lunch, and arrived at Rod's house in Moira at 3:15 p.m. Ania loved the house from the first minute.

We also saw an apartment within minutes of leaving Moira. It was so bad, we did not even bother going inside. The next day we saw a semi-detached house with gorgeous views of the river across the dolphin bay at Reis Magos.

It came down to the Portuguese villa at Moira, Goa, or a semi-detached villa with great views at Reis Magos, Goa. I was quite happy to go with either. Ania, however, was set on the Portuguese villa.

I thought about it, looked at my bank account several times, and thought I was within striking distance, but was just INR 20 lakhs or USD 40,000 short. I went to Rod the next day and asked him whether he would give me two months to find the INR 20 lakhs, to which he readily agreed. I paid a token deposit towards the villa the very next day.

We returned to Goa three weeks later to do the sale deed. Three months later, Ania came and took possession of the house, and I followed a few days later.

The year 2009 was pretty much consumed in settling in at Goa, not that it took a lot of time, as Ania was very organized and got things off the ground very fast. My mother came visiting exactly one month after Ania and I moved into the house.

The house was expanded, staff quarters built, a solid car port added, the boundary wall strengthened, and most important of all, the garden shed was converted into my office.

The following year, the house exterior was painted a brighter yellow and mango with white borders.

Ania's friends would visit often from Mumbai, and many people started asking me, "Can you find a house like this for me in Goa?" To humor them, I began asking what their budget was and would consider whether a deal was possible or not.

It took me about a year to complete my first property transaction, and thereafter, the pace started picking up. Now, nine years later, I am kind of established in the Goa property market. In 2011, Kunkun and Ajai decided to buy a home in Goa. I showed Kunkun what I thought was a beautiful property in Moira, situated bang on the river, down a very narrow driveway.

Ajai purchased the property a month later. I helped them renovate the house and built the fabulous deck that I had envisioned. What was an idea or vision, became the reality. Ajai and Kunkun now have a fabulous home on the river.

In November 2011, Udit, too, decided to purchase an investment property in Goa. Udit decided to purchase a run-down, broken house on the banks of a rivulet, just one kilometer from Mapusa.

In early 2012, the house was duly renovated and repainted indigo blue and white. The grounds were landscaped with fruit trees and a wooden deck was built on the banks of the rivulet.

Unfortunately, whereas the property business grew in Goa, Ania and I did not last. We parted ways in 2013 and continue to be friends.

In 2015, I bought a totally run down Portuguese villa in Nachinola, Goa, and restored it to its former glory. Once again, I tried my hand at something totally new, learning the art of renovation of old buildings. Not only did I complete the villa in record time, but also ensured that the work and interiors were done to exceptionally high standards, giving the Portuguese villa a grand old heritage look.

CHAPTER THIRTY-THREE

Jeeps

I have always had a passion for jeeps. I associate jeeps with my father. My clearest memories are of seeing him in his army jeeps, looking very smart and regal.

From about 2006, I had begun looking for my old white jeep, which my mother had sold. I wanted to buy it back. I sent my scouts looking for it. They went all over the place, to Dhanbad and beyond into West Bengal looking for my jeep, to no avail.

In early 2008, I was informed that there was a low bonnet Army jeep at Panagarh, West Bengal. I happened to be in Ranchi. I jumped into my car and immediately went to Panagarh where I saw the 1944 Ford GPW jeep.

I concluded the deal straight away, paid the money and set out back to Ranchi with the GPW jeep in tow. We drove all night and arrived at Tikratoli at 6 a.m. the next morning.

It took three months to put the jeep together. It was a painstakingly slow restoration. Several parts were not available and had to be sourced from Pune, Mumbai, and Jama Masjid, Delhi.

A few months later, I acquired a 1958 CJ3B jeep, which took only two months to restore. Two years later, I purchased a Jonga from the Army surplus and finally, last year, I bought a 1956 CJ3B jeep.

I now have three left-hand-drive petrol jeeps and one Jonga, all Indian Army issue vehicles, all beautifully restored and in good running condition.

A 1995 CJ3B jeep and a 1960 Mark 1 Ambassador are my latest additions, which are currently under restoration.

CHAPTER THIRTY-FOUR

SAP Revisited

I n late 2011, SAP AG's USA attorney sent me a notice that the sapcorp.com domain name that I had created way back in 1998 was an infringement.

I was forced to change the name SAPCorp to STLCorp in 1999. The domain, however, was kept alive. Anyone clicking sapcorp.com would be redirected to kleinstar.com, my parent SAP consulting company in New Zealand. SAP AG was not happy about that; they claimed that sapcorp.com was their domain, and a formal complaint was filed at the World Intellectual Property Organization (WIPO).

I was very annoyed about this and engaged a maverick lawyer in the USA to fight my case with WIPO.

I strongly believe and contend that I was done by the system. I came up against a judge from Australia, who, in my view, passed a totally biased judgment. The judge allowed and accepted additional submissions from the complainant, SAP AG, without informing us and when we added additional submissions ourselves, we were penalized. The judge was biased and went completely against established law.

I thought the judgment was grossly unfair. I had a discussion with my attorney at Tucson, Arizona, and decided to write a stern letter of complaint to the judge. The letter was composed thus:

Dear Mr. Rothnie:

I am the former owner of SAPCORP.COM, a domain name I owned from March 1998 until you decided to give it to SAP.

This letter is to notify you personally of my extreme disappointment with your decision that not only deprived me of ownership of a domain but impugned my integrity by implicitly finding that I had bad faith intent when I registered the name. I can scarcely state which aspect of the judgment offends me more.

You did not notify me that you would be accepting the additional submission from the complainant, nor accorded me the opportunity to respond to unsworn assertions that you found more credible than three mutually corroborative statements stated under oath by us. In this unseemly show of procedural favoritism, you concealed your denial of equal briefing opportunities to both parties with the disingenuous statement that my counsel did not request the opportunity. It is elementary neutral procedure to allow a party that objects to the admission of evidence the opportunity to submit surrebuttal, particularly where the allowance of a complainant's rebuttal is not even provided for under the rules.

But for the fact that there would be no financial sense to it, I would have filed an ACPA action simply to have the satisfaction of seeing a United States District Court judge reverse your decision. You are a severe disappointment to any person who would look to you for justice. Enjoy spending your thirty pieces of silver.

Eventually, I never did send this letter; perhaps, better sense prevailed. As someone said, better left alone, galling as that made me feel. I was extremely upset and angry at how this whole issue of the domain name had turned out. I thought it was grossly unfair. Who said life is fair?

CHAPTER THIRTY-FIVE

Reflections

So, here I am, in 2018, past 60 years of age. I was terrible in studies, passing as I did by the skin of my teeth. I opted for political science at college because it was the easiest course possible. Getting a Bachelor of Arts (BA) degree was a must.

I was 22 years old when I got my BA. I did not know what I wanted out of life or what to do in life. I had led a very sheltered existence until then. I really did not know much about life back then.

I started off as a shipping clerk in a containerized shipping company, Sea Land, in Tehran, and later, Madrid. This is where I learned that hard work and initiative pays off. My bosses went out of their way to keep me employed without a visa. When I returned from Iran and my European odyssey, I wanted to conquer the world. To accomplish that, I wanted to look a bit older, so I grew a beard, which I wore for a few years. When I turned 30, I wanted to look younger, so I shaved off my beard.

Following my return from Europe, I got my cousin Gokul's company up and running in Delhi. Subsequently, I joined a commodity-trading firm, again in Delhi. Later, I was a jetsetter trying to sell bulk cement out of Singapore, and then I tried my hand at farming in Ranchi. I realized that whatever I turned my hand to, I could get things done. It was focus, hard work and determination that led to success.

Pushing 30 plus, I did not want to get married; the idea then was to have a jolly good time, sow the oats, so to speak. But later when I thought I was ready to get married, I found no one ready to marry me. I guess the one thing I have learnt is, timing is everything in life as well as in business.

A chance meeting with Zoee changed my life and I went to New Zealand and imported and sold women's garments across the country. Then I began supplying people with knowledge and skills around the globe. I set up a SAP consulting company, opened offices in Auckland, Los Angeles, Bangalore, and Delhi, and provided SAP consultants to various companies in Australia, India, Indonesia, Malaysia, Singapore, the United Arab Emirates, the United States of America, and Qatar. I was one of the pioneers in structuring the reverse brain drain, that is, in bringing Indians who had been working abroad back to India, and that too at US dollar rates!

Around that time, I also bought a travel agency in New Zealand, which Zoee continues to run.

When I returned to India, I imported cashmere from Mongolia, and here I am now, 45 long years after I set out to change the world, living in Goa, renovating old Portuguese villas, and selling exclusive properties.

I always wanted to work and live on my own terms, to take risks, to take the blame for my decisions and to please only myself. The standards I set for myself were very high indeed. The women in my life were bright and smart, thorough professionals in their respective fields. They were all excellent cooks and very house proud. I think I can say with some authority that a good cook makes a very passionate lover. Without passion, life is insipid. If you are missing out on something and want to crank it up, get out there and get yourself a good cook, or otherwise, learn to cook. Believe me, the passion will follow.

Would I do something different? I sniff the air and think, maybe, why not, it sounds like an idea. I love the challenge, I love the journey, I just love being there.

Tikratoli remains an integral part of me. A large part of this book and reminiscing over my life was indeed done at Tikratoli.

Zoee remains a close friend. Ania sold the yellow-mango villa in Moira and continues to live in Goa. She has been a great source of love, encouragement and solace to me. I hope she will always be my friend.

I think of all the women in my life and feel that I did have my day in the sun. But I rue the fact that perhaps I did not go the distance with any of the women that played such a huge part in shaping my life. Perhaps, it was not meant to be. I strongly believe that when we think back, it is not what we did that we regret but what we always wanted to do but did not do. Perhaps, that is what one laments more than anything else.

As for me, I followed my heart and learnt that there would be adversity, there would be challenges, there would be broken relationships and loss of love. These things happen, and when they do, I say, accept them with full grace and dignity, as that is perhaps one thing that will tide you over all forms of hardship and difficulty.

Take the passion and the opportunities that come your way and give it everything you've got, be it your job or your interpersonal relationships. Love totally and infinitely, and above all, enjoy whatever you do. This will make the difference and will bring out the best in you.

For those of you who do not know what you want to do in life, take heart and be gentle on yourself. There is still time. Be patient, your day in the sun will surely come.

This book, my story, is especially for you.

CHAPTER THIRTY-SIX

Afterword

After a period of 39 long years of leaving Iran, I connected with my first ever boss, Mr. Hans Herdingh again. On a visit to London in 2017, I found Hans on Facebook and called him up. It was fantastic speaking to Hans after so many years; he remembered me well. He said, "You did a good job for me in Tehran." Hans and I had a long chat on the phone. I have promised him that one day in the near future, I will go and meet him in Holland.

Hans has now retired, and is living a quiet life with his wife, Lineke, in Wagenberg, Holland. Hans told me that Kar Sakhuja and Charles McCarthy did settle down together, after all, in Andorra. However, most unfortunately, Kar Sakhuja passed away about eight years ago. Matt Quartel, who had been living a retired life in Belgium, too, passed away a few years ago. Mr. Charles McCarthy and Mr. Dijksmann, too, have passed away.

Hans also informed me that Raja, the boy from Sri Lanka with whom I had shared a room in Tehran, is now living in London. I emailed Raja and we finally re-connected after 39 long years. Raja and I reminisced about our time in Sea Land, Tehran. Raja has two children, his daughter is married and lives in Paris, and his son lives with Raja and his wife in London. I promised Raja that I would meet him on my next visit to London. Raja remembered my friend Amarjit, the architect from Tehran, who is now leading a retired life in Brisbane, Australia.

I rue the fact I never got the opportunity to meet Kar Sakhuja and Matt Quartel ever again. I really would have liked that. But then, that's life, and what a life it's been.

My story would be totally incomplete without Hans Herdingh, Kar Sakhuja, Matt Quartel, and Raja Ayathuray. It's so fortuitous that I re-connected with Hans Herdingh and Raja Ayathuray again, after almost four decades, that too, whilst writing the final chapter of my life story!

www.ingramcontent.com/pod-product-compliance
Lightning Source LLC
Chambersburg PA
CBHW031258160726
47993CB00001B/212